UNI-WISSEN

John F. Davis

Phonetics
and Phonology

Klett Lerntraining

Bibliografische Information der Deutschen Nationalbibliothek
Die Deutsche Nationalbibliothek verzeichnet diese Publikation in der
Deutschen Nationalbibliografie; detaillierte bibliografische Daten sind
im Internet über http://dnb.dnb.de abrufbar.

Auflage 3 2 1 | 2017 2016 2015
Die letzten Zahlen bezeichnen jeweils die Auflage und das Jahr des Druckes.

Dieses Werk folgt der reformierten Rechtschreibung und Zeichensetzung. Ausnahmen
bilden Texte, bei denen künstlerische, philologische oder lizenzrechtliche oder andere
Gründe einer Änderung entgegenstehen.

© Klett Lerntraining, c/o PONS GmbH, Stuttgart 2015. Alle Rechte vorbehalten.
www.klett-lerntraining.de
Satz: Steffen Hahn GmbH Medienservice, Kornwestheim
Druck: medienhaus Plump GmbH, Rheinbreitbach
Printed in Germany
ISBN 978-3-12-939028-3

Contents

Preface

This volume is the fruit of many years of teaching phonetics and phonology to beginning students of English at Cologne University. It is aimed at readers who have no previous knowledge of the subject. For this reason I have confined myself to the structural approach in phonology (the phoneme and its realizations) as this provides a good foundation for the later study of other approaches and can be compared with the study of arithmetic before one goes on to mathematics. As phonetics is by nature associated with hearing rather than sight, a book of this kind is at a disadvantage, since the reader cannot hear the author, as students can their teacher. However, I have tried to make the text as simple and comprehensible as possible, providing examples that should partly compensate for this drawback.

I am very grateful to Professor Ansgar Nünning for inviting me to contribute to the Series he has edited, and a special word of thanks must be said to the staff of Ernst Klett Publishing House for coping so efficiently with the problems of printing a phonetic text and in particular to Manfred Ott for his patience and willing assistance in helping me to overcome the technical difficulties. My largest debt of gratitude, however, is to the many students who have asked me numerous interesting questions about phonetics and phonology over the years in the course of my teaching. It is from them that I have learnt a great deal which I hope to have passed on to others in this book.

John F. Davis
October 1998

Phonetics and Phonology

CHAPTER 1

Introduction

The aim of this book is to provide its readers with a short introduction to the phonetics and phonology of English within a structuralist framework and to give them a firm foundation from which they can proceed to other approaches to phonology. Limited space will allow consideration of only Standard British Pronunciation (RP) and General American (GA). Topics will usually be illustrated from RP, but where GA is different, these differences will be discussed and illustrated too.

1 Difference between Phonetics and Phonology

Definition

Phonetics is that part of linguistics in which we study the physical characteristics of the sounds which we hear in languages. It is interested in how we produce these sounds in the mouth, nose, throat and lungs, and in how the ear and the brain perceive and interpret them.

Phonology is the study of how particular languages use these sounds, e. g. what combinations of consonants a language allows at the beginning or end of a word or syllable, which sounds have a restricted distribution in the language, how some sounds affect neighbouring sounds in that language, etc.

Motivation

Of what use is a knowledge of phonetics and phonology to students and teachers of English?

Pronunciation

Students can improve their own pronunciation if they understand how the sounds of English (or another language) are produced physically (Phonetics) and how the sounds of English (or another language) function in that language (Phonology).

For example, German learners should be aware of the fact that the vowel in the German word *schön* is said with rounded lips and that it should not be substituted for the non-rounded vowel in the English words *learn* or *bird*. This is phonetic knowledge.

Another problem for German learners is not to use the glottal stop at the beginning of an English word starting with a vowel. German words with an initial vowel begin with a brief closing and opening of the vocal cords in the throat, as when a person strains slightly. This glottal stop is rare in English pronunciation and only used before word-initial vowels in very emphatic speech. There is thus a very big difference between the German sentence *Anna aß ein Ei*, where each word begins with a glottal stop, and the corresponding English sentence *Ann ate an egg*, where the last consonant in the first three words is run onto the beginning of the word following it, almost as if it were an initial consonant. Thus the function of the glottal stop in the two languages is very different. This is phonological knowledge.

Understanding

A knowledge of the phonetics and phonology of English can improve the student's understanding of native speakers of English. Similarly, the English of non-native speakers can be more easily understood if the student has some knowledge of how the phonetics and phonology of the non-native speakers' language works.

This kind of phonetic knowledge shows us why speakers of certain languages typically make certain kinds of mistakes.

Teaching

Phonetics and phonology are also important for teachers of English. They can help teachers to understand the ways in which their pupils are pronouncing wrongly and they allow them to offer suggestions for the improvement of a pupil's pronunciation.

2 Phonetics

1 Preliminaries

Goals

We said above that phonetics is the study of the physical properties of speech sounds. We must note carefully that we are not concerned here with the letters with which words are written but with the sounds which the letters stand for. The goals of phonetics are to determine and describe the properties of these sounds, how they are produced, how they pass physically from one person to another and how the speaker and the listener perceive them. For this purpose various kinds of phonetics are required.

2 Kinds of Phonetics

Articulatory

Articulatory Phonetics describes sounds with regard to the organs of speech, such as the lips, the tongue, the teeth, etc. We see which organs of speech are used to produce a certain sound, how they are manipulated, where they are moved to.

Acoustic

Acoustic Phonetics is concerned with what happens in the air between the speaker and the listener; in other words it is the study of the acoustic properties of speech sounds. For this, phoneticians use various kinds of technical apparatus, such as the sonograph, a kind of acoustic spectrograph, which analyses sound into its component frequencies and produces a graphical record of the results.

Auditory	**Auditory Phonetics** deals with the question of how sounds are perceived by the ear of the speaker or listener, what people think they hear, how the brain distinguishes sounds, how the brain segments sounds into understandable units. For example, if I replace the initial sound of the word *glass* by a *d* sound when I ask a native speaker of English *Would you like a **d**lass of beer?*, he will probably not notice that I have mispronounced the word *glass*, as his brain will have processed the erroneous initial sound as the *g* sound which he knows from experience to be at the beginning of this word.
Question	Another important question which can be asked here is: by what processes do people understand language? Clues and answers to this question may be given by the study of aphasia (the sudden loss of speech, e. g. through an accident to the brain), or by the study of how we learn our mother language or a foreign language as a child or as an adult. Other useful information can be gained from experiments on producing the sounds of a language synthetically, e. g. so as to make computers able to speak. Interesting as all these different kinds of phonetics are, we shall only have time and space to deal with one of them, namely articulatory phonetics, the most useful kind for students of English.

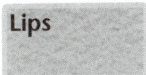 Articulatory Phonetics

1 Organs of Speech

Location	If we look on page 10 at the diagram of a head, nose and throat, we can distinguish eight parts which are important in the production of speech. Moving from the front of the mouth to the back, we find (1) the **lips**, (2) the **teeth**, (3) the **teeth-ridge** (a bump or protrusion of bone just behind the upper teeth), (4) the **hard palate** (the hard part of the roof of the mouth), (5) the **soft palate** (the soft part of the roof of the mouth) which ends in (6) the **uvula**. Behind the lower teeth lies (7) the **tongue**, and in the throat, inside the larynx (a hollow structure of cartilage and muscle forming the upper part of the air passage to and from the lungs) we have (8) the **vocal cords.**
Lips	The lips are used for consonants like [p] and [b][1], for the English semivowel [w] as in <u>w</u>ood or for rounded vowel sounds such as [u:] in the English word t<u>oo</u> or such as [ɔ:] in the English word l<u>aw</u>.

---

1 The phonetic symbols for sounds are usually written between square brackets. They should not be confused with letters used in the spelling of words.

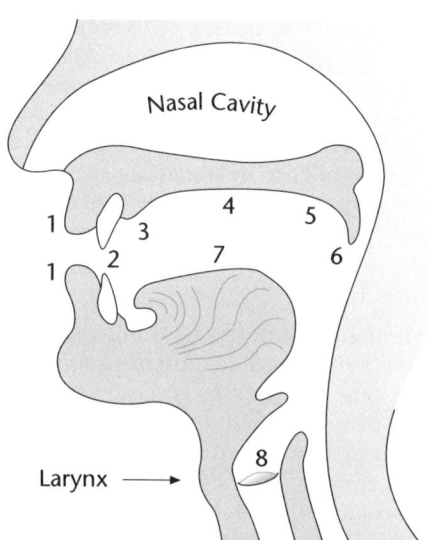

The lower lip in combination with the upper teeth can be used to produce the consonants [f] or [v] as in the words _fat_ or _very_.

Teeth   The teeth are needed for sounds like [θ] and [ð] where the tip of the tongue is placed between the teeth to make the initial sound of the words _thin_ and _then_ respectively.

Teeth-ridge   The teeth-ridge is a bony ridge immediately behind the upper teeth, containing their roots. As we shall see later, it is useful for the production of a large number of sounds such as [t], [d], [s], [z], [l] and [n], which are formed here with the help of the tip or blade of the tongue.

Hard Palate   The hard palate is the hard front part of the roof of the mouth, behind the teeth-ridge. The only English sound which is made on the hard palate is [j], the sound we hear at the beginning of _young_.

Soft Palate   The soft palate is the soft back part of the roof of the mouth and is important for the production of the nasal sounds [n] and [m], heard initially in the words _not_, _map_, and for the production of [ŋ], often spelt _ng_ in English and heard finally in the word _sing_. When the soft palate is lowered away from the wall at the back of the mouth, air from the lungs can escape through the nose producing the characteristic nasal quality of nasal sounds. In addition to nasal consonants some languages like French, Portuguese or Polish have nasalized vowels, which are also produced with the soft palate lowered. Nasalized vowels are not characteristic of English, though in American speech a vowel which occurs beside a nasal consonant is usually slightly nasalized.

Uvula

The uvula is the fleshy extension of the soft palate which can be seen hanging down at the back of the mouth when the mouth is opened wide. It can be made to vibrate as in the rolled *r* of Standard German, e. g. in the word d*rei (= three)*, but it is not used for any of the sounds in Standard English. This uvular *r* is heard, however, in place of the standard *r*-sound in some dialects of English, e. g. Geordie, which is spoken in Newcastle on the coast of northeast England.

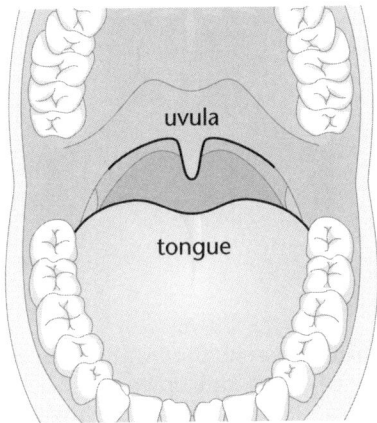

Tongue

Of all the organs of speech the tongue is probably the most useful. As it is very flexible, it can be moved around very easily and placed on other organs of speech to produce various consonants; in order to form vowels, the front, back and central parts of it can be raised to various heights without touching the roof of the mouth. When we come later to the classification of speech sounds it will be convenient to have some technical terms for the various parts of the tongue. The names for these can be seen in the diagrams on page 12. They are self-explanatory, but it should be noted that rather confusingly the front of the tongue is farther back than the blade of the tongue. The root plays no role in the production of speech sounds.

Vocal cords

The vocal cords are two pairs of membranes stretched across the larynx. It is only the lower pair which are used in speech. When these are held close together and air from the lungs is forced out through them they produce voice, just as when a child folds over a leaf and blows into it, noise is produced by the vibration of the edges of the leaf. The voicing produced by the vibrations of the vocal cords is very important as it is used by languages to distinguish between voiced and voiceless sounds, e. g. [p] and [b] differ from each other only insofar as the first sound is said with no vibrations of the vocal cords, whereas for the second sound they must vibrate. Theoretically, any sound which is voiced can also be made voiceless, but in most languages some sounds have no voiceless counterparts. Thus in English there are only voiced nasal sounds, like [n] and [m] which are always said with the vocal cords vibrating, and there are no corresponding voiceless nasal counterparts.

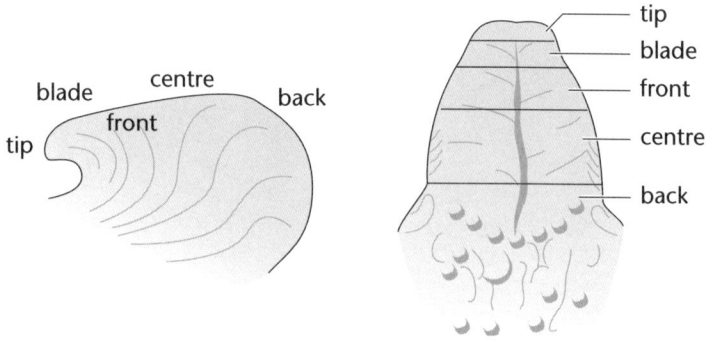

We can represent the vocal cords systematically, as seen from above when we look down the inside of the larynx. The diagram below shows three states of the **glottis** (the space between the vocal cords): with the vocal cords wide open as for normal breathing, with them closed and vibrating to produce voice, and with the back end of them slightly opened to produce whisper.

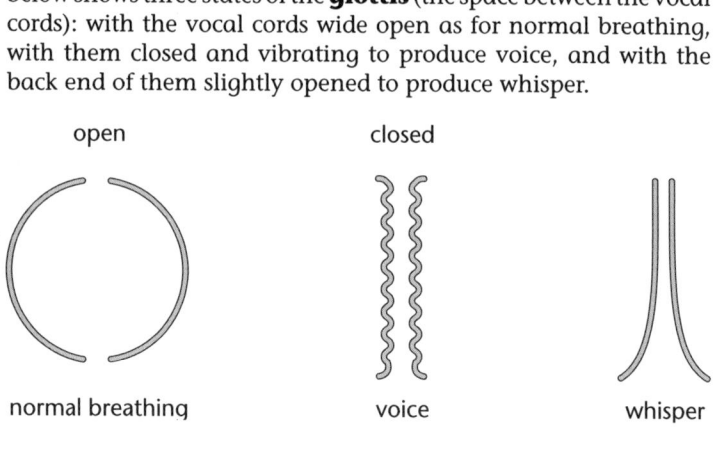

open	closed	
normal breathing	voice	whisper

2 Active and Passive Articulators

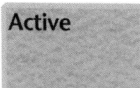

As we have seen above, some of the speech organs (or articulators, as they are usually called in this context) are controllable and can be actively moved. For example, the lips can be rounded, opened or placed together. The tongue can be raised to touch the teeth or various parts of the roof of the mouth. The vocal cords and the uvula can be made to vibrate. The soft palate can be lowered to produce nasal sounds or raised to produce oral (non-nasal) sounds.

Passive Other speech organs (the so-called passive articulators) are not movable and cannot be voluntarily controlled. These are the teeth, the teeth-ridge and the hard palate.

All these articulators are set out in the table below with the alternative names which are given to some of them. The numbers are from Diagram 1 on page 10.

Summary
Active articulators
1 lips
5 soft palate (velum)
6 uvula
7 tongue
8 vocal cords (vocal folds)

} All movable
All controllable

Passive Articulators
2 teeth
3 teeth-ridge (alveolar ridge, alveolum)
4 hard palate

} Not movable
Not controllable

After these general remarks, we are now in a position to make a detailed systematic examination of the various kinds of speech sounds and of the role which speech organs play in producing them.

Primary Function Before we do this, however, it must be pointed out that speech is not really the primary function of these organs. Long before speech and language were evolved, human beings used their lips for sucking and blowing and their tongues for moving food around beneath their teeth or for removing particles of food which had become lodged between their teeth. The teeth are primarily there for us to be able to bite off and chew food. We raise our soft palate to block off the entry to the nasal cavity primarily to prevent food from getting into our noses when we eat or swallow. And even though the vocal cords are more frequently used by humans now for producing voice, their primary function is to cut off the air leaving the lungs, so that we can strain (hold our breath), for example when we want to lift something heavy.

4 Classification of Speech Sounds

1 General Remarks

Broad Classification
The broadest classification of speech sounds is into **consonants**, **vowels** and **semivowels**.

Vowels
Vowels are sounds produced by opening the lips, vibrating the vocal cords, and raising various parts of the tongue to various heights in the mouth with no obstruction anywhere, i.e. with none of the articulators touching another. Vowels typically form the central, pulse-bearing part of syllables.

Consonants
Consonants, on the other hand, must be produced with some kind of obstruction, e. g. lip against lip (as for [p]), tongue between teeth (as for [θ]), tongue against teeth-ridge (as for [t] or [s]), tongue against soft palate (as for [k]). The obstruction may be complete and thus prevent lung air from leaving the mouth altogether for a moment (as when we say [p, t, k]) or it may be only partial so that the lung air can only escape with difficulty through a narrowly confined space and in so doing produces audible friction (as when we say [θ, s]).

Semivowels
Semivowels (also called glides) are sounds like [j] and [w] (heard at the beginning of *yes* and *wet* respectively), which have some of the characteristics of consonants and some of vowels. Like consonants they are found typically at the margins of syllables, i.e. on either side of a vowel, but they are vowel-like in the way they are produced. For example, if we artificially lengthen the initial sound of *yes* we get something close to the long vowel sound [i:] heard in the word *seen*, or if we similarly lengthen the [w] at the beginning of *wet*, it becomes the long vowel [u:] heard in *soon*.

Some languages treat semivowels as if they were consonants, others as if they were vowels. In English the form of the indefinite article before a consonant is *a*, but before a vowel *an*, e. g. *a tree* but *an egg*. If we look to see what happens when we use an indefinite article before a word beginning with a semivowel, we find that the form *a* is used, as in front of consonants, e. g. *a watch*, *a youth*, *a university*[2]. In French, on the other hand, semivowels are treated as vowels. The *n* of the French indefinite article *un* is silent before a consonant, e. g. *un choeur* [œ̃ kœr] *(= a chorus, choir)*, but not before a vowel, e. g. *un oeuf* [œ̃n œf] *(= an egg)*. When the article precedes a semivowel, the latter is treated as a vowel and pronounced with the *n*, e. g. *un oiseau* [œ̃n wazo] *(= a bird)*.

2 Phonetic Symbols

Need for Symbols

By now it will have become clear to the reader who is a beginner in phonetics that it is not easy to talk about sounds on paper unless we have some fixed way of referring to them. What we need is a set of symbols for consonants, semivowels and vowels where each symbol always stands for the same sound. In English spelling, the same sound can be represented by many different letters, or combinations of letters, e. g. the [iː] sound is spelt differently in each of the words *meet, meat, belief, conceive, concede*; similarly the same [t] sound which is spelt with a *t* at the beginning of the word *time* appears at the beginning of *thyme* and *Thames* spelt with *th*. On the other hand, the same spelling may represent many different sounds *(bread, bean* or *labour, land, above, what)*. This is very confusing. In phonetics, therefore, one sound must be represented by only one symbol and that symbol must always represent the same sound.

Symbols for English

We have already seen a few of these symbols in the paragraphs above. Now is the time (before undertaking a detailed classification of English sounds) to introduce the basic phonetic symbols for English consonants, semivowels and vowels. In the chart below, the phonetic symbols are placed in square brackets. They are not listed alphabetically, but divided into groups according to how they are produced phonetically. This will be the order in which we shall discuss their classification. Beside each symbol keywords are given showing underlined the commonest letter or combination of letters used for their spelling in British English. American pronunciations will be dealt with later. In accordance with our practice so far, these spellings (key words) are written in italics to differentiate them from phonetic script (in square brackets). Sometimes the phonetic sound is hidden in the spelling and cannot be underlined separately; e. g. in the word *use* the semivowel [j] at the beginning is combined with the sound [uː] in the single letter *u* of the spelling. In this case the letter containing both sounds has been underlined.

A phonetic symbol which is also used as a letter of the alphabet has the same name as that letter. The names of difficult symbols have been written in parentheses after the keywords. Alternative names are given in separate parentheses preceded by =.

---

2 Note that the semivowel [j] is hidden in the spelling. The word *university* is written with the vowel letter *u* initially, but phonetically it begins with the semivowel [j].

Chart 1	Symbols	Spellings	(Name)
	Consonants		
	1 [p]	_p_ack, ha_pp_y	
	2 [b]	_b_ig, lo_bb_y	
	3 [t]	_t_ip, le_tt_er, _Th_omas	
	4 [d]	_d_ig, la_dd_er	
	5 [k]	_c_o_ck_, a_cc_ount, _k_ill, _ch_aos, uni_qu_e	
	6 [g]	_g_un, e_gg_, _gh_ost, _gu_ess	
	7 [f]	_f_un, o_ff_, _ph_otogra_ph_, rou_gh_	
	8 [v]	_v_ery, Step_h_en, o_f_	
	9 [θ]	_th_ick, leng_th_	(theta)
	10 [ð]	_th_is, wor_th_y	(eth) = (edh)
	11 [s]	_s_un, pa_ss_, ni_c_e, _sc_ent	
	12 [z]	_z_oo, di_zz_y, wa_s_	
	13 [ʃ]	_sh_op, _s_ugar, na_ti_on, o_c_ean, cons_ci_ous, ten_si_on, mi_ssi_on, ma_ch_ine	(esh)
	14 [ʒ]	trea_s_ure, explo_si_on, u_s_ual, a_z_ure	(zhee) = (yogh)
	15 [h]	_h_ope, _wh_o	
	16 [tʃ]	_ch_ip, fe_tch_, _c_ello	(t, esh)
	17 [dʒ]	ju_dg_e, _g_entle, exa_gg_erate, a_dj_ective	(d, zhee)
	18 [m]	_m_y, ha_mm_er	
	19 [n]	_n_o, fu_nn_y	
	20 [ŋ]	si_ng_, u_n_cle	(eng)
	21 [l]	_l_ift, hi_ll_	
	22 [r]	_r_ed, che_rr_y	
	Semivowels		
	23 [w]	_w_et, q_u_een, _wh_y	
	24 [j]	_y_es, hidden in _u_se, f_ew_, f_eu_dal	
	Vowels (Monophthongs)		
	25 [i:]	b_e_, s_ee_, l_ea_ve, s_ei_ze, bel_ie_ve, p_eo_ple, encyclop_ae_dia, _oe_strogen	(i, colon)
	26 [ɪ]	h_i_t, w_o_men, carr_i_ed, s_y_mbol, handkerch_ie_f, b_u_sy, bisc_ui_t	(small capital i)
	27 [e]	m_e_t, s_ai_d, d_ea_d, _a_ny, fr_ie_nd, b_u_ry, G_eo_ffrey	

plosives

fricatives

affricates

nasals

long vowel sound (:)

long vowel

friend

Phonetics and Phonology

28 [æ]	f*a*t, pl*ai*t	(ash)
29 [ɜː]	h*er*, f*ir*, b*ur*n, w*or*d, j*our*ney	(reversed epsilon, colon)
30 [ə]	*a*bout, th*e*, p*er*haps, p*o*lite, s*ur*prise, fig*ure*	(shwa)
31 [ʌ]	f*u*n, s*o*n, bl*oo*d, c*ou*ntry	(inverted v)
32 [ɑː]	l*a*st, *au*nt, cl*er*k, h*ear*t	(script a, colon)
33 [ɒ]	st*o*p, c*ou*gh, kn*ow*ledge, wh*a*t, bec*au*se	(reversed script a)
34 [ɔː]	*a*ll, t*au*ght, s*aw*, f*ou*ght, d*oor*, f*or*d, b*o*red, b*oar*d	(open o)
35 [ʊ]	p*u*t, w*o*man, t*oo*k, w*ou*ld	(u without a tail) = (upsilon)
36 [uː]	d*o*, s*oo*n, w*ou*nd, f*ew*, n*eu*ter, s*ui*t	(u with a tail, colon)

Vowels (Diphthongs)		
37 [eɪ]	p*ay*, p*ai*d, l*a*ke, sk*ei*n, pr*ey*, gr*ea*t	(e, small capital i)
38 [aɪ]	l*i*ke, m*y*, t*ie*, d*ye*, n*ei*ther	(lower case a, small capital i)
39 [ɔɪ]	b*oi*l, b*oy*	(open o, small capital i)
40 [əʊ]	n*o*, l*oa*d, t*oe*, bel*ow*, br*oo*ch	(shwa, u without a tail)
41 [aʊ]	n*ou*n, t*ow*n, pl*ough*	(a, u without a tail)
42 [ɪə]	st*eer*, *ear*, h*ere*, w*eir*d, p*ier*ce	(small capital i, shwa)
43 [eə]	st*are*, th*ere*, th*eir*, b*ear*, h*air*	(e, shwa)
44 [ʊə]	s*ure*, p*oor*, t*our*	(u without a tail, shwa)

The symbols given above are those of the International Phonetic Association (IPA), which are used to indicate pronunciation in most British and European dictionaries and books on phonetics and phonology.

5 Detailed Classification of English Consonants and Semivowels

General Remarks

If we wish to refer to a particular consonant sound so that another person knows exactly which one we mean, we need a unique description which cannot be confused with that for any other consonant. In phonetics this can be achieved by using **four parameters** or characteristics, which play an important role in the production of consonants.

Parameters

Manner of Articulation
(How is the sound produced? With an obstruction in the mouth? With friction caused by escaping lung air?
Through the nose? Down the sides of the tongue? etc.)
Voiceless versus Voiced
(Is the sound said without or with vibration of the vocal cords?)
Fortis versus Lenis
(Is the sound said with relatively strong tension in the muscles of the mouth and throat and with relatively strong breath force or are both relatively weak?)
Place of Articulation
(Where is the sound produced, using which organs of speech?)

Let us now consider each of these parameters in detail and look at the kinds of English consonants to which they can refer.

1 Manner of Articulation

Kinds of Consonant

It will be convenient to differentiate between seven different kinds of consonants according to the manner in which they are articulated; and since semivowels are treated as consonants in English we can add these as an eighth kind:

1 **plosives**, 2 **fricatives**, 3 **affricates**, 4 **r-sounds**, 5 **laterals**, 6 **nasals**, 7 **frictionless continuants**, 8 **semivowels**

Plosives

Starting at the front of the mouth and working backwards along the roof, we can look first at sounds 1-6 in the chart on page 16. These are the so-called **plosives** or **stops.** They are produced by blocking the air expelled from the lungs at the lips for [p, b], at the teeth-ridge for [t, d], and at the soft palate for [k, g]. The air builds up pressure behind the lips or the tongue at these points and when the pressure is strong enough it is released with a small explosion (or 'popping' sound). In phonetics this is referred to as a **plosion**, hence the name: **plosive manner of articulation**:

Plosives [p   t   k]
            [b   d   g]

Glottal Stop

Although in English it is used only in very emphatic speech before word-initial vowels, we could also add to this chart the plosive produced by completely closing the space between the vocal cords (the so-called *glottis*) and then by releasing with a plosion the air trapped behind the closure. This plosive is usually referred to as the *glottal stop* and is written in phonetics with the symbol [ʔ]. On the first page of this book we encountered this sound at the beginning of each word in the German sentence *Anna aß ein Ei*.

Fricatives

Fricatives are the sounds 7–15 in the chart on page 16. Unlike the plosives, they are not produced with a complete closure at some point in the mouth but with only a partial blockage. The air from the lungs is not completely held back, but escapes with difficulty through a narrow opening, generating friction in the process. Starting at the front of the mouth we find [f, v] produced with this **fricative manner of articulation**: a small part of the bottom lip is placed just under the top teeth and air from the lungs is forced between them causing friction. Similarly, the tip of the tongue can be placed between the upper and lower teeth so that it touches both, and lung air can be forced over the tongue between it and the upper teeth producing the two fricative sounds [θ, ð] heard in *thin* and *thus* respectively. Farther back in the mouth, the blade of the tongue can be raised to the teeth-ridge leaving only a narrow space between the two, through which air can be forced to generate friction. This gives us another pair of fricative sounds [s, z] as in *miss* and *froze* respectively. Farther back still along the roof of the mouth, a little before we reach the position for [j] (No. 24 in the chart), air can be forced over the blade or front of the raised tongue giving us the fricative pair [ʃ, ʒ] as in *wish* and *leisure* respectively. Finally, the vocal cords can be pressed together, not completely so as to produce the closure we called the glottal stop, but close enough to produce the fricative sound [h] as in *hop*.

There are two other fricative sounds which we could mention here: [ç] (called: c cedilla) and [x]. The sound [ç] is heard regularly in Standard German as the final sound in words like *ich, weich, Pech* and it sometimes replaces [hj] in English at the beginning of words like *huge, humid, humour*. The sound [x] is also common in German, e. g. as the final sound in *hoch*, but in English it occurs only in words borrowed from other languages, e. g. word-finally in *loch* (Scottish: *Loch Ness*) or in the name of the German composer *Bach*.

Fricatives
[f   θ   s   ʃ   ç   x   h]
[v   ð   z   ʒ   ]

Affricates	The **affricate manner of articulation** is a combination of plosive and fricative. Affricates are single sounds but they begin as plosives and continue as fricatives. For this reason they are usually represented phonetically by two symbols, the first representing the initial plosive and the second representing the fricative. English possesses only two affricates: [tʃ] and [dʒ] (Nos. 16 and 17 in the chart on page 16), which can be heard at the beginning of *chop* and *job* respectively. As we shall see later when we look at places of articulation, the plosive-like beginning of [tʃ] and [dʒ] are not pronounced with the tip of the tongue on the teeth-ridge as for the normal plosives [t] and [d] but with the blade or front of the tongue forming first a complete closure at a position along the roof of the mouth a little before the position for [j]. Then in this so-called alveo-palatal position the tongue is pulled away from the roof of the mouth just enough for each affricate to continue with the fricative quality of [ʃ] and [ʒ] respectively. To emphasize that this is only one process and not two, the phonetic symbols for each affricate are often written together as a ligature [ʧ, ʤ] and not as two separate symbols for each sound [tʃ, dʒ].

We may note that German is richer in affricates than English: in addition to [tʃ], German has [pf] as in *Pferd*, and [ts] as in *zehn*.

Affricates English: [tʃ]   German: [pf]   [ts]   [tʃ]
[dʒ]

***r*-Sounds**	The manner of articulation to which we are referring here is associated only with kinds of *r* which are not characteristic of Standard British or American pronunciation. These are the **rolls** (= **trills**) and **flaps**.
rolls	A roll is a series of rapid plosions caused either by vibrating the tip of the tongue for the **lingual roll** (IPA symbol [r]) or by vibrating the uvula for the **uvular roll** (IPA symbol [ʀ], called *small capital r*). The lingual roll is not usually heard in Standard English, but it occurs in dialects such as Scottish and may also be used by singers of classical music to improve comprehension. The uvular roll also is not found in Standard English, but it is common in the speech of some German speakers in words such as *arbeiten*. Other Standard German speakers replace it by a sound with another manner of articulation, the uvular fricative (IPA symbol [ʁ], called *inverted small capital r*).
flaps	The **lingual flap** (IPA symbol [ɾ], called *fish-hook r*) is produced by only one downward and upward movement of the tip of the tongue. In Spanish the rolled lingual *r* and the flapped *r* constitute two different sounds and cause differences of meaning, e. g. *perro* (= *dog*) is said with a lingual roll, whereas *pero* (= *but*) is said with a lingual flap. In Standard English the flapped *r* is used by some

speakers after the fricative [θ] in words like *three, thread, thrust* and also between vowels in words like *very, marry, lorry*. In normal English speech frequent use of the flap often sounds pedantic, as for example if it is used in each word in the phrase *three very merry married heroes*, but it can be heard on the stage from the mouths of actors who wish their speech to be easily comprehensible at a distance.

Although rolls and flaps play a very minor part in English pronunciation, it is important to discuss them and to see how they are articulated since, like the German uvular fricative, they are frequently used by non-native speakers in place of the typical English *r*, which has quite a different manner of articulation as we shall see below.

Rolls lingual: [r][3]   uvular: [ʀ]
Flap lingual: [ɾ]

Laterals

Sounds pronounced with a **lateral manner of articulation** are the *l* sounds. Here a partial closure is made with the tip or blade of the tongue at the teeth-ridge with the air-stream escaping either on one side or both sides of the tongue. In English there is only one *l* sound (No. 21 in the chart on page 16), but it has two variants depending on the context in which it occurs: one is the so-called **clear** *l*, which is always heard before a vowel as in the words *leave* or *hollow*, and the other is the so-called **dark** *l*, which occurs everywhere else, e. g. before a consonant or at the end of a word before a silence, as in the words *held* and *fall*.

Clear & Dark *l*

The clear *l* is pronounced with the back of the tongue in its normal low position, whereas the dark *l* is pronounced with the back of the tongue raised. Thus the dark *l* sounds as if one were articulating an [ʊ] (the vowel in *put*) at the same time. This [ʊ]-coloured *l* is written in phonetics with a swung dash (a wavy line, called a *tilde*) through the middle of it [ɫ] and the symbol is called *tilde l*. Most European languages use only the clear variant of *l*, e. g. German, French, Spanish, Italian, but the dark variety can be heard too, e. g. in the Cologne dialect of German.

It is important for students to be able to differentiate between these two variants of [l], as the wrong use of them makes English pronunciation sound foreign.

---

3 It should be noted that the symbol [r], used correctly here for the lingual *r*, is often used laxly in the phonetic transcription of English for the frictionless continuant *r*, the typical English *r*-sound, which as we shall see below is more accurately written with the symbol [ɹ].

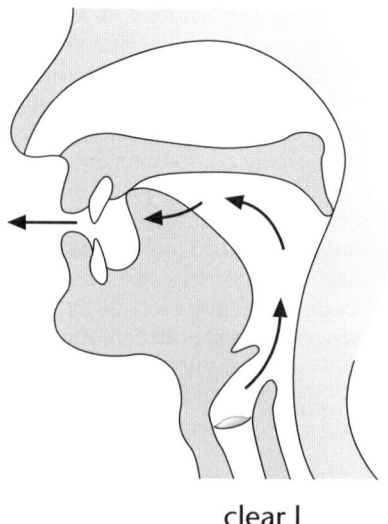

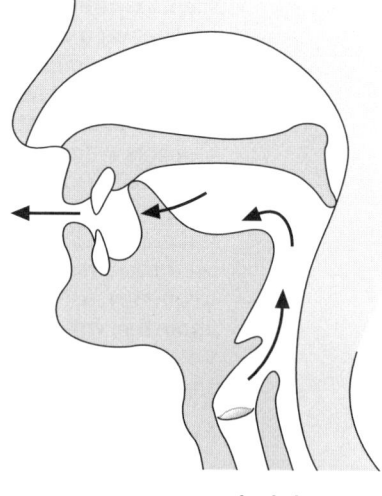

clear l   dark l

Nasals

In our discussion of the organs of speech above we saw that it is the soft palate which is responsible for the **nasal manner of articulation.** When the soft palate is lowered away from the back wall of the mouth the air-stream can escape through the nose giving the characteristic quality which nasal sounds have. In English there are three nasal consonants (Nos. 18, 19, 20 in the chart):

[m] produced by making a closure with both lips, lowering the soft palate and allowing the air-stream to pass through the nose;

[n] produced in the same way except that the closure is made with the tip of the tongue on the teeth-ridge; and

[ŋ] similarly except that the closure here is made with the back of the tongue on the lowered soft palate.

Many languages, e. g. French, Spanish, Italian, have another nasal consonant which has the closure on the hard palate, producing a palatalized n, which sounds as if it has a little [j] after it and which is symbolized in phonetics as [ɲ]. This is heard in French *oignon*, Spanish *señor*, Italian *montagna*. The sound does occur in English, but is treated as a combination of [n] + [j] both in phonetics and in the spelling, e. g. [kænjən] *canyon*, [ʌnjən] *onion*.

Nasals [m n (ɲ) ŋ]

Frictionless Continuants

We shall use the term **frictionless continuant** to describe the manner of articulation of the English r, not to be confused with the r-sounds we talked about above. Frictionless continuants are not produced with the amount of closure characteristic of other consonants and, as their name says, no friction is generated dur-

CHAPTER **1** Phonetics and Phonology

ing their articulation and their voicing can be made to continue for as long as one wishes. They are also called *approximants* and often made to include the semivowels [j] and [w]. We shall reserve the term *frictionless continuant* just for the *r*-sound (No. 22 in the chart) and consider the semivowels as a separate manner of articulation. In fact, like [j] and [w], the English *r*-sound has a vowel-like quality and is produced by articulating the non-rounded vowel heard in *bird* while at the same time curling back the tip of the tongue to a position just behind the teeth-ridge. No contact is made, however, between the tongue and the roof of the mouth. The correct IPA symbol for this sound is [ɹ] (called *turned r*), but for convenience English phoneticians and the makers of English dictionaries often replace it by [r], as we have done in the chart on page 16.

Frictionless Continuant [ɹ]
usually written in English phonetics as [r]

Semivowels As we saw above, the two English semivowels [j] and [w] (Nos. 23 and 24 in the chart) are both approximants and vowel-like, with the tongue position for [j] a little higher than for the vowel [iː] (which we can hear in *seen*), and for [w] a little higher than for [uː] (the vowel we hear in *soon*), but with no contact between the tongue and the roof of the mouth. When we come to look at the phonology of English we shall discover that these two sounds also have consonantal variants which are fricative.

Semivowels [j w]

It is now time for us to turn to the second of the four parameters needed for the classification of consonants and semivowels.

2 Voiceless versus Voiced

Voicing The **parameter of voicing** (whether a sound is said with or without voice) plays a very important role in phonetics. When we discussed the function of the vocal cords earlier we noted that any sound which can be articulated **with the vocal cords vibrating** can also be said **with no vibrations**. In most languages there are pairs of consonants which make differences in meaning but which differ only in being said without or with voice. Thus the words *pig* and *big* each begin with a plosive made with both lips but in the first word this sound is voiceless whereas in the second it is voiced.

Although this parameter is used in all languages, it is not always easy for the beginner in phonetics to hear the difference between voiceless and voiced clearly. At this point it will therefore be useful to give a few tips on how to make the distinction more prominent.

Test

Let us begin with the fricative pair [s] and [z]. As fricatives can be produced for as long as we can expel air from the lungs, we can also sing them on various notes if they are voiced. Thus we can stretch out [z] over the first line of the English national anthem, singing a continuous [z] in place of the words *God save our gracious Queen* and the melody can be clearly heard. If we try doing the same thing for [s], the familiar melody cannot be heard, because the sound is voiceless.

Test

Another test is to repeat a pair of voiceless and voiced fricatives one after another several times in one breath, at the same time holding a finger in each ear: [s z s z s z]. For the [s] one can only hear the friction between the tongue and the teeth-ridge, but for the [z] there is a surprisingly loud booming noise in the ears, rather like the fog-horn of an ocean-going ship. This is the vibration of the vocal cords, namely voice. The experiment can be repeated with pairs such as [f v], [θ ð] and [ʃ ʒ] with the same result.

Test

For plosive sounds this test does not work as the plosion is momentary and the sound cannot be extended. However, one can produce the voicing of a voiced sound for a short while before the plosion is made. This pre-voicing sounds rather strange, a little as if one is trying to vomit: thus to pronounce a [b] in this way, one vibrates the vocal cords keeping the lips closed and at the same time gradually blowing out the cheeks until the plosion. In this way one can clearly hear the voicing before the air escapes between the lips. This cannot be done for the voiceless counterpart [p]: when the cheeks are blown out, no voicing is audible. This pre-voicing test is possible for both the other plosive pairs [t d] and [k g] and for the affricate pair [tʃ dʒ], though the cheeks cannot be blown out for these.

Distinctive Voicing

The attentive student will have noticed that in our discussion of the various manners of articulation on pages 19–20, we listed the consonants showing each manner in pairs with one sound below the other, e. g. with [b] below [p], [d] below [t], and [g] below [k] in the list of plosive consonants, and similarly with the lists for fricatives and affricates. In each case the upper member of the pair is voiceless and the lower voiced.

Non-Distinctive Voicing

When we come to the phonology of English we shall see that in some of the manners of articulation, e. g. lateral, frictionless continuant and semivowels, the sounds usually occur voiced but they may have voiceless variants which do not, however, make differences in meaning of the kind we saw with [p] and [b] in *pig* and *big*. In the case of the English nasals, these sounds occur only in a voiced form and there are no voiceless variants.

3 Fortis versus Lenis

Intensity of Articulation

This third parameter is the most difficult to perceive, as it is connected with the intensity of the articulation. In English, voiceless sounds are said with much greater tenseness in the muscles of the mouth, tongue and throat, and with relatively strong breath force. Voiced sounds, on the other hand, are pronounced with weaker tenseness and weaker breath force. The technical terms used in phonetics to indicate this difference are taken from Latin: **fortis** *(= strong)* and **lenis** *(= weak)*.

Need for Fortis/Lenis

As this distinction is coupled with voicelessness and voicedness in English, one might think at first that the parameter of fortis versus lenis is not really necessary. However, there are situations where distinguishing between fortis and lenis articulation is the only way to keep two consonant sounds apart. This happens when speech is whispered, i.e. articulated with a special use of the vocal cords without any vibrations to produce voicing. If I whisper the two words *pig*, *big* alternately several times and concentrate my attention on the initial consonant, I can feel the difference in intensity quite clearly. In whispering, the [p] and [b] are no longer differentiated by being voiceless and voiced respectively but by being fortis and lenis respectively. Another situation where fortis and lenis articulation is all that keeps two consonants apart is when the two affricate consonants [tʃ] and [dʒ] occur before silence, as when the words *larch* and *large* are said in isolation. Here the final [dʒ] of *large* becomes totally devoiced, i.e. it is now voiceless like the [tʃ] in *larch*, but remains lenis whereas [tʃ] is fortis.

4 Place of Articulation

Ordered Groups

If we look again at the numbered phonetic symbols for consonants in the chart beginning on page 16, we can see that they are not only arranged in pairs according to whether they are voiceless or voiced, and not only in groups according to their manner of articulation, but also according to their **place of articulation**. In order to be able to consider these groups in detail, let us make a list of the various places of articulation, showing the English consonants which are produced there with their manner of articulation and their voicing.

Chart 2	Place of Articulation	Manner	Voicing	
	1 **labial**	plosive	voiceless	[p]
			voiced	[b]
		nasal	voiced	[m]
		semivowel	voiced	[w]
		(	voiceless	[w̥])
	2 **labiodental**	fricative	voiceless	[f]
			voiced	[v]
	3 **dental**	fricative	voiceless	[θ]
			voiced	[ð]
	4 **alveolar**	plosive	voiceless	[t]
			voiced	[d]
		fricative	voiceless	[s]
			voiced	[z]
		(lingual roll	voiced	[r])
		(lingual flap	voiced	[ɾ])
		lateral	voiced	[l]
		nasal	voiced	[n]
	5 **post-alveolar**	frictionless continuant	voiced	[ɹ]
	6 **palato-alveolar**	fricative	voiceless	[ʃ]
			voiced	[ʒ]
		affricate	voiceless	[tʃ]
			voiced	[dʒ]
	7 **palatal**	semivowel	voiced	[j]
		(fricative	voiceless	[ç])
	8 **velar**	plosive	voiceless	[k]
			voiced	[g]
		(fricative	voiceless	[x])
		nasal	voiced	[ŋ]
	(9 **uvular**	roll	voiced	[ʀ])
		(fricative	voiceless	[ʁ)
	10 **glottal**	(stop	voiceless	[ʔ])
		fricative	voiceless	[h]

In the list above we have put brackets around those consonants or their variants which are not usual in Standard English or which are found only in dialect speech.

Labial

The **labial place of articulation** needs little explanation. Sounds which are formed at the **lips** are called labial sounds, and when **both lips** are involved it is customary to call them **bilabial**.

[p, b]

The chart above shows us that English possesses both a voiceless and a voiced bilabial plosive, namely [p] and [b], where the air-stream from the lungs is expelled orally.

[m]	It also possesses a voiced bilabial nasal [m], where the soft palate is lowered and the air-stream escapes through the nose. The close relationship between the oral voiced bilabial and the nasal voiced bilabial can be clearly heard when a person has a heavy cold and the soft palate and the back wall of the mouth are inflamed and swollen. The soft palate can no longer be lowered, with the result that no air can pass through the nose, and the nasal consonants are therefore replaced by oral ones: so for a sentence like *I'm coming tomorrow* we hear something like *I'b cubbing toborrow*.
[w, ẉ]	Another bilabial sound is the voiced semivowel [w], which is said with strong rounding of the lips. There is also a voiceless variety of this sound, which is used in Scottish dialects and some kinds of American English wherever the spelling *wh* occurs. In these cases it really constitutes a new sound since the difference in voicing is all that distinguishes between words such as *witch* [wɪtʃ] and *which* [ẉ ɪtʃ]. This same voiceless bilabial semivowel can sometimes also be heard for the *wh* spelling in very formal English and on the stage. It can be written phonetically with a special symbol, an inverted *w* [ʍ], or, as in the list above, the semivowel can be shown to be voiceless by writing a small ring below it [ẉ].
Diacritics	Symbols, like the small ring, which are written above or below a phonetic symbol, are referred to as diacritic symbols or **diacritics**.
Labiodental	**Labiodental** is the term for the place of articulation of those sounds which are made with the **lower lip** against the bottom of the **upper teeth**.
[f, v]	As we see in the chart, there are only fricative labiodentals in English: [f] and [v] (as in *fine* and *vine* respectively). Usually we can tell from English spelling which one is to be pronounced: the letter *v* in a word always indicates the voiced labiodental fricative [v], whereas the voiceless labiodental fricative is represented by *f*, *ff* or *ph* (see chart 1 on page 16). Note, however, the common little word *of*, which is the only one in the language where an *f* in the spelling is pronounced [v], and the word *nephew*, where we can sometimes hear the older pronunciation with [v] for *ph*, instead of the commoner [f].
Dental	**Dental** sounds are pronounced with the tip of the tongue either **between the teeth** or just **behind the upper teeth**.
[θ, ð]	English has only fricatives at this place of articulation and these are both **interdental**: voiceless [θ] and voiced [ð] (as in *through* and *though* respectively).
Others	There are, however, some variants of the voiceless and voiced alveolar plosives [t] and [d] and of the voiced alveolar nasal [n] in Eng-

lish which are formed behind the upper teeth instead of on the teeth-ridge. We can indicate these dental variants in phonetics by writing under them a diacritic (called *a subscript inverted bridge*) which looks like a small upside-down bridge or goal-post: [t̪], [d̪], [n̪]. Where these occur will be discussed later when we talk about consonant allophones in phonology (see page 91). It is interesting that in the Romance languages like French, Spanish and Italian the dental [t̪], [d̪] and [n̪] are the regular forms and not positional variants as in English.

Alveolar

Of all the places of articulation in English it is the **alveolar** region in which the largest number of consonants are produced. Alveolar consonants occur when the **teeth-ridge** (also called the **alveolum** or **alveolar ridge**) is touched by the tip or blade of the tongue.

[t, d, s, z, l, n]

In our discussion of manners of articulation we noted the voiceless and voiced alveolar plosives [t] and [d], the voiceless and voiced alveolar fricatives [s] and [z], the voiced alveolar lateral [l] with its clear and dark variants, and the voiced alveolar nasal [n]. This nasal sound is related to the voiced alveolar plosive [d] in the same way as the bilabial nasal [m] is related to the voiced bilabial plosive [b]: each pair has identical articulation except that for the nasal sound the soft palate is lowered to allow the air to escape through the nose.

Others

We also noted the voiced alveolar rolled *r* [r], which appears so strikingly in the pronunciation of each *r* and *rr* in the Spanish sentence *Que rapido ruedan las ruedas del ferrocarril (How rapidly the wheels of the railway turn)* and which in Scottish English and sometimes in the singing of English classical music can be heard replacing the usual voiced post-alveolar frictionless continuant *r* [ɹ].

Another uncommon variant of the usual English *r* (which we discussed above under *r*-sounds) is the voiced alveolar lingual flap [ɾ], sometimes heard in a sentence like *Mary married Harry.*

Post-Alveolar

The **post-alveolar** position is one of three places of articulation which lie quite close together between the teeth and the hard palate: alveolar, post-alveolar and palato-alveolar. As rather a large number of English consonants are articulated here, it will make the description of them easier to understand if we look at the diagram on p. 29, which also shows all the other English consonants at their respective places of articulation.

[ɹ]

In this diagram we see that there is only one English consonant that is articulated in the post-alveolar position and that is the common English frictionless continuant *r*-sound [ɹ] (here shown as r). We may recall that it is pronounced with the tip of the tongue raised towards a position on the roof of the mouth **slightly behind the teeth-ridge** (or **alveolum**); hence the term **post-alveolar**. The tongue tip is slightly curled back, but with no contact between the underside of it and the alveolar ridge.

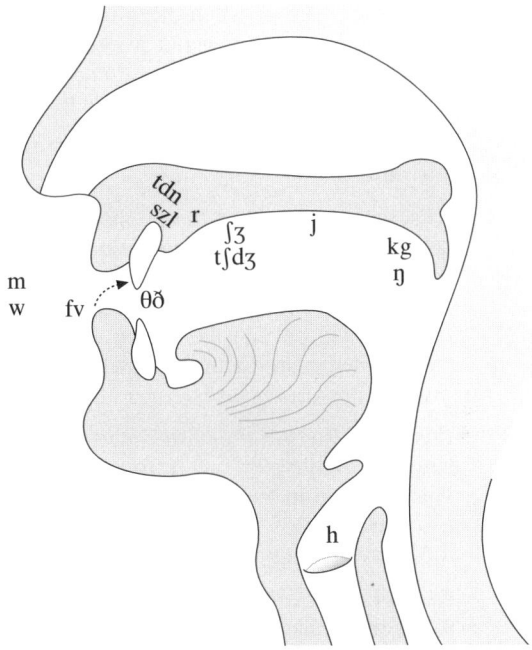

Palato-Alveolar

The place of articulation referred to as **palato-alveolar** lies a little farther back than post-alveolar but just before we come to the palatal area.

[ʃ, ʒ, tʃ, dʒ]

Here we find two pairs of English sounds: the voiceless and voiced fricatives [ʃ] and [ʒ], and the voiceless and voiced affricates [tʃ] and [dʒ], all of which we discussed in detail under their respective manners of articulation.

Palatal

The **hard palate** is the place of articulation of only one English **palatal** sound.

[j]

This is the voiced palatal semivowel [j], which can be seen represented by the letter *y* in the spelling of the word *year*, or by the letter *i* in the spelling of *onion*. The phonetic combination [j] plus the vowel [uː] is frequently spelt with a single letter *u* before one written consonant, as in *stupid*, or before one written consonant followed by the letter *e*, as in *cute* or *use*. When we deal with the phonology of this combination (see Ch. 3, page 112), we shall see that there are some environments in which the alveolar semivowel is dropped by some speakers: thus in place of the [ju:] pronunciation for the *u* in *stupid* [stju:pɪd] we can also hear just [u:]: [stu:pɪd].

| **Others** | Students of Romance languages may also note that the hard palate is the place of articulation for the type of *n* which we referred to under the nasal manner of articulation and which is found in such words as French *agneau (lamb)*, Spanish *niño (boy)* or Italian *signora (Mrs.)* and is written phonetically as [ɲ]. |

| **Velar** | The **soft palate** or **velum** is the farthest back part of the roof of the mouth. |

| **[k, g, ŋ]** | It is here that we find the English voiceless and voiced velar plosives [k] and [g] respectively, and the related voiced velar nasal [ŋ], all three of which can be heard in the word *kangaroo* [kæŋgə'ru:]. We saw that it is not only important as a place of articulation, but also plays a special role in manners of articulation since it can be raised for the production of oral sounds and lowered for the production of nasal sounds. |

| **Others** | It is here also that the voiceless velar fricative [x] is formed, a rare sound in English (heard in the name for Scottish lakes, e. g. *Loch Lomond*, and in some people's pronunciation of the name of the German composer *Bach*), but a common one in many Germanic and Slav languages. |

| **Uvular** | As a place of articulation the **uvular position** is of no importance in English as no sounds in the standard language are produced using the **uvula**, the fleshy, finger-like extension of the soft palate which hangs down at the back of the mouth above the tongue. In some dialect pronunciations, however, the post-alveolar frictionless continuant kind of *r* is replaced by a uvular roll or a uvular fricative, the two sounds which are common pronunciations of the letter *r* in German and French. Foreign learners of English should be warned against using this uvular pronunciation for the English *r*, as it sounds rather unnatural to native speakers. |

| **Glottal** | The **glottis** is the opening between the vocal cords in the larynx and is used for the production of the English *h*-sound. |

| **[h]** | This is phonetically the voiceless glottal fricative [h]. Here the vocal cords are held far enough apart for the airstream from the lungs to escape only with friction. |

| **[ʔ]** | We pointed out in our discussion of plosives under manners of articulation that there is also a glottal plosive, which is usually referred to as the glottal stop [ʔ]. It plays no active role in English, but it can be used to give more emphasis to words beginning with a vowel. If a politician utters the sentence !*I* !*am* !*totally* !*and* !*utterly* |

!*against* !*invasion* !*of* !*an* !*independent country* using the glottal stop where we have written exclamation marks, it sounds as if he is banging the table with his fist as he says each of these words. For this reason it is particularly important for speakers of German, where the glottal stop is normal in front of word-initial vowels in non-emphatic speech, to be careful not to use this sound in that position in English.

Final Remarks

We have now completed our tour of the four parameters needed for the classification of consonants. With their aid we can comfortably refer unambiguously to any individual consonant, and anybody familiar with the parameters will know exactly which sound we mean. So if we talk of the voiceless fortis labiodental fricative this can only be the sound [f] and no other. As was mentioned earlier, the specifications fortis and lenis can usually be left out in English, as naturally voiceless sounds are always fortis and voiced sounds are always lenis. (Note that if a voiced sound loses its voicing, e. g. word-finally, it usually remains lenis, as we shall see in Chapter 3.) If we look again at the specification just given for [f], we see that the usual order of the parameters in a consonant specification is: Voicing, (Fortis/Lenis), Place of Articulation, Manner of Articulation.

Finally we may note that these parameters are useful for defining natural groups of consonants. Using only one parameter we can conveniently refer to large groups of consonants, e. g. with Manner to such natural groups as *the plosives* or *the nasals* in a language, or similarly with the parameter of Place to such natural groups as *the labials* or *the alveolar sounds*. Notice that the more parameters we use, the smaller the group becomes until we eventually reach the individual sound. Thus with two parameters, Place and Manner, we can reduce the larger natural group of all the *plosives* in a language to the rather smaller group of *the bilabial plosives*; and with three parameters, Voicing, Place and Manner, as in *the voiceless bilabial plosive*, we arrive at the individual consonant [p].

Obstruents & Sonorants

Before we leave the topic of consonants and devote our attention to the classification of vowels, we should mention that there are two other useful terms which are often used in the literature of phonetics and phonology to designate broad consonantal groups: obstruent and sonorant. **Obstruents** are those consonants which require some kind of obstruction in the mouth that restricts the air-stream: these are the plosives, the fricatives and the affricates. **Sonorants**, on the other hand, are the voiced speech sounds which are uttered with a comparatively free flow of air through the mouth or nose and include all the remaining speech sounds: namely the nasals, laterals, frictionless continuants, semivowels and also the vowels. This sonorant group is rather large and unwieldy, but it is sometimes very useful to have a phonetic term like *obstruent* to cover the plosives, fricatives, and affricates, which in phonology may all behave together as a group. For instance, the obstruents in English all occur in voiceless and voiced pairs, where the voicing is important for making differences of meaning (compare the pairs *to, do; Sue, zoo; chain, Jane*). The sonorants, on the other hand, are all basically voiced, but if in a certain context a voiceless variant occurs this makes no difference to the meaning (see the discussion of /l, r, j, w/ in Chapter 3).

6 Detailed Classification of Vowels

1 Preliminary Classification

Monoph-thongs/ Diphthongs

Before we consider the phonetic classification of vowels, we must differentiate between **monophthongs** (simple vowels) and **diph-thongs** (vowels which glide from one position to another). Monophthongs are written phonetically with only one symbol e. g. [ɪ] as in *sit*, [ʊ] as in *put*; whereas diphthongs are written with two symbols, the first showing the position from which the vowel starts and the second the position at which it ends, e. g. [aɪ] as in *buy*, [aʊ] as in *loud*.

Let us begin with the monophthongs and postpone our discussion of diphthongs until later.

New Parameters

For **the classification of monophthongs** we shall need a completely different set of parameters from those we used for consonants. It is customary to consider monophthongs in terms of their length, and to ask whether they are pronounced with the front, centre or back of the tongue, whether that part of the tongue is raised to a high or mid position or remains low, and whether they are rounded. For some languages, like French, Portuguese or Polish, it is also important to note whether the vowel is nasal or not.

We can refer to these parameters with the terms set out in the list below, omitting nasality as this plays no role in English.

2 Parameters

Defining Questions

Length of Vowel (Is the vowel long or short?)
Height of Tongue (Is the tongue raised? To what height?)
Part of Tongue (Which part of the tongue is used?)
Lip Rounding (Are the lips rounded or in a neutral position?)

Let us now look at each parameter separately and in detail. As with the parameters for consonants, here too it will be necessary sometimes to anticipate some of the features of parameters other than the one under discussion in order to make the explanation clear.

Length of Vowel

Monophthongs may be either long or short, whereas diphthongs because of the nature of their articulation are always long. Some languages have pairs of monophthongs which are identical except for one being short and the other long. English also has long and short monophthongs but, as we shall see below, these pairs also differ slightly in respect to tongue height and tongue part: thus in a pair of words like *lid* and *lead* we can clearly hear not only the difference in the length of the vowel in each word but also a distinct difference in the quality of each vowel.

Height of Tongue

Theoretically we could imagine many different heights to which a particular part of the tongue could be raised but in practice phoneticians usually only recognise **three**. The most convenient way to refer to these is by using the terms **high**, **mid** and **low**. However, as we see from the diagram below, some people use a binary set of terms: *close* and *open*, where *close* (= high) refers to the closeness of the tongue to the roof of the mouth when it is raised to a high position (the gap here is closed), and *open* (= low) refers to the openness of this gap when the tongue is in a low position. For users of this binary system the mid height has rather awkwardly to be called *half-close to half-open*.

	front	central	back
high			
mid			
low			

Part of Tongue

This diagram shows us that three parts of the tongue are relevant for the production of vowels: the **front**, **central** and **back** areas. It also shows us all three of these areas raised to a high position. The high front position is used for the English vowel [i:] heard in *green*, and the high back position for the vowel [u:] heard in *spoon*. No English vowels occur in the high central area, but speakers of Northern Welsh use it for their pronunciation of the vowel in Welsh words like *dyn* (= *man*) or *tŷ* (= *house*). In Welsh this vowel is non-rounded and as we would expect sounds like a cross between [i:] and [u:].

When the tongue is raised to the mid height, all three parts of the tongue are used for British English vowels: front mid as in [e] heard in *wet*, central mid as in [ɜ:] heard in *bird*, and back mid as in [ɔ:] heard in *saw*.

When the tongue is not raised but kept in a low position, the front area is not used in English, but the central area is needed for the initial position of the gliding diphthongs [aɪ] and [aʊ] as in *cry* and *sound* respectively. For the production of vowels in the low area with the back part of the tongue, the latter is usually slightly drawn back and only very slightly raised. The vowel [ɑ:] heard in *father* is said in this position.

Lip Rounding

In the classification of consonants we saw that the lips are the place at which a number of them can be made. For vowels, however, the lips are used in a different manner: any vowel can be said with the lips relaxed in a neutral position or with the lips pursed as when we blow at something. Vowels said with neutral lip position are non-rounded and those said with pursed lips are rounded. Some languages like German or French have pairs of vowels which are identical except that one is rounded and the other is non-rounded, e. g. German *Flöte (= flute)* and *flehte (= begged)*, *Tüte (= bag)* and *tute (= hoot)*, *Kölner (= inhabitant of Cologne)* and *Kellner (= waiter)*. In English there are no pairs of this kind: instead roundedness is associated with the back part of the tongue, with the result that except for the low back vowel [ɑ:] all the back vowels occur only in a rounded form.

It is interesting to notice in this connection that the semivowel [w] also has lip rounding like the vowel [u:] with which it is related, thus showing that although English treats it as a consonant it nevertheless retains some vowel-like characteristics. We may also note that most native English speakers also pronounce their frictionless continuant *r* with slight lip rounding. In Modern English the *w* in front of the *r* in the spelling of words like *write*, *wrong* or *wren* has dropped out of the pronunciation, but in Old English it was pronounced and led to the rounding of the *r* sound following it. Maybe when the [w] was lost, the rounding it had caused was generalized and transferred to every pronounced *r* in the language.

3 Cardinal Vowels

Background

Although we can use the four parameters to distinguish between many of the vowels of English, the language possesses some pairs like [i:] and [ɪ], both of which are high and front, or [u:] and [ʊ], both of which are high and back. Furthermore, we have no way of adequately comparing tongue heights and tongue parts in two or more languages: a high front vowel in one language may be lower than the corresponding high front vowel in another. In order to show relative positions on these parameters we need some kind of fixed points against which the tongue height and tongue part of any vowel can be measured. This problem was solved by the English phonetician Daniel Jones, who taught at London University from 1907 until 1949 and was Emeritus Professor of Phonetics until his death in 1967.

Cardinal Vowels

He put forward the **system of cardinal vowels**, vowels having a fixed position with which any naturally occurring vowels can be compared. He started with the two most extreme positions for vowels: the **highest possible front vowel** with the front of the tongue raised as close as possible to the hard palate without producing any friction or turbulence (cardinal [i]), and the **lowest possible back vowel** (cardinal [ɑ]). These two positions were established by X-raying the tongue and recorded as shown in the diagram below.

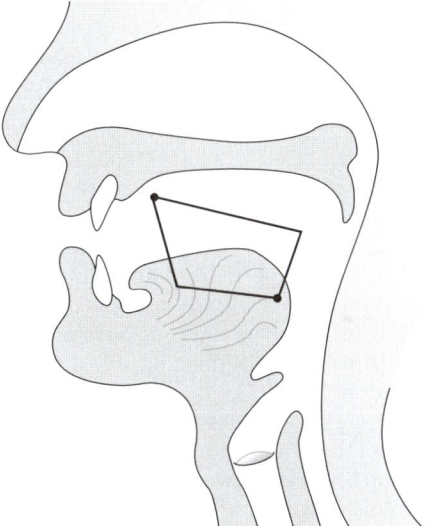

Three further front cardinal vowels were established by lowering the front of the tongue down from the cardinal [i] position to the lowest possible front vowel position, stopping at two intermediate points where each vowel seemed acoustically to be at the same distance from the one above it. The X-ray record of the tongue positions for these four cardinal vowels showed them also to be roughly the same distance apart spatially. Using the same procedure, this time raising the back of his tongue to three equal heights from cardinal [ɑ] up to the highest possible back vowel, he was able to establish three more cardinal vowels.

Vowel Quadrilateral

When the positions for these eight cardinal vowels are joined together by lines, we get the rather irregular figure shown in the diagram on page 35. It is customary in phonetics to show this as a **regularized quadrilateral**, as seen in the diagram below, where the cardinal vowel positions are shown as numbered dots at the outer intersections of the lines.

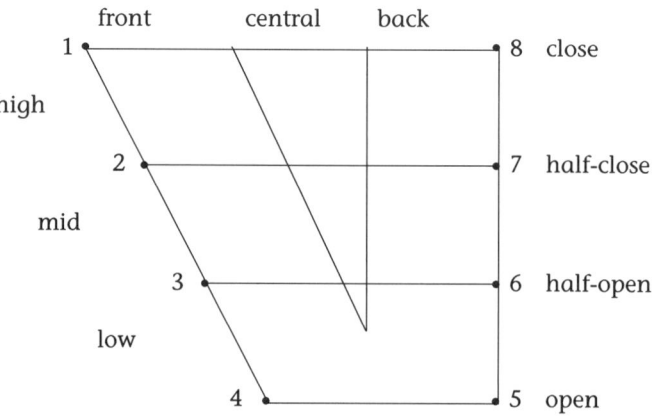

Regularized Quadrilateral

It will be noticed that the regularized quadrilateral is so drawn that the top and bottom lines are parallel to each other and that the back line is at right angles to these two. The front line retains the slope of Jones' irregular quadrilateral, which we saw in the diagram on page 35. Two horizontal lines (joining position 2 with 7 and position 3 with 6) are now drawn across the figure at equal distances from the top and bottom, and divide the quadrilateral into three areas: high, mid and low, corresponding to the three tongue heights. The figure is completed by dividing the top line into three equal parts corresponding to the front, central and back parts of the tongue and by drawing at a third of the distance along the top line a downwards sloping line parallel to the front line and then at two thirds of the distance a second line parallel to the vertical back line. These two new lines join together at a point just below the horizontal line which separates the low area from the mid area.

Terminology

As we saw above, **two sets of terminology** can be used in connection with the vowel quadrilateral. That shown on the left-hand side of the numbers in the diagram above has the advantage that one can easily talk about areas like *high, mid* and *low,* where various tongue heights are used by different languages. In the set of terms shown on the right-hand side these areas have to be referred to rather awkwardly as *close to half-close, half-close to half-open,*

and *half-open to open*. For the exact positions of the eight cardinal vowels in the diagram both sets are adequate: the tongue height for cardinal vowels 1 and 8 can be called *high* or *close*, for cardinals 2 and 7 *high-mid* or *half-close*, for cardinals 3 and 6 *low-mid* or *half-open*, and for cardinals 4 and 5 *low* or *open*.

More Cardinal Vowels

When Daniel Jones devised the cardinal vowels he presumably had the languages of Europe in the forefront of his mind with the result that the three highest of the back cardinal vowels are all rounded, whereas the lowest back and the four front cardinal vowels are all non-rounded. However, if we look at the languages outside Europe especially in Asia, we discover that non-rounded back vowels are just as common as rounded ones. Furthermore, quite a number of European languages have rounded front vowels. Daniel Jones solved this problem by positing **two sets of cardinal vowels**: (a) the **primary cardinals** 1–8, which have 1–5 non-rounded and 6–8 rounded, and (b) the **secondary cardinal** vowels 9–16, where the rounding feature for each primary cardinal is reversed.

Theoretically it would be more logical to have all the primary cardinal vowels non-rounded and all the secondary ones rounded, but Daniel Jones' system has been retained as it has proved to be more convenient for European phoneticians. In the diagram on page 38 the two quadrilaterals are shown with the 16 positions for the primary and secondary cardinal vowels and the symbols which are used for them. As most of the symbols for the secondary cardinals are irrelevant for English we can conveniently ignore them, but it should be noticed that the inverted *v* symbol [ʌ] and the inverted script *a* symbol [ɒ] are used for two English vowels which have slightly different positions from the corresponding cardinals.

Compared with German & French

So that the reader can obtain some idea of the primary cardinals we can compare them here with some German and French vowels and leave the English ones for detailed description below. Cardinal 1 [i] is very like the French vowel heard in *gris (= grey)* or *si (= if)*, or with the tongue a little higher than the German sound in *Sieb (= sieve)*. Similarly, cardinal 2 [e] can be compared with the French vowel which occurs twice in the word *été (= summer)* or with the German vowel in *See (= sea, lake)*. Cardinal 3 [ɛ] is similar to the French vowel in *raide (= stiff)* or the German one in *Netz (= net)*. The French vowel in *bague (= ring)* and the German one in *Mann (= man)* are said a little farther towards the centre of the tongue than the low front cardinal 4 [a]. Note that this cardinal vowel and the French and German sounds are quite different from the English sound [æ] heard in *man!*

If we turn now to the back cardinals, we find that cardinal 5 [ɑ] sounds like the vowel in northern French *bas (= low)* and is farther back than the first vowel in English *father*. Cardinal 6 [ɔ] is roughly the same vowel as the one heard in German *Klotz (= block)*, whereas cardinal 7 [o] can be compared to the French vowel in *eau (= water)* or the German one in *Floh (= flea)*. Finally, cardinal 8 [u] is close to the French sound in *chou (= cabbage)* and to the German one in *Hut (= hat)*.

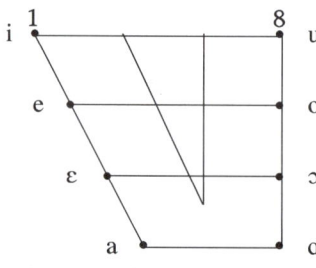

Primary Cardinal Vowels (1–8)

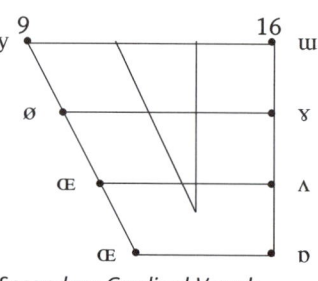

Secondary Cardinal Vowels (9–16)

Usefulness The big advantage of the cardinal vowels is that they are independent of any language. They can be learned from the recordings which Jones made of them or from any phonetician who has learned them. For the readers of this book, who cannot hear what is written on the page, this is of course not very useful, but they will discover that it does help them to understand the differences between the vowels in their own language and those of English if they can see these plotted against the nearest cardinal vowels and thus visualize the differences in tongue height and tongue part.

❼ Detailed Classification of English Vowels

Preliminaries In the diagram below we have set out the positions for each of the English monophthongs as a black dot with an area enclosing it. The dot shows the position in which most speakers with standard British pronunciation produce the sound, whereas the area around the dot (enclosed by a full circle or part of a circle) shows the wider positions which the sound may sometimes have. It is clear that when we utter sounds repeatedly as in speech, there must be slight variations in tongue position for each repetition. Furthermore, when we compare the speech of one person with that of another, even if both speakers use standard pronunciation, one may have a higher tongue position for a particular vowel and the other may have a lower position. It is for these minor variations that the circle around the dot caters.

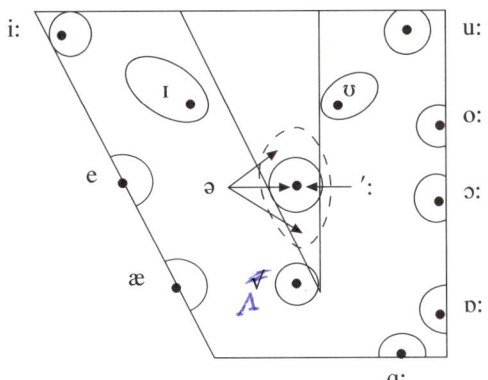

1 High Vowels

If we take a careful look at the diagram above we notice that the dots showing the standard pronunciation of the vowels in the high and mid layers of the quadrilateral are arranged symmetrically. The long non-rounded, high front vowel [i:] (as in *feast*) is usually articulated a little below the position for cardinal [i], while the long rounded high back vowel [u:] (as in *food*) assumes a correspondingly symmetrical position just below that for cardinal [u]. In the same high layer we see a second pair of symmetrical vowels, this time both short and both with a position that is lower and more towards the centre of the tongue: [ɪ] as in *sin* and [ʊ] as in *foot*. In a very careful differentiation of the two high front vowels we can specify the higher one as we did above as *long, non-rounded, high, front* and the lower one as *short, non-rounded, high towards mid, front towards central*. Similarly, the higher back one can be specified as *long, rounded, high, back* and the lower one as *short, non-rounded, high towards mid, back towards central*. On the other hand, for normal purposes (when we already know the exact position of the lower vowels relative to the higher pair) it is sufficient to refer to the front pair as the *long and short high front vowels* and to the back pair as the *long and short high back vowels*, although as we saw above it is not just the length which makes the difference between them.

2 Mid Vowels

Front/
Central/
Back

In the mid layer of the quadrilateral there are four more symmetrical vowels. The short non-rounded front mid vowel in *met* should in careful phonetic representation be written with the symbol [ɛ] but English phonetics for convenience' sake usually employs [e] instead. This vowel is uttered with the front of the tongue raised to a position midway between cardinal [e] and cardinal [ɛ]. Corresponding to it at the back of the mouth is the long rounded back mid vowel [ɔ:], heard in British English *taught*. This occupies a position midway between cardinal [o] and cardinal [ɔ]. In exactly the centre of the vowel quadrilateral we find at this mid height two more vowels: the short non-rounded mid central vowel [ə] (heard in the first syllable of *about* and usually called *shwa*, though this is really the name of the symbol representing it) and the long non-rounded mid central vowel [ɜ:] (heard in *nurse*). The name for the symbol representing this latter vowel is technically *reversed epsilon with a colon*. Beginning students tend to confuse reversed epsilon with normal (non-reversed) epsilon (the Greek letter used above for cardinal [ɛ]). It is therefore more easy to remember *reversed epsilon with a colon* if it is referred to as *little round three, two dots*. As these two English mid central vowels appear to differ only in length, we might ask why both are not written with the same symbol. If we look at older books on phonetics we discover that it was indeed the practice to write both with shwa (i.e. [ə] and [ə:]). For example, Daniel Jones does this in all the editions of his famous *English Pronouncing Dictionary* from 1917 onwards. However, this practice was changed by his successor to the chair of phonetics at London University, Professor A. C. Gimson, when he published the revised 14th edition of the dictionary in 1977, using [ə] for the short mid central vowel and [ɜ:] for the long one. Since then modern phoneticians have continued to use these two different symbols because the two vowels behave differently in English. The long one does not usually vary in tongue height whereas the short one does. The latter has variants that are both higher and lower than [ɜ:], which we can describe when we come later to the phonology of vowels.

3 Low Vowels

Front/ Central/ Back

In contrast to the positions for the high and mid vowels, those for the vowels in the low layer of the quadrilateral are asymmetrical. The long non-rounded low back vowel [ɑ:] is pronounced with the tongue as low as for cardinal [ɑ] but with a tongue part which is not quite as far back. The other low back vowel [ɒ] is rounded, produced a little higher than the primary cardinal [ɑ] or its rounded counterpart cardinal [ɒ], but just as far back as both. On the other hand, at the front of this layer we find only the one vowel [æ]. This is pronounced with a higher tongue position than for the two low back vowels and a little less than halfway down between cardinal [ɛ] and the lowest front cardinal [a]. Most learners of English whose mother tongue does not contain this vowel usually substitute for it a vowel from their own language which may be as high or even higher than cardinal [ɛ]. Starting with the position for their own vowel, they should be encouraged to lower the front of the tongue until they reach the correct height for English [æ].

In the centre of the low layer we see the remaining low vowel [ʌ]. This too is articulated with a higher tongue position than for either of the two low back vowels. When Daniel Jones began his recordings in the early years of this century, the vowel was said farther back than the central position which it occupies in the speech of young modern speakers. This more retracted position can still be heard, however, in the pronunciation of older speakers.

Asymmetry When a vowel system is symmetrical, this suggests that pronunciation is stable: when it is asymmetrical, like that of English, this usually indicates that the pronunciation is changing. As we saw above, this diagnosis is correct for modern English in the low layer of the quadrilateral. The vowel [ʌ] has gradually moved from farther back to a central position in modern British English, and in some kinds of modern American English it has moved from here upwards into the mid layer, with the result that for speakers of this variety it has merged with the mid central vowel [ɜː], although it may not be as long. This pronunciation can often be heard in pop songs, where even British singers generally assume an American accent. Older generation British speakers may thus have been a little surprised to hear the Beatles singing *love, love, love* as [lɜːv lɜːv lɜːv] rather than with their native Liverpool pronunciation [lʊv lʊv lʊv].

4 Varieties of English

Need for More Terms We have now reached a point where we shall have to distinguish between different varieties of English in order to label more clearly the type we are describing, in particular with regard to vowels. Up to now, especially for our classification of consonants, we have contented ourselves with the term *Standard English* for the most acceptable kind of British and American pronunciation, but strictly speaking this term should be reserved for the grammar of English and not for its pronunciation.

RP There is one dialect of British English of which the pronunciation is not associated with any particular region of Great Britain but which is characteristically heard from educated speakers. This is commonly referred to as **Received Pronuncia-**

tion[4] (= **RP**), which is not a particularly satisfactory term as it seems to suggest some kind of value judgement. However, it is widely used by phoneticians. RP is the one British pronunciation which is understandable to almost all other types of native English speakers throughout Britain and the world. It should be noted that the terms *Queen's English* and *BBC English* which are sometimes heard in this context really refer to grammar and lexicon. They are inaccurate if used to label the pronunciation we are describing, as the Queen's type of pronunciation shows certain characteristics which are not found in RP and as the English pronunciations heard on the BBC may be very varied. In view of its general acceptance and universal comprehensibility, RP is clearly the most suitable kind of British accent to teach to foreign learners.

General American

In the case of American accents, there is no one clearly delimited type which can be compared to RP, but the name **General American**[5] **(GA)** is usually given to the accent which is most acceptable and seems to have the fewest or none of the features which are disapproved of in the pronunciation of some of the other dialects. This is the type of pronunciation in which all the r's in the spelling are pronounced and which is given in all the good American dictionaries.

5 Diphthongs and Triphthongs

Diphthongs

For **the classification of diphthongs** we shall have to differentiate more sharply between RP and General American than we could for monophthongs. All the RP monophthong positions can be found in General American (though they may be used for different vowels), but in the case of the diphthongs there is one in RP, namely [əʊ], which has rather a different counterpart [oʊ] in General American. However, before we discuss this, there are **several general characteristics** of English diphthongs which we must make clear first.

Charac-teristic

Production: Diphthongs are produced by moving the tongue from one vowel position to another, by changing the tongue height, sometimes the tongue part and sometimes the lip rounding. For example, for the English diphthong [ʊə] the back of the tongue is raised first to a high-towards-mid position, the lips are rounded and the vocal cords begin to vibrate. The back of the tongue is then lowered and the centre raised to mid height while the lips are gradually unrounded. As the tongue produces this diphthong it moves, of course, through numerous other vowel positions intermediate between those of the initial and final vowel.

**Charac-
teristic**

Graphic Representation: Although a diphthong is really a glide through numerous vowel positions, it is represented phonetically by writing side by side the vowel with which it begins and the vowel with which it ends.

**Charac-
teristic**

Closing/Centring: In English, diphthongs either rise to a final high (= close) position (**closing diphthongs**) or they move to a central vowel position (**centring diphthongs**). If we look back at the list of symbols given on page 17, we see that there are five closing diphthongs, three of which end in the front high vowel position for [ɪ], namely [eɪ, aɪ, ɔɪ], and two which end in the back high position for [ʊ], namely [əʊ] in RP or [oʊ] in GA, and [aʊ] in both RP and GA. The three remaining diphthongs all move to the mid central position for schwa [ə] and are therefore centring diphthongs [ɪə, eə, ʊə]. To these we could add [ɔə], which can still be heard in the pronunciation of some older RP speakers.

Before we consider all these in more detail, let us look at the graphic representation of their tongue movements shown in the first two quadrilaterals in the following diagram.

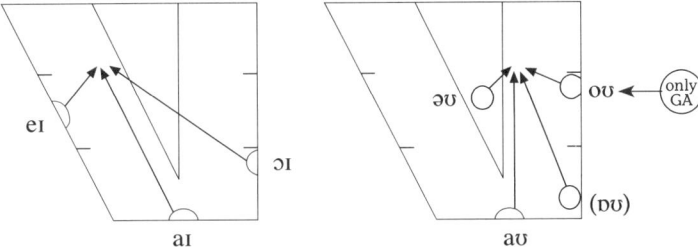

Closing Diphthongs (rising to ɪ)   Closing Diphthongs (rising to ʊ)

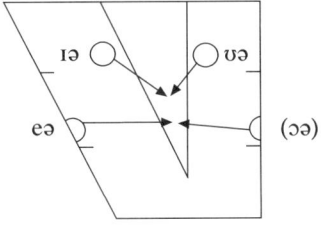

Centring Diphthongs

---

4 For a brief summary of the history of the term RP and the accent to which it refers see A. C. Gimson's introduction (especially pages x and xi) to the Fourteenth Edition of Jones, *English Pronouncing Dictionary* ...

5 For a brief discussion of the variation within General American pronunciation see the Introduction to Wells, *Longman Pronunciation Dictionary* ..., p. xiv, or for a detailed treatment Wells, *The Accents of English* ..., vol.3.

[aɪ, aʊ]	It is important to notice that the closing diphthongs [aɪ, aʊ], which we hear in the words *pie* and *cow* respectively,begin with a vowel using a part of the tongue which is not used for any of the low monophthongs in English. This initial non-rounded low central vowel [a] position is roughly that used by Standard German speakers for the letter *a* in German words like *Mann* (= *man*) or *fand* (= *found*). As we see from the diagram, the initial position for [aɪ] may be slightly farther forward, anticipating the frontness of the high vowel position in which the diphthong ends; similarly the diphthong [aʊ] may begin a little farther back, anticipating the backness of the high vowel position to which the tongue glides finally.
[eɪ, ɔɪ]	As the symbols for the diphthong [eɪ] suggest, the tongue rises from an initial position close to or very slightly higher than that of the front mid monophthong [e] and rises to the position for the short high front monophthong [ɪ]. This diphthong is the vowel we hear in the word *plate*. In the case of [ɔɪ], as in *toy*, the initial symbol [ɔ] suggests that this diphthong starts in the same position as for the long monophthong [ɔː] heard in *fork* but in fact it usually begins rather lower, though not quite as low as for the monophthong [ɒ] which we hear in *pot*.
[əʊ]	As we mentioned earlier, the diphthong [əʊ], which is found in the RP pronunciation of words like *bone* and *load*, does not occur in General American. The diagram shows us that it begins in the upper part of the mid central area where the higher varieties of [ə] occur, i.e. a little higher than for the long central vowel [ɜː]. This is to be expected of a diphthong that rises to a final back position which is high: it anticipates the final high position by beginning a little higher, just as the closing diphthongs which begin low anticipate the frontness or backness of the vowel positions with which they end by beginning a little farther forward or back respectively. Before looking at its GA counterpart, we should note that in place of [əʊ] many modern RP speakers have a variant [ɒʊ] which they use before [l] in words like *gold, rolled, boulder*. This variant will be mentioned again when we come later in this book to the phonology of diphthongs.
[oʊ]	The GA diphthong [oʊ] begins a little below the high-mid back cardinal vowel [o] and rises to the same short high front vowel position as its RP counterpart. Thus whereas the rounding of the lips does not set in for [əʊ] until the middle of the diphthong, the GA diphthong is rounded throughout. Most American speakers do not have a separate variant before [l].

[ɪə, eə, ʊə]	Of the three centring diphthongs only [eə] needs more careful description. Both [ɪə] and [ʊə] have initial positions corresponding to those of the monophthong represented by their initial symbol; [eə] on the other hand begins much lower than the RP monophthong [e], roughly in the position for cardinal [ɛ] and for some speakers it may be even lower than the cardinal vowel. In older types of phonetic representation of RP the difference between the higher initial position for the diphthong [eɪ] and this lower initial position for the diphthong [eə] was visible in the script: thus the former was written [eɪ] whereas the latter appeared as [ɛə]. However, nowadays, since the epsilon was only needed for this one diphthong and since a lower initial position can be expected of a centring diphthong than of a closing one, the use of the epsilon has been abandoned and both diphthongs are written with initial [e].

([ɔə]) In some kinds of RP particularly among older speakers a fourth centring diphthong may be heard in words like *pour, sore, floor*. This is written as [ɔə] and, as the script suggests, it begins roughly with the tongue position for the monophthong [ɔː]. In the pronunciation of most middle and younger generation RP speakers this diphthong no longer exists and has been replaced by the long monophthong [ɔː], which interestingly has also ousted the [ʊə] diphthong for most of these speakers in many common words like *poor, sure, your*. Thus whereas the older generation of speakers had three differing pronunciations [pɔː, pɔə, pʊə] respectively for the three words *paw, pour, poor*, most middle and younger generation speakers have only one for all three: [pɔː].

RP versus GA Historically all the RP diphthongs were originally a combination of their initial monophthong plus [r], as can be seen from the spelling. When the [r] sound was dropped before a consonant or before a silence, it left behind a reflex in the form of [ə]. It is therefore not surprising to find that in most kinds of General American, in which the r-sounds are still pronounced wherever they occur in the spelling, these centring diphthongs do not exist. However, some GA speakers do have the diphthong even in front of the [r]. We thus see the following correspondences between RP and GA:

RP [ɪə]   = GA [ɪr] or [ɪər] as in *here*
[eə]   =   [er] or [eər] as in *there*
[ʊə] (→ [ɔː]) =   [ʊr] or [ʊər] as in *moor*

(These correspondences and others are given in more detail in Chapter 5.)

Final Notes To complete the picture of the centring RP diphthongs two points must be added. First, the [r] which is dropped before a consonant or a silence in words like *here, there, moor* reappears in these words when the next word begins with a vowel sound, e. g. as in *he̲re and the̲re in England* (this is the so-called linking *r*). In this case RP retains the diphthong and does not reduce it to the monophthong plus [r] which is heard in GA. Second, in RP the final [ə] position of these diphthongs like that of the monophthong [ə] may vary considerably in tongue height depending on where each diphthong occurs in a word. As this is a phonological matter it will be dealt with later under the phonology of vowels.

Triphthongs Triphthongs are vowels which glide directly from one vowel height to another (as for a diphthong) and then change direction and move to a third vowel height. In English this third vowel is always shwa and can only be preceded by one of the five closing diphthongs. So only the following triphthongs are possible:

[aɪə]	as in	*fire, iron*
[eɪə]	as in	*layer, player*
[ɔɪə]	as in	*buoyant, royal*
[aʊə]	as in	*our, power*
[əʊə]	as in	*Noah, lower*

Triphthongs are monosyllabic. However, some analysts do not recognize them as one syllable, but analyse them as two, i.e. as a diphthong followed by the vowel /ə/.

⑧ Syllabic Consonants

Nasals/ Liquids Before we leave the topic of phonetics and the classification of consonants, semivowels and vowels, we must look again at some of the nasal consonants and the two sounds [l] and [r], which are sometimes referred to as liquids. When [n] and [l] are preceded by [ə] in an unstressed syllable, the shwa usually drops out in fast speech and the [n] and [l] become syllabic, i.e. they receive the pulse of the syllable in which they stood. Let us take as an example the word *sudden*. In very careful speech it would be pronounced ['sʌdən], i.e. with two syllables, the first of which is stressed (as shown by the sign ['] placed in front of it) and the second unstressed. In less careful faster speech the pronunciation is usually ['sʌdn̩], where the shwa is dropped but the pulses of the two syllables are kept. To show that a consonant has become syllabic a small upright line is used as a diacritic below it. Another example is the word *bottle*, which in very careful RP would be pronounced ['bɒtəl] but which is usually said as ['bɒtl̩], i.e. with syllabic [l̩].

[l̩] & [n̩] Syllabic [l̩] and [n̩] are the two commonest syllabic consonants in both British and American English and, as they themselves are alveolar, they occur regularly after other alveolar sounds (e. g. [t] and [d], [s] and [z]) but not after another [l] or [n]. Thus even in fast speech such words as *canon* or the masculine forename *Alan* always retain the shwa before the final nasal: ['kænən, 'ælən].

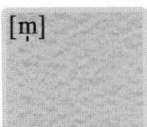

Syllabic [m̩] occurs in a few very common words which are pronounced weakly in certain contexts in normal English, e. g. *them, some, from* as in the sentence *One of them bought some cheese from the farmer*, which in RP would be ['wʌn əv ðm̩ 'bɔːt sm̩ 'tʃiːz frm̩ ðə ðə 'fɑːmə]. Syllabic [ŋ] is not usually found in English.

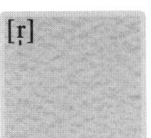

In American speech syllabic [ɹ̩] often replaces unstressed [ər] in words like *perhaps, manner, sender, letter* and may even be used in stressed syllables in such words as *stirring, furnish.*

More details of these syllabic consonants and their distribution can be found in Ch. 3, pages 100, 103, 109.

2

CHAPTER Phonology

❶ Structural Phonology

1 Preliminary Considerations

Phonetics

At the beginning of this book we defined phonetics as the study of the non-functional properties of sounds in languages. In Chapter 1 we looked in detail at the sounds of English, examining the way in which they are produced and seeing how we could classify them. In the course of describing the phonetics of these sounds, we had sometimes to refer to variants and the contexts in which they occur. Here we had already begun to enter the field of phonology, the study of how the sounds which a language uses function within that language. We shall see below that just as it was impossible to talk about the phonetics of English without taking some phonological features into consideration, it will also be impossible to examine the phonology of English without referring to some of the phonetic features of English sounds. The two studies go very closely hand in hand.

Meaning

Phonetics is not concerned with the functional use of sounds to construct words that have meanings: that is part of what phonology is about. However, before we leave phonetics we should notice that in every language there are some phonetic sounds which are connected with meaning but which can only be heard in one particular word, usually an exclamation, and nowhere else in that language. Although words of this kind have meaning, the phonetic sounds in them to which we are referring are not productive, i. e. are not functional in word formation, and are therefore not part of the regular phonology of that language. They exist in a sort of no-man's-land between phonetics and phonology.

tut-tut

A sound of this kind in English is the so-called dental click [ǃ] (also written [|]), which is used to express disapproval, e. g. of a child's behaviour. It is then often accompanied by a wagging of the index finger in the direction of the child. This sound is made by placing the tip of the tongue against the bottom teeth, the blade of the tongue against the upper teeth, and by sucking inwards causing a vacuum which is then released with an audible noise. It is usually uttered twice and in novels is represented in spelling by the word *tut-tut*. The double nature of this spelling becomes obvious when we hear people reading it aloud as [tʌt tʌt], not using the dental click, but replacing it with consonants and vowels which do function elsewhere in English.

Another example of this phenomenon is the word *ugh,* which is used as an exclamation of disgust, e. g. when one sees or hears something revolting. One quite common pronunciation of it is [ɯə] with a vowel close to the high back non-rounded secondary cardinal vowel, followed by shwa; another pronunciation of it is [ɯx] with the same vowel followed by the voiceless velar fricative.

Phonology

Just as in phonetics we were able to discuss the phonetic aspects of speech sounds either in general or in relation to a particular language, so in phonology we can take the same two approaches in talking about the functional aspects of speech sounds. In modern linguistics there are various schools of phonology, e. g. generative phonology, natural phonology, metrical phonology, autosegmental phonology, to name only a few; and each has its own methods of explaining and accounting for phonological phenomena. In this little book we shall have time to look at the ideas of only one of these schools, namely those of structural phonology. Historically this is the school out of which most of the others have developed. Therefore for beginners in the subject this is the most useful approach as it forms a good basis from which to go on to the study of other approaches. To get some idea of the scope of structural phonology and the kinds of things that it deals with, here are a number of typical questions that we can ask.

Scope

(a) Which sounds contrast in a language to produce changes in meaning? Which do not?
We shall see below that for the first of these two kinds of sounds the term **phoneme** is used, and the contrast into which two phonemes enter (when they produce a change in meaning) is called a **phonological opposition.**
(b) How many sounds does a language possess?
We are referring here to its **phoneme inventory**.
(c) Which sounds vary in different positions in words?
Here we can talk about **positional variants or allophones.**
(d) Where do the sounds occur in the words of a language? Where do they not occur? What combinations are possible?
The technical term used here is **phonological distribution.**
(e) What can happen to sounds in certain positions in a language?
There are four important **phonological processes** which we can describe briefly here and discuss in detail later: assimilation, coalescence, elision and epenthesis.
1. **Assimilation:** This is where one sound influences another so as to make the two more alike. We often see this happen in the common pronunciation of *good morning* in fast speech, where the alveolar plosive [d] at the end of *good* is influenced by (i. e. assimilated to) the bilabial nasal [m] at the beginning

of *morning* and changes to the corresponding bilabial plosive [b]. Thus instead of the careful pronunciation [gʊd 'mɔːnɪŋ] we now hear the assimilated pronunciation [gʊb 'mɔːnɪŋ].

2. Coalescence: Two sounds combine to produce a single new one. In the fast pronunciation of the words *this year* it often happens that the final [s] of the word *this* fuses with the initial [j] of *year* and in place of the two we hear [ʃ], i. e. instead of the careful pronunciation [ðɪs 'jɪə] we hear [ðɪ 'ʃɪə].

3. Elision: One sound in a word drops out. For example, very few native speakers of English pronounce the [t] that occurs between two other consonants in a word like *Christmas* or in a combination of words like *last week*. Instead of ['krɪstməs] we usually hear ['krɪsməs], and instead of [lɑːst 'wiːk] a common pronunciation is [lɑːs 'wiːk].

4. Epenthesis: A sound which is not indicated in the spelling is inserted into a word. This happens, for example, in the pronunciation of the word *length*, which should be ['leŋθ] but is very often ['leŋkθ].

All the changes which we see in these phonological processes are not arbitrary but occur in accordance with rules which can be explicitly formulated.

❷ Phonemic Analysis

1 Phonological Opposition

Questions

Let us now reconsider the questions which we asked above about the scope of phonology in general and apply them specifically to English. The first of them can be reformulated as follows: of all the possible sounds which languages can use to form their words, which sounds does English use for this purpose? Of course, in the first chapter of this book we indirectly answered this question when we set out the list of phonetic symbols for English: logically each symbol must refer to a separate sound which English uses. The picture was not absolutely clear, however, as we also included symbols for some sounds which we called variants. Two important questions which we did not ask at that stage now arise. How was this list of sounds determined? How do we decide which sounds are variants of others?

Method

In order to discover which sounds a language employs for its word formation, structural phonology uses the **minimal pair** (or **substitution) test.** Two words are chosen such as *head* and *red*, which must satisfy the following conditions:
(a) they must have the same number of segments;

(b) all their segments must be identical except for one;
(c) the differing segment must be at the same place in each word;
(d) the two words must be different in meaning.
Let us look at the phonetic representation of *head* and *red* and number the segments:

Minimal Pair

```
            1 2 3
           [h  e  d]
           [r  e  d]
```

Opposition

Each of the two words has three segments, in both words segments 2 and 3 are identical and only segment 1 is different, and each word has a different meaning. This difference in meaning must be a result of the opposition between [h] and [r] in the first segment. Therefore we can claim that in English there is an [h] sound and an [r] sound. In order to establish the remaining sounds of the language, we will have to find other suitable minimal pairs. This may not always be very easy, as the language may allow certain sounds to occur only in certain positions, where it is difficult to find an opposing sound in the second member of a minimal pair. However, we are not limited to just the first segment in a word: the opposition between the two sounds can be in any segment. Consider for example the following four minimal pairs using the word *flock* where the opposition is found in a different segment in each pair.

```
 1 2 3 4      1 2 3 4      1 2 3 4      1 2 3 4
[f  l  ɒ  k]  [f  l  ɒ  k]  [f  l  ɒ  k]  [f  l  ɒ  k]
[f  l  ɒ  g]  [f  l  ɪ  k]  [f  r  ɒ  k]  [k  l  ɒ  k]
```

In the first pair where *flock* is contrasted with *flog*, the opposition occurs in the fourth segment and we see that it is the sounds [k] and [g] which are causing the difference in meaning. In the next pair where *flick* is the second member, we now have an opposition in the third segment between the vowels [ɒ] and [ɪ]. In the second segment of the third pair it is the [r] of *frock* which is in opposition to the [l] of *flock*. Finally, in the fourth pair with *clock* as its second member, it can only be the sounds [f] and [k] in the first segment which make the difference in meaning between the two words.

Inventory

Using the five minimal pairs discussed above we can now begin a list or inventory of the sounds of English: so far we have established

the consonants: [h, r, k, g, l, k] and
the vowels: [ɒ, ɪ].

Note that a sound which we have already established, e. g. the [k] at the end of *flock*, may have to be used again in another pair,

e. g. *flock, clock* to establish a further sound, in this case [f]. Since we already have [k] once in our list, there is no necessity for it to be added again.

In this way we can continue to find minimal pairs which will provide us with the remaining sounds of the language and so complete our inventory. Having now answered the question about which sounds English uses to construct its words and how these sounds can be determined, we can turn to the other question asked at the beginning of this sub-chapter: How do we decide which sounds are variants of others?

2 Sounds and their Variants

Problem

In the minimal pair test we have so far assumed that the sounds which we find in opposition in the same segment are fully fledged (i. e. full sounds in their own right), but how can we be sure that they are not variants of certain sounds? For example, if we consider the minimal pairs *wing, will* and *get, let*

1	2	3		1	2	3
[w	ɪ	ŋ]		[g	e	t]
[w	ɪ	l]		[l	e	t]

we see that the *l* which contrasts with [ŋ] in the third segment of the first pair is the dark *l* we referred to in Ch.1, page 21, whereas the *l* which contrasts with [g] in the first segment of the second pair is the clear *l*. Are these two *l* sounds two fully-fledged sounds in English? Or are they two variants of just one sound? We could put these two questions in another way. When we establish our inventory of sounds using the minimal pair test, do we add two kinds of *l* to the list? Or should we add just one. The two kinds of *l* both seem to make differences in meaning and yet if we were to ask an unsophisticated native speaker of English he would probably tell us that there is only one *l* sound in the language. In other words most native speakers have never noticed that they use two varieties of *l* when they speak. The reason for this, of course is that the two sounds are phonetically almost identical. Both are voiced and alveolar and lateral: the only difference is that the dark *l* is velarized, i. e. the back of the tongue is raised during the articulation. All this must lead us to the conclusion that it is not possible to decide from the minimal pair test whether a sound is a variant or not. This can only be determined later when we know a lot more about the language.

Phonetic Similarity

The question of phonetic similarity does not provide us with any additional help in deciding the status of contrasting sounds in minimal pairs. To appreciate this, let us look again at the [k] and [g] in the fourth segments of *flock* and *flog*, which as we have seen contrast to make a difference in meaning. Phonetically they are just as similar as the two kinds of *l*: each pair differs in only one feature. The two kinds of *l* are distinguished from each other only by the feature of velarization, whereas [k] and [g] differ only in respect of voicing. However, in this latter pair, it can only be this difference in voicing which produces the difference in meaning. The [k] and [g] seem therefore to be two full sounds in their own right. Let us suppose on the other hand that we are analysing a language in which voicing is not distinctive. If we were to pronounce a word in this language with a [k] at one time and then later with a [g], nobody would notice as there would be no change of meaning. So, unlike the two English sounds, the [k] and [g] in this language are variants of one sound. We would now have to consider the voiceless velar plosive as a variant of the voiced one, or vice versa.

Non-Contrasting Variants

In addition to these two cases, a third arises where variants may be used in the same segment with no change of meaning at all. Let us look once again at the final [k] in *flock*. In our analysis above we have assumed the normal pronunciation of this word when it is said in isolation or before a silence. For the [k] here the back of the tongue is raised to touch the velum and there is a normal release of air from the mouth when the plosion occurs. Another variation of this sound can be heard in this position when people are taking extra care with their speech. Here the velar plosive is pronounced in the same way but with a more forceful release so that the plosion is followed by a small puff of air sounding as if an [h] has been added. Phoneticians call this phenomenon **aspiration** and more will be said about it when we deal with the phonology of plosives later. In addition to this aspirated variant of the [k] sound there is a third variant which is heard word-finally before a consonant at the beginning of the next word. Here, except in very careful speech, the plosive is unreleased, i. e. the air which should escape at the plosion is held back and not released until the plosion of the following consonant occurs. The [k] pronounced in this way sounds very like a glottal stop, but the speaker can feel the difference. Whereas for the [k] the back of the tongue must be raised to the hard palate, there is no tongue movement associated with the glottal stop as the plosion is made at the vocal cords. It must be stressed that this unreleased kind of plosive and the unaspirated and aspirated kinds are all optional variants, and the speaker's choice produces no change in the meaning.

Summary

As the argument above has required us to go into a considerable amount of detail, let us summarize briefly the conclusions we have reached so far. There seem to be three different kinds of sounds which English can use in the pronunciation of words:

(a) those which contrast with each other in the same segment in a minimal pair to produce a difference in meaning, like the [k] and [g] in the fourth segment of *flock* and *flog*, and which seem to be full sounds in their own right;

(b) those like the dark *l* (which contrasts with [ŋ] in the minimal pair *wing, will*) and the clear *l* (which contrasts with [g] in the minimal pair *get, let*), both of which seem to be variants of one sound and produce changes in meaning;

(c) those like the three different kinds of [k] in the third segment of *lock* which appear to be optional variants of one sound and which do not contrast with one another to make differences in meaning.

Let us now consider what methods structural phonology uses to cope with this situation.

3 Phonemes and their Phones

Phoneme

In our discussion above we talked rather loosely about fully fledged sounds or full sounds in their own right. Now is the time to introduce the concept of the **phoneme.** Various scholars have put forward different theories about what a phoneme really is, but for our purposes the most useful approach is to define it as **the smallest unit of sound that differentiates meaning** and to treat it as **an abstraction.** It is this latter idea, namely that the phoneme is an abstraction, which needs some explanation.

Ideal Sound

Let us consider for a moment the English *l* sound. Whenever English speakers utter a word with an *l* in it, they will have an ideal picture in their minds of this particular sound. This goal, the ideal *l*, that they are aiming at is an abstraction. The realization of this abstraction, i. e. the sound that actually comes out of their mouths, may vary considerably with each utterance and from person to person. Thus the abstract sound is one thing and the realizations of it are another.

Phone

We have reserved the term phoneme for the abstract entity, so let us now introduce the term **phone** for any concrete realization of a phoneme, i. e. for any actual physical utterance of the abstraction. We can compare the phoneme with a note in music. If a musician talks about 'middle C', the note he is referring to is an abstraction. We cannot hear it unless he plays it on a musical instrument or realizes it in some other way, e. g. by singing or whistling it. The sound which we hear from the musical instrument or which he sings or whistles can be compared with the phone.

The comparison can be taken farther, for just as 'middle C' can be written as a note on one of the five ledger lines on a sheet of music, so we can also write phonemes as black marks on a sheet of paper. They are usually indicated by placing the phonetic symbol for the sound between slashes, e. g. /ŋ/, /f/, etc. Just as the notation for 'middle C' on the sheet of music makes no sound on its own but must be realized in some way, so the representation of the phoneme on paper is equally silent but can be realized by a speaker as an audible phone.

If we return for a moment to our discussion of the sounds of English and their variants in the preceding section, we can now see that we were really talking about abstract phonemes and their concrete realizations. The dark *l* [ɫ] that contrasted with [ŋ] in the minimal pair *wing, will*, and the clear *l* [l] that contrasted with [g] in the minimal pair *get, let* can now be analysed as two phones realizing the phoneme /l/. Similarly, the three kinds of *k* [k, kʰ, k˥] (normal, aspirated, unreleased) which we discovered at the end of *flock* are all phones realizing the phoneme /k/. Notice, however, that we must now correct our analysis of the [k] and [g] which we found in opposition to each other in the minimal pair *flock, flog* and which we thought to be sounds in their own right. These sounds in their own right are really the abstract phonemes /k/ and /g/. What we found in the minimal pair are their respective realizations, i. e. the phones [k] and [g]. This situation can be seen more clearly in the following diagram.

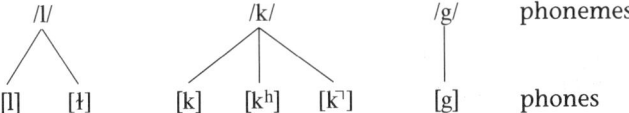

Unfortunately, the reader cannot hear me pronounce the phones in the diagram above: I am obliged to represent them graphically as symbols between square brackets. However, it must be emphasized that phones are audible sounds, whereas phonemes are inaudible abstractions.

4 Complementary Distribution and Free Variation: Allophones and Free Variants

In the diagram above we see that some phonemes have several different realizations. We must now turn to the important topic of distribution, which we mentioned right at the beginning of this chapter in connection with the scope of phonology. Where do these phonic variants occur? Are there contexts which allow the use of only one of the realizations? Are there contexts where the speaker has the choice of more than one? We shall see below that both kinds of context occur in English.

Comple-mentary Distribution

In the case of the phoneme /l/ we saw that it has two realizations: the phone clear *l* which is used before a vowel, and the phone dark *l* which is used everywhere else, i. e. before a consonant or before silence. Here the speaker has no choice: the two kinds of *l* are mutually exclusive, i. e. where I find one I never find the other. This kind of distribution is referred to in phonology as **complementary distribution.**

Allophones

Phones which occur in this kind of context are said to be in complementary distribution and for the moment we can call them **allophones.** However, this definition will have to be refined, as not all sounds which appear in complementary distribution are necessarily allophones. For example, the phone [ŋ] always occurs at the end of a word or syllable in English and never at the beginning, whereas the phone [h] is always found at he beginning of a word or syllable and never at the end. In the case of clear and dark *l* it is obvious that the two phones are realizations of the one and the same phoneme /l/, as depicted in the diagram above. If we try to treat [ŋ] and [h] in this same manner, we run into trouble immediately. If these two phones are realizations of one and the same phoneme, what can we call this phoneme?

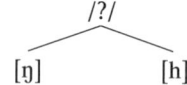

/?/

[ŋ]   [h]

For native speakers such a phoneme does not seem to have any psychological reality in the way that /l/ does. It would be very strange for a language to have a sound that is sometimes pronounced as a [ŋ] and sometimes as a [h]. These two phones are phonetically too dissimilar. Whereas clear and dark *l* are identical in voicing, manner of articulation and place of articulation and differ only in that dark *l* is velarized, the two phones [ŋ] and [h] have no phonetic features in common. We can see this clearly from the following two tables where '+' indicates the presence of a feature and '–' its absence.

	[l]	[ɫ]		[ŋ]	[h]
Voicing	+	+	Voicing	+	–
Alveolar	+	+	Velar	+	–
Lateral	+	+	Glottal	–	+
Velarized	–	+	Nasal	+	–
			Fricative	–	+

Since [ŋ] and [h] seem to be totally unrelated phonetically it is only logical to allot each phone to a separate phoneme, i. e. to treat [ŋ] as a realization of the phoneme /ŋ/, and [h] as a realization of the phoneme /h/.

Allophone Redefined
Let us now attempt a more careful definition of the allophone. An allophone is one of two or more phones which must satisfy the following conditions:

(a) they must contrast with another phone in the same segment of a minimal pair to produce a change in meaning;
(b) they must be in complementary distribution with one another;
(c) they must be phonetically similar to one another.

Condition (a) is necessary in order to exclude those phones like the three realizations of the phoneme /k/ at the end of *lock*, which are optional and do not produce differences in meaning. We shall return to these in a moment. Condition (b) states the primary characteristic of allophones, and condition (c) is required in order to exclude phones like [ŋ] and [h], which satisfy conditions (a) and (b) but which are phonetically too disparate to be thought of as realizations of one and the same phoneme.

Free Variation
Where there is a choice between two or more phones in the same segment in a word, the term **free variation** is used to describe this phenomenon, and the phones which are involved are called **free variants.** The three phones of /k/ at the end of *lock* fit into this category.

We should notice that free variation occurs not only between the phones realizing one phoneme but also between two distinct phonemes. For example, whereas /i:/ (with its phonic realization [i:]) and /e/ (with its phonic realization [e]) contrast to produce a change of meaning in minimal pairs like *seat, set* and *heed, head*, they are in free variation in the first syllable of the word *economics*, the RP pronunciation of which can be represented phonemically either as /i:kə'nɒmɪks/ or /ekə'nɒmɪks/. The same situation is found with the phonemes /eɪ/ and /e/, which contrast in the words *pain* and *pen* but which are free variants in the second syllable of *again* ([ə'geɪn, ə'gen]). A third example, this time with consonants, can be seen with /ʃ/ and /s/, which as phonemes in a minimal pair like *shell, sell* serve to keep the two meanings apart, whereas in the word *appreciate*, either sound can be used with no change of meaning (/ə'pri:ʃieɪt/ or /ə'pri:sieɪt/), showing them here to be free variants.

Terminology
Let us look back for a moment and review the terminology which we have used so far. We have seen that there are two kinds of sound: abstract phonemes and their audible phones. Most phonemes have several phones realizing them but it is conceivable that a

phoneme may have only one realization, e. g. [f] seems to be the only realization of /f/. When several phones realize one phoneme we have referred to them as variants or, more exactly, positional variants. These are of two kinds: allophones and free variants. Allophones are positional variants where the speaker has no choice: one allophone must be used in one context, and another allophone in a different context. Free variants are positional variants where the speaker has the choice of using more than one of the phones in the same context.

Unfortunately this careful distinction which we have made above is not always adhered to and we sometimes find the term *allophone* being used for any realization of a phoneme, i. e. as a synonym of *phone*. This analysis, shown as Analysis 2 in the diagram below, requires more complicated formulation than the one we have recommended above (Analysis 1). For the free variants we have chosen the two phones of /r/ described on pages 20 and 23 (the frictionless continuant [ɹ] and the lingual flap [r]).

	1	2	3
Phoneme	/f/ ǀ [f]	/l/ ⌃ [l] [ɫ]	/r/ ⌃ [ɹ] [r]
Analysis 1	↑ phone	↖ ↗ allophones	↖ ↗ free variants
Analysis 2	single allophone of one phoneme	allophones in complementary distribution	allophones in free variation

5 Neutralization

Three Cases

Another aspect of the topic of phonemes and their realizations is the phenomenon of neutralization. Neutralization takes several forms, three of which we can examine here.

Case 1

The first is best illustrated from German, where the opposition between related voiced and voiceless phonemes is neutralized. In this language voiced plosives and fricatives normally contrast with their voiceless counterparts, but when they occur word-finally they become totally devoiced and change from lenis to fortis, i. e. they are replaced by their voiceless counterparts. For example pairs like *Rat* (= advice) and *Rad* (= wheel), *bunt* (= colourful) and *Bund* (= alliance) are not minimal pairs when said in isolation as they have identical segments:

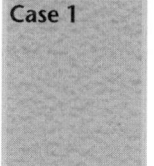

	1 2 3			1 2 3 4
Rat	[r a: t]		*bunt*	[b ʊ n t]
Rad	[r a: t]		*Bund*	[b ʊ n t]

However, when genitive suffixes are added, the underlying /t/ or /d/ reappears and the words are now minimal pairs:

	1 2 3 4 5			1 2 3 4 5 6
Rates	[r a: t ə s]		*buntes*	[b ʊ n t ə s]
Rades	[r a: d ə s]		*Bundes*	[b ʊ n d ə s]

If we think of this again in terms of phonemes and their realizations, we face a problem. The final segment of *Rad* and of *Bund* is realized by a phone of the phoneme /t/, whereas when the suffix follows, the same segment of each word is realized by a phone of the phoneme /d/. This is not the situation we encountered above in the case of the English word *economics*, where the speaker is free to choose between two phonemes in the first segment of the word. Word-finally in German the speaker has no choice: the word *Rad* must end with /t/, and before a suffix this same segment must be /d/. In other words the two phonemes are in complementary distribution. Furthermore, native speakers of the language feel that they are realizations of one and the same sound. If this is so, this entity must be even more abstract, or (put in another way) be at an even deeper level, than the phonemes which realize it.

Archi-phoneme

A useful label for a sound which in one context is realized by one phoneme and in another context by another phoneme is the term **archiphoneme.** An archiphoneme can be symbolized by a capital letter written between phoneme slashes. Usually the voiced sound in a pair like neutralized word-final /t/ and /d/ in German is chosen for the capital symbol, e. g. /D/. In the following diagram we see this archiphoneme and its realizations, together with some further examples which are described below.

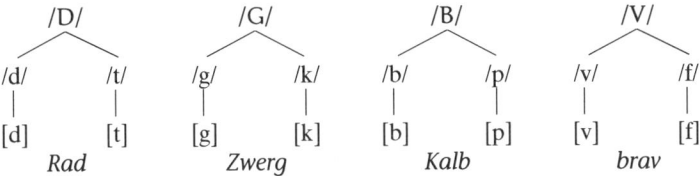

Zwerg (= *dwarf*) is realized as /tsvɜrk/, but in the genitive case as /'tsvɜrgəs/; similarly *Kalb* (= *calf*) is /kalp/ but with the genitive ending /'kalbəs/; and the adjective *brav* (= *well-behaved*) is /braːf/ but when declined for case and gender the *v* of the spelling reappears, e. g. /'braːvəs/ in *ein braves Kind* (= nominative of *a well-behaved child*).

Thus we can represent *Rat* phonemically as /raːt/ where the final phoneme /t/ never changes, but *Rad* with the sound which in final position is sometimes /t/ and sometimes /d/ can be represented phonemically as /ra:D/. Similarly, *Werk* (= work), *Skalp* (= scalp) and *Graf* (= count, earl), which all have unchanging final segments, will appear phonemically as /vɜrk, skalp, gra:f/, whereas *Zwerg, Kalb, brav* can be distinguished from them by writing the archiphoneme in final position: /tsvɜrG, kalB, bra:V/.

Case 2	A second kind of neutralization can be illustrated from English. We have seen that English possesses two vowel phonemes /i:/ and /ɪ/, which contrast in a minimal pair such as *scenic, cynic*, where they occur in stressed syllables. One of these two sounds also occurs unstressed, either directly in front of another vowel as in *obvious* or word-finally as in *happy*. In present-day RP and General American pronunciation it is impossible to tell whether this sound is a phone of /i:/ or a phone of /ɪ/. In this environment the distinction between the two phonemes has been neutralized. Phonetically the sound has the high front tongue position of /i:/ but the shortness of /ɪ/. Is it then a short positional variant of the phoneme /i:/? Or a slightly higher positional variant of the phoneme /ɪ/? We may note that in older kinds of English, e. g. that of Daniel Jones in the early years of this century, the pronunciation in these two unstressed positions was clearly [ɪ], as it still is in Midland and Northern dialects of British English. So in words like *silly, busy, fishy* both syllables of each word were pronounced identically and this pronunciation can still be found in the phonetic representations of many older English dictionaries. In modern RP and GA, however, the second vowel in each word is clearly different from the first and is represented phonetically as [i], e. g. ['sɪli, 'bɪzi, 'fɪʃi]. The same kind of neutralization is also found between the two English high back phonemes /u:/ and /ʊ/, which contrast in a minimal pair like *pool, pull* where they are stressed, but which seem to have only one common realization when unstressed before another vowel, e. g. in *influence, situation, strenuous*. Similar to /i:/, the vowel here has the higher tongue position of the phoneme /u:/ but the shortness of the lower phoneme /ʊ/. It is therefore written phonetically as [u], e. g. in ['ɪnfluəns, sɪtju'eɪʃn, 'strenjuəs]. This phone does not occur word-finally except in the weak pronunciation of a few very common monosyllables like *to, you, who, do* (see the weak forms in Ch. 5 on pages 145–147, 154).

Problem	In this kind of neutralization no archiphoneme is involved; the problem is not that one already existent phone is shared by two phonemes, but that we have a new phone which could justifiably be considered as a realization of either of two phonemes. Diagrammatically we can show this as follows:

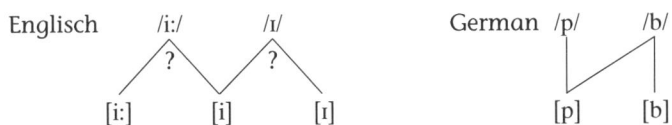

Englisch /iː/ /ɪ/   German /p/ /b/

[iː]   [i]   [ɪ]   [p]   [b]

In the German case we chose to solve this problem by positing an archiphoneme /B/ with two phonemes /p/ and /b/ which are realized on the phone level as [p] and [b] respectively (see the diagram on page 59); for the English case we can only make an arbitrary choice, either we allot [i] to the phoneme /iː/ or we allot it to /ɪ/.

Case 3

A third kind of neutralization is found where a whole group of related sounds which are normally contrastive are no longer in opposition to one another in a certain context. As an example let us consider the group of English nasal phonemes /m, n, ŋ/. At the end of a morpheme (i. e. the smallest meaningful functional unit in a language which may be a word or part of a word) they contrast to change meanings, e. g. in *some, sun, sung,* but when they occur before a plosive in the middle of a morpheme, the opposition between the three is neutralized. For example, in the words *temper, wonder* and *anger* the nasal before the plosive in each morpheme must have the same place of articulation as the following plosive: before bilabial /p/ only bilabial /m/ is possible, before alveolar /d/ only alveolar /n/, and before velar /g/ only velar /ŋ/. With very rare exceptions, no other combinations of nasal plus plosive are allowed in this morpheme-medial position in English. There are no morphemes with bilabial /m/ before an alveolar plosive such as we see in German in the words *Amt (= office)* and *Hemd (= shirt).* Notice that English words like *sometimes, sunburnt* and *longboat* are only apparent exceptions, as they consist of two morphemes, not one: /sʌm + taɪmz/, /sʌn + bɜːnt/ and /lɒŋ + bəʊt/. The bilabial nasal before the alveolar plosive in *sometimes* is thus not morpheme-medial but morpheme-final where the three nasals can legitimately contrast. The situation is similar for the apparently offending alveolar /n/ before bilabial /b/ in *sunburnt* and for the velar /ŋ/ before bilabial /b/ in *longboat.*

Summarizing this third kind of neutralization, we can say that all the characteristic features of the three English nasal sounds except their nasality are neutralized before a morpheme-medial plosive. In words like *temper, ember, hunter, wonder* and *anchor, anger* we need only to specify that there is a nasal consonant before the plosive and the context determines which nasal it will be: the speaker has no choice.

6 Other Approaches

Criticisms Some phonologists have criticized the analysis put forward above and pointed out several weaknesses in the concepts of the phoneme, allophone and archiphoneme. A famous example was given by the phonologist Halle in 1959, who shows that in Russian, where voiceless [t] becomes voiced [d] word-finally before a following voiced sound, we have to posit both a /t/ and a /d/ phoneme because these contrast elsewhere in the language, whereas in exactly the same context we have to classify the phones [tʃ] and [dʒ] as allophones of one phoneme because they do not contrast in Russian. We have the **same situation** twice, but a **different analysis** in each case: the pairs of sounds in question differ only in voicing, yet one pair consist of two phonemes, and the other of only one.

Another criticism is one that can be levelled against the condition of **phonetic similarity,** which was specified above for allophones in English in order to exclude the complementarily distributed pair [ŋ] and [h]. To be allophones of one phoneme, phones must be phonetically similar, but how do we determine the point on the scale at which two sounds cease to be phonetically similar? How do we know where to make the cut-off?

Another problem for phonemic analysis in English is that of **phonological alternation.** The language possesses large numbers of closely related pairs or groups of words where the same segment in each member of the pair or group is realized sometimes by one phoneme and sometimes by another. For example, from the noun *critic* we can derive the adjective *critical* which has /k/ in the sixth segment like the noun, whereas the same segment in another derivative, the verb *criticise*, despite the same spelling has /s/. The root *critic* seems to have two forms: one with /k/ and another with /s/. Morphologically the two forms are obviously closely related; yet the two phonemes in their sixth segment are phonetically clearly not related. Similarly, the relationship between the words *allege* and its derivative *allegation* is not reflected in the analysis of the sound represented by the *g* in each word as /dʒ/ and /g/, which are phonetically unrelated. Put in another way, the problem could be stated as follows: if we think in terms of phonemes, the words *allege* and *allegation* seem to be no more related than the words *badge* and *bag*, which also have the phonemes /dʒ/ and /g/ in the same segment. Yet there is clearly a relationship between these two phonemes, as the alternation between them occurs in many other words and their derivatives: *oblige, obligation; legislate, legal; regicide, regal; purge, purgation; etc.*

Finally, there is the problem of the lack of functional difference between phonemes in the environments where neutralization takes place. By definition phonemes should be phonetically functional, in fact phonology is sometimes referred to as functional phonetics, yet when they are neutralized this primary characteristic is removed.

Alternative This state of affairs has led some phonologists to reject the concept of the phoneme and to seek other methods of explaining the phonological phenomena we have been examining. The restricted space we have in this little book will not allow us to look in detail at these other approaches, but we can for a moment consider how a model like that of Generative Phonology could cope with the problem of the neutralization of voicing in word-final plosives and fricatives in German. Instead of an abstract archiphoneme with two phonemes which have to be realized by phones, we could posit a single **underlying** *d*-sound upon which certain phonological rules operate. In this case a rule which takes the voicing out of plosive and fricative sounds before a word-boundary would be required. A primitive form of this rule could be written using the following symbolism:

Rule: $\qquad$ [+ voice] $\rightarrow$ [– voice] / _____ #

The square brackets enclose distinctive features with a plus or minus value, the arrow indicates a change from what is on the left to what is on the right of it, the slash means 'in the following environment', the low horizontal line shows where the sound which is to be changed occurs and the double cross indicates a word-boundary, i. e. where a word begins or ends. The rule therefore reads as follows: a voiced sound changes to a voiceless sound in the following environment, viz. at the end of a word. As it stands, the rule is too powerful, for it would make every voiced sound at the end of a word voiceless and in German the change takes place only with plosives and fricatives. We could refine the rule by specifying which voiced sounds undergo the change, e. g. we could add the features 'plus plosive' and 'plus fricative' using curly brackets to indicate an obligatory choice between these two:

Revised Rule: $\begin{bmatrix} + \text{voice} \\ \left\{ \begin{matrix} + \text{plos} \\ + \text{fric} \end{matrix} \right\} \end{bmatrix} \rightarrow$ [– voice]/_____#

The rule now says that any sound that is voiced and either a plosive or a fricative will change to voiceless at the end of a word. The change is in fact more complicated than this in German as it also occurs at the ends of some morphemes but not all. We do not need to go into the details here. It is important only for us to have seen how this type of situation can be dealt with using a model which posits underlying sounds and which uses distinctive features and rules. In comparison with the model using archiphonemes, phonemes and their realizations which merely lists these units and cannot show any relationships between them, this generative model has the advantage that the phonological rule operating on a sound to produce another does clearly show the relationship between the two.

The rule we have given above not only simplifies the situation in German but also uses features which we have taken from articulatory phonetics so that the reader can follow more easily. The kind of features normally used in the rules of Generative Phonology are of a more complicated kind and need careful explanation, for which we have no time here.

Despite the problems which the phonemic approach encounters, we shall continue to use this throughout the rest of this book, for it is historically the oldest, as we already mentioned earlier, and the one from which most others are derived. A knowledge of it is therefore essential in order to understand what came later. Furthermore it will provide us with many interesting and valuable insights into the phonological structure of English.

3 Suprasegmental Phonemes (Prosodic Features)

1 Preliminaries

Stress

In our analysis of English words up to now we have considered only the phonemes in each segment (segmental phonemes) and how they are realized. It is clear, however, that this is not the complete picture. When we utter an English sentence there are other phonetic aspects of the words (beyond the segments) which also contribute to the understanding of the sentence by the hearer. One of these is **stress**. For example, before we can pronounce the word written as *import*, we have to know whether it is a verb or a noun in order to determine which syllable is stressed and which is not. If it is a verb the stress is on the second syllable /ɪm 'pɔːt/; if it is a noun the stress is on the first /'ɪm pɔːt/. As the words in this pair are semantically related, a foreigner's wrong use of stress here would not be very confusing to a native speaker. However, with a word like *entrance* where stress on the second syllable gives us a verb with the meaning of *to delight, enchant* /ɪn 'trɑːns/, whereas stress on the first syllable produces a noun with the meaning of *way in, door, gate* /'en trəns/, the likelihood of misunderstanding is very much greater. Stress in English is an important feature in the structure not only of words but also of phrases and sentences, as we shall see below.

Intonation/ Tone	Another feature of the pronunciation of English, and indeed of all languages, is the melody to which the syllables of words are said. This is referred to in phonology as **intonation.** Here we can talk about changes of voice pitch, i. e. whether a syllable is on a higher or a lower tone than its neighbours or remains on the same tone. Notice that differences in this kind of height are produced by the vocal cords and are not the same thing as differences in the height of vowels, which are produced by the tongue. A simple example to show that intonation is in addition to the segments in an utterance is the following sentence: *John has gone.* Said with falling intonation, i. e. with each syllable on a progressively lower pitch than its predecessor, the sentence is a statement (e. g. in answer to the question *Where's John?*); but said with rising intonation, i. e. with progressively higher pitched syllables, it is either a question asking whether John has left or it is an exclamation of surprise at the fact that John is no longer here. These changes in meaning have nothing to do with the phonemes in each segment of the utterance but are produced by the suprasegmental feature of intonation. As we shall see below, we can distinguish between **tone,** which is suprasegmental with respect to only one syllable, and **intonation,** which is suprasegmental over a stretch of utterance.
Prosody	Phenomena such as stress, tone and intonation can be collectively referred to as the **prosody** of a sentence or utterance. They can be thought of as phonemes or as prosodic features depending on the phonologist's approach. Let us now examine each of them in more detail.

2 Stress

Nature of Stress	Phonetically, stress is concerned with the degree of force with which a syllable is uttered: a stressed syllable is said with more energy than its neighbours and is therefore usually louder, sometimes longer, and may even be on a higher pitch. These factors make it more prominent. Phonologically we can distinguish between four kinds of stress: (a) **word stress,** (b) **sentence stress,** (c) **shift stress,** and (d) **contrastive stress.**
Word Stress	In English any words of two syllables or more will have one syllable more prominent than the others when the word is said in isolation, e. g. when quoted or talked about. Even one-syllable words carry stress when said by themselves. Since **word stress** can also be the feature which, as we saw above in the case of *entrance*, can help us to distinguish between two words that have the same segmental structure but differ in meaning, it is also referred to as **lexical stress.**

Degrees of Stress

Notice too that there may be different degrees of stress or, looked at in another way, different phonemes of stress. Long polysyllabic words may have more than one prominent syllable: the most prominent one of these is said to carry **primary stress**, but another syllable though weaker may also be more prominent than the rest and can be said to carry **secondary stress**. For example, the word *catastrophic* has primary stress on the third syllable, but there is clearly a weaker stress on the first syllable: /ˌkæ tə ˈstrɒf ɪk/. Primary stress is usually indicated by a small raised vertical line in front of the stressed syllable, whereas secondary stress is shown by means of a small vertical line placed low before the stressed syllable. The syllables which carry neither primary nor secondary stress can be thought of as weak, i. e. having no stress on them. To understand this, let us first look again at *catastrophic* and the word from which it is derived *catastrophe*. This pair is remarkable insofar as all the vowels in each segment of one word are different from those in the corresponding segment of the other:

1	2	3	4	
/ˌkæ	tə	ˈstrɒf	ɪk/	*catastrophic*
/ kə	ˈtæ	strə	fi/	*catastrophe*

Though this metamorphosis seems at first sight to be chaotic, it is in fact quite regular. Languages which use stress are of two kinds: those which retain the full value of their vowels in unstressed syllables (e. g. German: /katastroˈfaːl/ and /kataˈstroːfə/) and those which **weaken** these vowels (e. g. English, Russian). In English we find that /ə/ and /ɪ/ are the typical weak vowels used to replace full vowels in unstressed syllables. Thus where *catastrophic* has /æ/ and /ɒ/ in the stressed first and third syllables, *catastrophe* has both of these weakened to /ə/ as they are now unstressed. Similarly, where *catastrophe* has /æ/ in the stressed second syllable, the corresponding syllable of *catastrophic* has /ə/, because the stress has shifted and this syllable is now weak.

A pair in which we can see both the weak vowels /ə/ and /ɪ/ are the words *advantage* and *advantageous*, which are set out for comparison below.

1	2	3	4	
/ˌæd	vən	ˈteɪ	dʒəs/	*advantageous*
/əd	ˈvaːn	tɪdʒ/		*advantage*

Here again we find stressed /æ/ in one word being replaced by weak /ə/ in the other (in the first segment), but a different replacement occurs in the third syllable of these two words. The stressed full vowel /eɪ/ in *advantageous* is replaced by the weak vowel /ɪ/ in *advantage*.

To return to our consideration of degrees of stress, we can now see that English words are characterized by having **full vowels in stressed syllables** and (usually) one of the **weak vowels** (/ə/ or /ɪ/) **in unstressed syllables.** If a word has both a primary and a secondary stress and also contains a third syllable with a full vowel, some phonologists analyse out a third degree of stress (tertiary stress) for this syllable. For example, the third syllable of the word *recommendation*/ˌrek ə men 'deɪ ʃən/would be a candidate for tertiary stress, especially as the /e/ of this syllable is not weakened compared with the corresponding syllable in the parent word *recommend*, which carries primary stress. Although such arguments seem to be in favour of positing a third degree (or third phoneme) of stress, it is very difficult to hear any difference in the force between a syllable with tertiary stress and one with no stress. Furthermore, there do seem to be a few words in English where full vowels genuinely occur unstressed: for example, words ending in *-ow (pillow, window, sorrow,* etc.) clearly have no stress on this syllable, yet the full vowel /əʊ/ is retained. Thus it seems more practical to distinguish only primary and secondary stress and to consider any further full-vowel syllables in a word to be unstressed. To determine the stress pattern of an English word we can use the following rule of thumb: as English words containing unstressed full vowels are rather rare, we can usually assume that a syllable with a full vowel will carry stress and that a syllable containing /ə/ will not. We should notice that in the case of a syllable containing /ɪ/, we must be more careful, for whereas /ə/ can never be stressed, /ɪ/ though common in unstressed syllables does also occur quite often in stressed ones. In the word *women*, for example, we see it both stressed and unstressed: /'wɪm ɪn/.

We must also remember that an unstressed syllable may also contain one of the two phones [i] and [u], which we discussed in connection with neutralization on page 60.

Finally we may note that there are some differences in word stress between American and British English, though very few. Among these are adverbs ending in *-arily*, which have primary stress on this ending in GA and secondary stress on an earlier syllable. In RP this earlier syllable usually has the primary stress and there is no secondary stress in the word at all. Consider the transcription of the words *customarily, ordinarily, temporarily* below. As is to be expected, the vowel in the syllable with secondary stress in GA is full, whereas the unstressed vowel in the corresponding RP syllable is weakened to shwa. Notice too that some RP speakers have /ɪ/ in place of shwa in the weak syllable before the final *-ly*.

GA: /ˌkʌs tə 'mer ə li, ˌɔːr də 'ner ə li, ˌtem pə 'rer ə li/
RP: /'kʌs tə mə rə li, 'ɔː də nə rə li, 'tem pə rə rə li/

In the pronunciation of the adjectives from which these adverbs are derived, American also has a full vowel in the third syllable: /'kʌs tə mer i, 'ɔːr də ner i, 'tem pə rer i/. Most American dictionaries mark this vowel too as carrying secondary stress, but Wells in LPD and Roach & Hartman in EPD leave it unmarked. RP again has a weak vowel here. Interestingly some of these American pronunciations are finding their way into modern British English, presumably because of the large amount of American speech which can be heard on British television nowadays. One noteworthy imported American pronunciation of this kind is /ˌpraɪ 'mer ə li/ in place of native British /'praɪ mə rə li/.

Sentence Stress

Let us now turn from the stress which each word has in isolation and examine how stress behaves when words are strung together in larger units such as phrases and sentences. It will be convenient to refer to this kind as **sentence stress.** When incorporated in a sentence, many common English function words (words which are often monosyllabic and belong to small closed sets of grammatical words such as the personal pronouns, the prepositions and the conjunctions) may carry no stress at all and the strong vowel which they had in isolation is replaced by one of the weak vowels we mentioned above. As we shall be examining words with strong and weak forms in detail later, in Ch. 5, let us consider just one monosyllabic example here. The conjunction *but* when quoted or said in isolation is stressed and pronounced /'bʌt/; far more common, however, is its normal pronunciation within a sentence where it is unstressed with the strong vowel weakened to shwa: /bət/. Similarly two-syllable function words, which must have a stressed syllable in isolation, may lose this stress when incorporated in a sentence, although the strong vowel will be retained. For example, the preposition *between* when said by itself must have the second syllable stressed /bɪ 'twiːn/, but when used in a sentence such as *they walked between the trees*, both syllables will usually be unstressed: /ðeɪ 'wɔːkt bɪtwiːn ðə 'triːz/. We see then that it is the lexical words in the sentence, i. e. those that carry the main semantic content (the nouns, adjectives, verbs, adverbs), which take stress, whereas the function words are left unstressed.

Shift Stress

One particularly interesting stress phenomenon is **shift stress** (or **switch stress**), which is very characteristic of English and involves both word and sentence stress. There are a large number of words (mostly adjectives) which have two stresses (a secondary and a primary) when they are said in isolation or are single constituents in a sentence, but which switch the primary stress to the syllable with secondary stress when they form part of a larger construction, e. g. a noun phrase. When this shift takes place, the syllable that originally carried the primary stress now becomes unstressed. The following examples will make this clear.

1. Adjectives ending in -ese indicating nationalities: *Chinese, Japanese, Burmese, Portuguese ...*
   e. g. *The guide is Chinese* /ˌtʃaɪˈniːz/
   A Chinese guide /ˈtʃaɪ niːz ˈgaɪd/
2. Numbers above *twelve*: *thirteen, fifteen, twenty-two, fifty-six ...*
   e. g. *Jane's thirteen* /ˌθɜː ˈtiːn/
   John's twenty-two /ˌtwen ti ˈtuː/
   Thirteen books /ˈθɜː tiːn ˈbʊks/ *with*
   twenty-two pages /ˈtwen ti tuː ˈpeɪ dʒɪz/ *in colour*
   He died in 1313 /ˈθɜː tiːn θɜː ˈtiːn/
3. Many adjectives starting with *un-*: *unhappy, unarmed, unclear ...*
   e. g. *She felt unhappy* /ˌʌn ˈhæp i/
   An unhappy feeling /ˈʌn hæp i ˈfiː lɪŋ/
4. Many compound adjectives of the kind ADJ+NOUN+ed: *red-haired, blue-eyed, two-faced ...*
   e. g. *They're all red-haired* /ˌred ˈheəd/
   A red-haired youth appeared /ˈred heəd ˈjuːθ/
5. Some common adverbs which can also be used adjectivally: *outside, inside, next-door, upstairs, downstairs ...*
   e. g. *They live next-door* /ˌnekst ˈdɔː/
   Our next-door neighbour /ˈnekst dɔː ˈneɪ bə/
6. Names of some cities and other geographical landmarks which can also be used adjectivally: *Berlin, Budapest, Hyde Park, Notting Hill ...*
   e. g. *They went to Berlin yesterday* /ˌbɜː ˈlɪn/
   The Berlin Police have arrested him /ˈbɜː lɪn pə ˈliːs/
   Hyde Park /ˌhaɪd ˈpɑːk/
   Hyde Park Corner /ˈhaɪd pɑːk ˈkɔː nə/

This kind of stress is not shown in dictionaries intended for native speakers, but can usually be found in the better modern didactic ones and also in dictionaries of pronunciation, e. g. LPD and EPD. Sometimes it is indicated merely by giving examples of the kind we have seen above. Sometimes a label such as 'stress shift' is placed after the transcription of the pronunciation with both secondary and primary stress. A third method is to use a symbol after this transcription (usually a black wedge [◄] pointing in the direction in which the primary stress moves), e. g.

Japanese /ˌdʒæp ə ˈniːz◄/   *unarmed* /ˌʌn ˈɑːmd◄/

Before we leave the topic of stress, there is one further kind which we must consider. This is **contrastive** or **emphatic** stress. Normally when we utter a phrase or sentence the last stressed word is the one we consider most important, the one we want listeners to concentrate their attention on. For example, in the sentence *She gave him a small piece of cake*, it is this final word *cake* which is the most important part of the message and which therefore has the most prominence. On the other hand, when two elements in a sentence are contrasted, they are usually given special stress, which runs counter to the generalization we have just made. Thus the person to whom the cake was given might protest with the statement: *I didn't want a small piece of cake, I wanted a large piece.* Now there is a contrast between the words *small* and *large* and these therefore receive special stress. This may consist in making the stress extra loud but it is usually associated with a fall in pitch, i. e. the syllable with contrastive or emphatic stress is started higher and the pitch falls so that the following syllable or syllables are considerably lower. A change in pitch of this kind is often referred to as **accent** and some phonologists therefore call syllables with contrastive stress **accented** syllables. This can be shown in transcription by doubling the vertical line before the syllable with contrastive stress, but more commonly nowadays it is indicated by replacing the stress sign by a long grave accent [`],which shows the direction of the fall in pitch. This symbol can also be used just like the stress sign not only in the transcription of the phonemes of a sentence, but also together with the orthography. Thus the sentence above with contrasted *small* and *large* could be written as follows:

I 'didn't 'want a `small 'piece of 'cake, I 'wanted a `large 'piece.

We have considered contrastive stress to be the same thing as emphatic stress, for whenever a word is emphasized there is invariably a contrast implied although not always expressed. For example, if I say *Harry is a 'bad loser* emphasizing *bad*, this implies that he is not a good one. Similarly if I say *Harry 'can be very charming* emphasizing *can*, this statement implies a contrast with Harry's normal behaviour: at the back of my mind I am probably thinking *Usually he is not very charming.* It is conceivable, however, that there may be some cases where emphasis is not connected with contrast.

3 Tone and Intonation

Tone

Just as English uses the suprasegmental phoneme (or prosodic feature) of stress to differentiate between two words with the same syllabic structure but with different meanings, so some languages use **tone** for this purpose. Each syllable is then associated with a certain level of pitch (e. g. high, mid, low if the language has level tones, or high-falling, low-falling, high-rising, low-rising, etc. if the language uses moving tones). A simple example of this can be seen in the Nigerian language called Igbo, which uses two tone phonemes, a high and a low one, to mark the syllables of its words. Thus, four Igbo words with otherwise identical segments in their two syllables can have their meanings kept separate by a different combination of these two tones. Four such words are shown below with a grave accent over the vowel for a low tone, an acute accent over the vowel for a high one and with the English meaning written beneath each word.

Igbo

àkwà	ákwá	ákwà	àkwá
'bed'	'weep'	'cloth'	'egg'

For the speakers of European languages this may seem an exotic way to distinguish between meanings but in fact tone languages are widespread throughout the world, being found not only in Africa and East Asia but also in the Americas. Some of them have level tones at different pitches like Igbo, some have falling and rising tones beginning at different pitches, and some have a combination of these like Chinese.

Intonation

If we think of tone as the pitch on which a single syllable is uttered or as the change in pitch within a single syllable, we see that it can be used in two different ways: (a) as in Igbo, within single words to make contrasts in meaning, and (b) as in English, over groups of words, especially sentences, to show their grammatical structure and also to signalize the emotions and attitudes of the speaker. We can refer to this latter use of pitch and pitch changes as **intonation.** These stretches of intonation take the form of patterns or tunes and are very closely connected with stress, for the most significant changes in pitch (e. g. a step up in a rising tune or a step down in a falling tune) usually occur on stressed syllables.

Simple Tune

A simple **tune** (or **pattern**) usually consists of a **head** (the first stressed syllable in an intonation group), and a **nucleus** (the last and most strongly stressed syllable in an intonation group, also called the **tonic syllable**). If there are any stressed syllables between the head and the nucleus these are referred to as the **body**. A very short utterance may consist of a nucleus alone (e. g. a monosyllable like *yes* and *no*) or of a nucleus followed by one or more unstressed syllables, as in *possibly*. When there is no head, one or more unstressed syllables may precede the nucleus, as when a person being hurried says *just a moment*).

Exception

This is the usual way in which English uses tones. Before turning our attention to some of the details of normal English intonation, however, we may point out that there are some cases of the use of tone in English which seem to be more like what happens in tone languages. For example, in colloquial speech if we wish to show that we understand or agree with what is being said to us, we may utter a long [m] (syllabic 'em') starting on a low tone and rising to a slightly higher one. Its meaning here is *yes*. If on the other hand I use the same sound but start at a higher pitch and make a bigger rise, the utterance now means *what did you say?* or *please repeat what you have just said.*

m̩ ⟋ *yes*

m̩ ⌐ *what did you say?*

The normal use of tones in English, however, as we saw above, would be for the fall or rise in pitch to be a falling or rising tune, or a combination of these, spread over the whole utterance. For example, in the sentence *the dogs have smelt the meat* a falling tune would be normal with the highest pitch on the head *(dogs)*, a slightly lower pitch on the body *(smelt)* and a low fall on the nucleus *(meat)*. Just as when we scan a line of poetry we can talk about a foot in the metre of the verse, so we can also talk about a **foot** in intonation as a stretch of speech which consists of an initial stressed syllable and any subsequent unstressed syllables. These feet combine to form an **intonation group (tone group)**, i. e. the stretch of words over which a tune operates. Thus the sentence we have just examined contains three feet, the first beginning at *dogs*, the second beginning at *smelt* and the third beginning at *meat*. This leaves us with one unstressed syllable at the very beginning of the sentence: the word *the* in front of *dogs*. Initial unstressed syllables of this kind are not infrequent and will have to be treated as a foot despite the absence of stress. We will call them the **pre-head.** They may begin high or low, and this can sometimes make a surprising difference to the meaning. Consider for a moment the expression *there you are*. It can be used as a polite set phrase of goodwill when we hand something to somebody. It then has a high falling pre-head (i. e. a high unstressed first syllable and a lower unstressed second syllable in the first foot) and the second foot consists of a nucleus with rising pitch. Notice that although we have no head in this sentence we must still refer to the initial unstressed syllables as the pre-head, since it is after them that the head would appear if it were present. The same set phrase changes its meaning, however, when uttered with a low rising pre-head (i. e. a low unstressed first syllable and a slightly higher unstressed second syllable) with the stressed third syllable (the nucleus) rising even higher. When this intonation is used, the sentence suggests that what somebody has just said confirms your own opinion or proves a statement you have just made on that subject. It may even be sarcastic.

There you are. ⟋ (= *This is for you.*)

There you are. ⟋ (= *That proves what I said.*)

As the study of the intonation patterns of English is a large and complicated field, we shall limit ourselves to the consideration of only a few characteristic cases, viz. simple statements and questions.

Statements

Statements are usually characterized by having a low **pre-head** (i. e. one or more sentence-initial unstressed syllables) followed by a falling tune which starts with a high tone on the first stressed syllable (the **head**), and then steps down on each further stressed syllable (the **body**) until the last (the **nucleus**), which is then said with a low fall. As this last stress is the most prominent we will show it below in the orthography of the sentence by a double stress mark, which we shall use here to differentiate it from contrastive or emphatic stress (also characterized by pitch movement (accent) plus stress over one syllable).

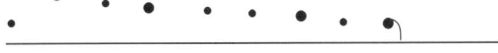

The 'dog was 'gnawing an e'normous ''bone.

This kind of pitch movement, which we have referred to as a falling tune or pattern, can also be thought of as a falling phoneme of intonation. In the sentence above we have shown the pitch of unstressed syllables by a small dot and that of stressed syllables by a larger dot. The low fall (or glide) over the nucleus is represented by adding a tail to the larger dot showing the direction of the pitch movement.

Questions

Depending on their grammatical structure, English questions may have either a falling intonation pattern or a rising one. They fall into three main categories: (a) **question-word questions,** (b) **yes-no questions** and (c) **echo questions**.

Q-Word Q's

(a) When questions begin with one of the interrogative adverbs such as *where? when? why?* or with one of the interrogative pronouns or determiners such as *who? whose? which? what?*, they have the same falling pattern as we find in statements. The reason for this is probably that since the initial interrogative word immediately marks the utterance as a question no further signal is required. Besides being called a **question-word question** this type of sentence is also referred to as a **wh-word question**, since with the exception of the interrogative adverb *how?* all the initial interrogative words begin with *wh*. To illustrate this falling intonation pattern in questions, let us convert the statement above about the dog and the bone into a *wh*-word question and set it out below:

'Why was the 'dog 'gnawing an e'normous ''bone?

(b) A sentence of a different kind is the yes-no question. As its name suggests, it does not ask for information as question-word questions do, but requires the answer *yes* or *no*. Questions of this type do not begin with an interrogative word but show that they are questions by inverting the subject and the verb when the latter is a modal verb or by introducing the auxiliary verb *do* for this inversion when the verb has no other auxiliary or modal verb accompanying it. This type of question is characterized by having a falling pattern of intonation with a final rise beginning on the nucleus. Let us now change the statement about the dog and the bone into this type of question. One pronunciation of this would be as follows:

Was the 'dog 'gnawing an e'normous ''bone?

Here we have first a low rising pre-head and then the falling tune begins high on the head *(dog)*, descends on each of the intermediate stressed syllables *gnaw-* and *-nor-* (the body) and the prominent monosyllabic nucleus *bone* has a low rise.

Another pronunciation of this sentence could have the initial auxiliary verb stressed: *was* would then become the head and begin on a higher pitch than *dog* but the falling pattern of the rest of the question with the final rise on *bone* would be retained.

Before we leave yes-no questions, it should be mentioned that American English differs from British English in usually having a rising pattern throughout all the feet of this kind of sentence: for Americans yes-no questions start low and each successive stressed syllable is said on a higher pitch until the final rise begins on the nucleus. Compare the following:

GA:

RP:

Did you 'see all those 'spots on the ''tablecloth?

(c) A third type of question is the echo-question, which begins with a wh-word but does not ask for information. By echoing another speaker's words it signals to him that the listener has not understood and requires him to repeat what he has just said. This kind of question, unlike the normal question-word question, has a rising intonation pattern with a final rise on the nucleus, just like the American version of the yes-no question.

'Why did your 'brother 'go on the "stage?

The person to whom this question is addressed has just said that his brother has become an actor, but the questioner has either not understood the reason for the brother's decision or is so surprised that he needs to be told the reason a second time.

Tails

In all the sentences which we have given above to illustrate different intonation patterns the most prominent stress in the sentence has always fallen on the final word and in each case (except for *tablecloth*) this has been a monosyllable. As this syllable also has to accommodate the final rise or final fall, the vowel in it, even when short, may be lengthened. When, however, this final word consists of a stressed syllable (nucleus) followed by one or more unstressed syllables there is usually no noticeable lengthening of the nucleus vowel and the direction of the rise or fall in pitch is continued over these unstressed syllables, i. e. they become increasingly lower in a falling tune or increasingly higher in a rising one. We saw this happening with the last two syllables of *tablecloth*, but it is particularly striking when one of these questions occurs between inverted commas in explicit dialogue in a book and the author adds a few words to inform the reader how they are uttered and by whom. When sentences of this kind are read aloud, the whole of this tail (i. e. the syllables and words following the nucleus of the question) follows the direction of the pitch movement on the nucleus. Thus after a nucleus with a final rise the tail will continue to rise, i. e. each stressed syllable of the tail will be said on a successively higher pitch and the final stressed word of the tail may even have a rise of its own if it is a monosyllable. Similarly, a tail that comes after a question or a statement ending with a falling nucleus will have all its syllables on a lower tone than that with which the nucleus ends, and if its own last stressed word is monosyllabic this also may have a fall in pitch. The following examples should make this clear.

Yes-No Q Rising Tail

"'Can you "sing?" 'asked the 'vicar with a 'pleasant 'smile.

Echo Q Rising Tail

"'What's the "time?" in'quired 'Jane in 'great dis'may.

(Somebody has just told Jane that it is past midnight and she now realizes that she has lost her train.)

Statement Falling Tail

"I 'want to 'go "home," said 'Jack to his 'younger 'brother.

Q-Word Q Falling Tail

"'When can you 'pay the "bill?" 'asked the 'owner of the shop.

Tag-Q's

As the reader has no doubt begun to realize from these examples, intonation is a rather complex area of phonology. The complexity lies in the fact that there are many different variants of the basic tunes and that these can be used in different ways for different purposes.

In the sentences above we have barely scratched the surface: even in our brief consideration of questions we have not mentioned those which have the grammatical structure of ordinary statements but are said with rising intonation. Nor have we mentioned **tag-questions,** which consist of a statement followed by a tag such as *do you, can they, haven't we, wasn't I*. These tags repeat any auxiliary or modal verb found in the statement or else they introduce a form of the auxiliary verb *do* and then they pick up the person and number of the subject of the statement as a personal pronoun following the tag verb. If the statement is in the negative, the tag will be affirmative, e. g. *You didn't open the door, did you?* or *I wasn't rude, was I?* If the statement is affirmative, then the tag will be negative, e. g. *We have paid, haven't we?* or *They can come, can't they?* The intonation of tag-questions is notoriously complex as both the tag and the statement it follows can have a variety of different intonation patterns, each of which lends a different meaning to the sentence or makes it have different implications. This area of phonology overlaps with pragmatics, which amongst other things studies the meanings that a statement can have other than the face meaning of the words it contains.

Other Types

Unfortunately, time and space will not allow us to examine this aspect of intonation in detail but we should notice that besides the two types of intonation which we have referred to as the rise and the fall or as rising and falling tunes, we can distinguish two others which also have pragmatic significance: the **fall-rise** (or **falling-rising tune**) and the **rise-fall** (or **rising-falling tune**). Just like the simple rise and the simple fall, each of these can occur on a single stressed syllable, which then is usually lengthened to accommodate the pitch movement. Let us consider first the fall-rise. An example of this tune over a stressed monosyllable is the word *yes* used as a comment during a conversation:

Fall-Rise

"Yes...   (but I don't fully agree with you)

The fall-rise tune tells the listener that the speaker has mental reservations, i. e. there is a *but* at the back of his mind. In the example above, although by using the word *yes* the speaker seems to accept what the listener has just said, the intonation indicates that he is having some problems with it. Notice that the words in parentheses do not have to be spoken aloud.

Rise-Fall

The rise-fall tune has quite different implications. It always indicates sarcasm, irony or impatience. For example, if somebody says: "*Isn't Bill Smith a clever fellow!*" and you consider him to be a complete idiot, you might be tempted to reply:

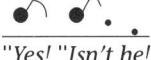

"Yes! "Isn't he!   (= I couldn't agree less!)

This last example, although probably said without a pause, contains two intonation groups, each with its own rise-fall tune: one over a monosyllabic nucleus and one over a nucleus followed by two unstressed syllables. In the latter case there is first a short rise of pitch on the nucleus (the pitch movement being restricted because of the shortness of the vowel) and then the fall is so rapid that the following unstressed syllable seems to begin straight away on a low tone with the final unstressed syllable being even lower.

In the same way the fall-rise may also be spread over a nucleus followed by one or more unstressed syllables. In this case only the falling part of the fall-rise occurs on the nucleus. The rising part begins on the first unstressed syllable following the nucleus and, as we would expect, continues over any subsequent unstressed syllables. Quite often the fall-rise is preceded by a falling tune over the syllables of the feet preceding it. When this occurs it is usual for the nucleus to begin the falling part of the fall-rise a little higher than the end of the fall of the preceding feet. The following examples should make this clear.

**Fall +
Fall-Rise**

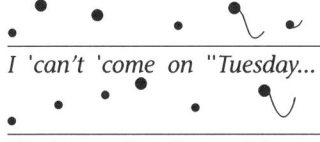

I 'can't 'come on "Tuesday...   (but maybe on Thursday)

He has a 'handsome "face...   (but I don't admire much else)

**Final
Remarks**

To sum up, we can say that, whether we consider them as phonemes or find another analysis for them, English has four kinds of intonational pitch movements (tunes or patterns): the fall, the rise, the fall-rise and the rise-fall. We have seen that these are found in association with stressed syllables in the feet of an intonation group and are characteristically used (a) to clarify the information which the speaker gives, e. g. by signalling grammatical structures such as statements and questions, and (b) to reflect the emotional attitudes of the speaker.

Intonation is a particularly difficult area for foreign learners as each language has its own characteristic patterns and these may be quite different from those in the target language, or even if they are similar they may not be used for the same purposes.

For a fuller account of intonation with an examination of various different analyses and approaches the reader is recommended to consult Cruttenden's *Intonation*.

4 Length

General Remarks

Before we return in Chapter 3 to segmental phonemes and examine in detail their allophones in English, we must spend a little time looking at two other phonological features, which are sometimes considered to be suprasegmental: one is length (in vowels and in consonants) and the other is juncture (where and how morphemes or words begin and end). They resemble each other insofar as it is usually more satisfactory not to treat them as suprasegmental phonemes, but to explain their presence in other ways. Let us look first at length and postpone juncture until the following section.

One could argue that if stress can be considered as a separate feature over and above the segments of a word, so can vowel length and consonant length too. After all, just as we can show stress by using an additional sign (the little upright stroke before the stressed syllable), so we can also indicate length by writing a separate length sign (the colon) after vowels.

Vowel Length

Thus instead of classifying English vowels into long and short-phonemes, we could analyse the long ones as being the corresponding short vowels plus the phoneme of length. So, for example, the long vowel /iː/ would then really be the phoneme /ɪ/ with the length taken out of it and this length could itself be considered as the phoneme /ː/. Although this analysis would reduce the number of vowel phonemes, it presents certain problems. First of all, the high short vowels of English (/ɪ/ and /ʊ/) differ phonetically from the long vowels by having a lower tongue height. We could get round this by saying that they are raised when combined with the phoneme of stress, but then why does this not happen with the phoneme /ə/, whose tongue height is usually the same as that of its long counterpart /ɜː/? Another awkward question is why does the short vowel /ɒ/ become more rounded when it combines with the phoneme of stress to produce /ɔː/. Even more embarrass-ing for this analysis is the vowel /ɑː/, which does not seem to have any corresponding short vowel. The nearest candidate would be /æ/, but this is phonetically too different. In the face of all these difficulties it is not surprising that phonologists have rejected a phoneme of length for English and choose to analyse its vowels into individual long and short ones. Notice, however, that for a language with pairs of otherwise phonetically identical long and short vowels the analysis with a phoneme of stress would be more economical and quite acceptable.

Consonant Length

In the case of long consonants we again run into difficulties in English. Certainly in a word like *wholly* the *l* sound is normally longer than that in the word *holy* and we might feel tempted at first sight to posit a phoneme of length accompanying the pho-neme /l/ in the first word, but on looking more closely we discover that there are two occurrences of the phoneme /l/ in *wholly*: the first marks the end of the morpheme *whole* and the second the begin-ning of the adverbial suffix *-ly*, which is also a morpheme. Although these two *l*'s when side by side may be realized phonetically as a long *l* [lː], there seems to be no justification for an analysis of them as only one phoneme /l/ plus a phoneme of length.

A somewhat different case is presented by the /n/ in *send*, which is phonetically longer than that in *sent*, but this too can be explained in another way. As we shall see in Chapter 3, nasal phonemes occurring before obstruents (plosives, fricatives and affricates) which are voiced are realized by a lengthened allo-phone. Thus we can write *send* phonetically as [senːd] compared with *sent* [sent], but on the phonemic level we have no need for a phoneme of length. Length here is not a phoneme in its own right but merely a feature of the realization of a phoneme. Notice also that in *send* it has nothing to do with the morphological structure of the word as was the case in *wholly*.

5 Juncture and Boundary Phenomena

Use of Term

The word **juncture** is ambiguously used to refer both to the joints between words or morphemes, i. e. their boundaries, and to the phonological phenomena which occur there. When a person utters a sentence, a listener must somehow recognize where words (or morphemes) begin and end in order to be able to understand the meaning of the whole.

Juncture Mechanisms

Languages have many mechanisms to help the listener make these decisions. Take, for example, the glottal stop in German. We saw when we were considering the phonetics of this sound in

Chapter 1 (pages 7–8, 19) that it occurs at the beginning of a word (or morpheme) before a vowel and nowhere else. It is therefore a clear signal to the hearer that the word (or morpheme) that the speaker is using begins here. In other words it marks a boundary between two words (or morphemes). Notice that there does not have to be a pause before the glottal stop: the utterance may be a continuous stream of sounds. German uses the glottal stop as a kind of mental signal to listeners to help them to break up the utterance into its component parts.

English

We saw a similar situation in English phonology where the glottal stop is used for a same purpose but only in emphatic speech at the beginnings of words that have an initial vowel. Thus in addition to signalling emphasis it also signals the boundary between the word it is attached to and the preceding word. Again it helps the hearer to locate the end of one word and the beginning of another.

A better example in English is the phoneme /h/, which is found only at the beginning of a morpheme and not confined to emphatic speech. Here again we have a signal that a boundary is present, in this case a morpheme boundary. Note that we may also have negative signals about the location of boundaries, e. g. a listener hearing the phoneme /ŋ/ will know immediately that this cannot be the beginning of a morpheme, as /ŋ/ never occurs in this position in English. A similar negative signal is given by one of the short vowels /æ, ɒ, e, ʌ/, which the language does not allow to occur syllable-finally and which therefore can never mark the end of a word.

Phoneme?

As we saw above, boundaries between words or morphemes are sometimes referred to as junctures and in some older analyses, where grammmatical or morphological facts were allowed to play no role whatever in phonology, the juncture was thought of as a suprasegmental or even segmental phoneme, a kind of inaudible segment in the stream of utterance which conditioned the presence or absence of certain phonemes, such as the glottal stop in German or the /h/ in English, or which gave rise to other phonological phenomena which occur at and mark the ends of words and morphemes. In more modern analyses phonological boundaries are still required and the phenomena found there must still be accounted for, but this is now done by recognizing the grammatical and morphological structure of words and groups of words alongside their phonological structure. Although the need to posit various phonemes of juncture is no longer felt, two of the symbols which were used in this kind of analysis are still current: the plus sign (+) for a morpheme boundary and the double cross sign (#) for a word boundary.

Other Mechanisms	In the two cases which we described above, the boundary marking was effected by the presence or absence of a particular phoneme. However, it is not common for phonemes to be used in this way; in the majority of cases boundaries between words or morphemes are indicated by the use of certain allophones of segmental phonemes or by prosodic features such as stress, pitch and length.
Example	A good example of this is provided by the comparison of the two phrases *a spice candle* (a candle that burns aromatically) and *a spy scandal* (a scandal involving a spy). In the careful enunciation of these phrases the boundary between the last two words is phonetically clearly marked. On the phonemic level both phrases have an identical sequence of segmental phonemes /əspaɪskændl/. On the phonetic (allophonic) level, however, there are a number of differences which show where the boundaries between the two nouns occur and which therefore help to keep the two meanings separate.
Length	First, the vowel in *spice* is shorter than that in *spy*. English vowels are clipped, i. e. made shorter, when they occur in syllables which close with a voiceless (fortis) consonant (**pre-fortis clipping**). In an open syllable, i. e. one that ends in a vowel, as is the case with *spy*, they will have their normal length. When a stressed open syllable marks the boundary of a sentence (e. g. at the end in the nucleus of an intonation group) it may even be longer than usual: so in the sentence *They've caught the spy* the vowel of the last word will be even longer than in *spy scandal*.
Allophones	Second, the voiceless alveolar fricative /s/ at the end of *spice* will be said relatively weakly as the syllable is dying away at this point, whereas the same consonant at the beginning of *scandal* will be said relatively strongly, as the syllable must increase in intensity from here onwards until it reaches its peak in the middle of the word. In other words the boundary phoneme /s/ is realized here by two allophones, one which increases in intensity at the beginning of the word and one which decreases in intensity at the end of a word. If we compare this phenomenon to the waxing and waning of the moon, we can call the former allophone **waxing** [s] and the latter **waning** [s].
Allophones	There is also a third feature which signals the position of the boundary in our two phrases, viz. **aspiration.** The velar plosive /k/ can be realized either by an aspirated allophone, i. e. one followed by a short puff of air, or by an unaspirated one, i. e. without the short puff of air after it. Aspiration is found in English only when a voiceless plosive occurs alone before a stressed vowel at the beginning of a syllable. Thus the presence of the aspirated allo-

phone [kʰ] at the beginning of *candle* tells the listener that the preceding [s] must belong to the preceding word. In the case of the word *scandal*, however, although the allophone [k] occurs before a stressed vowel it is not aspirated as it is not alone in initial position but preceded by [s]. So here the unaspirated [k] tells the listener that the [s] and the [k] form a word-initial consonant cluster, and this clue will be reinforced, of course, by the fact that the [s] is a waxing [s].

Prosody

We said above that juncture can be indicated not only by the use of certain allophones but also by the stress and intonation. If we look again at the sentence *They've caught the spy*, not only the longer vowel in *spy* signals the end of the sentence but also both the more prominent stress on that syllable and the low-fall in the intonation. Again, even if the speaker continues and makes no pause between this sentence and a following one, these three signals will still be there to help the listener to analyse the utterance as two sentences by showing the boundary between them.

Other Examples

To round off this section on juncture we can quote one or two of the famous examples that have been used in the literature of phonology, naming the kinds of allophones we find at the boundaries. Full details will be given of these allophones in the next chapter.

ice cream, I scream: clipped [aɪ] in *ice*, normal length [aɪ] in *I*; waning [s] in *ice*, waxing [s] in *scream*; voiceless fricative [r] in *cream*, voiceless non-fricative [r] in *scream*.

the waiter cut it, the way to cut it: clipped [eɪ] in *waiter*, normal length [eɪ] in *way*.

white shoes, why choose: unreleased [t] in *white* followed by relatively strong [ʃ] in *shoes*; the [t] part of [tʃ] released and the [ʃ] as part of the affricate not as strongly articulated as fricative [ʃ] alone.

an aim, a name: waning [n] in *an*, waxing [n] in *name*.

Historical Notes

As an historical note we can mention that since waxing and waning [n] are difficult to tell apart this has sometimes in the course of the development of English led to a reallocation of the boundary between the indefinite article *an* and the noun following it. Thus in modern English we say *an orange*, but this should really be *a norange* since the noun is ultimately derived from the Arabic *naranj* and the Persian *narang*. Another example is the modern noun *apron*, which has suffered a similar fate. It is derived from the Old French word *naperon* and ought really to be *napron*, but a misinterpretation of the boundary signals led in the 16th century to a reanalysis of *a napron* as *an apron*. Sometimes this phenomenon is found working in the other direction. Shakespeare has the Fool in *King Lear* calling his master *nuncle*, which resulted from a reanalysis of *mine uncle* as *my nuncle*. The reallocation of boundaries has also taken place in modern English: for example the word *another* is clearly made up of the morphemes *an + other*, yet most modern speakers pronounce this word as if its structure were *a + nother*: [ə 'nʌðə]. This new phonological boundary becomes even more apparent when the word is given emphatic stress. Here the first syllable is sometimes pronounced with the strong form of the indefinite article [eɪ], which can only occur before another word beginning with a consonant [eɪ + ''nʌðə]. A slightly different modern example is provided by the word *beetroot*, in which the morpheme boundary is clearly between *beet* and *root*. This is always pronounced with a voiceless fricative [r], an allophone which can only occur after a voiceless plosive in the same syllable. Here again the phonological boundary no longer coincides with the morphological one.

For further reading on Juncture, see Gimson Ch. 2, and Lass Ch. 2.

Consonant Phonemes
CHAPTER and their Phones

① Plosives

**Prelimi-
naries**

In this chapter we shall examine more carefully the distribution and phonetic characteristics of the different realizations of consonant and vowel phonemes in English. As many of these realizations are free variants and not always allophones in complementary distribution we shall continue to refer to them as phones and not follow the common practice of using the term *allophone* loosely to cover all the realizations of a phoneme. In some respects this will be a continuation of the last topic in Ch. 2, as many of these phones are associated with boundaries of various kinds. Let us turn first to the plosive phonemes.

Four Criteria

There are four main features which we can use to distinguish between the phones of the plosive phonemes: **aspiration, degree of voicing, kind of release** (plosion), and **place of articulation.** Let us consider each of these separately.

1 Aspiration

Definition

As we saw in Ch. 2, page 81, **aspiration** is the term used to refer to the small puff of air which occurs between certain consonants and the vowel which follows them. In phonetic transcription it is represented by a small superscript *h* written after the aspirated consonant.

/p, t, k/

In English only the voiceless plosives /p, t, k/ can have aspirated phones. The plosive phone occurs before a stressed vowel and must be the only consonant in this position. If the stressed vowel has primary stress the plosive is relatively strongly aspirated; if the vowel has secondary stress the aspiration is usually weaker. If a voiceless plosive is part of a consonant cluster (i. e. not alone) before a stressed vowel, it is not aspirated. A few examples will make this clear: In the word *territorial* both *t*'s will be aspirated. The first comes before a vowel with secondary stress and will therefore be a little less aspirated than the second, which is followed by a vowel with primary stress: [ˌtʰerɪ'tʰɔːrɪəl]. Examples of aspirated *p* and *k* can be seen in the words *pour* ['pʰɔː] or *compare* [kəm'pʰeə] and *call* ['kʰɔːl] or *occur* [ə'kʰɜː]. Unaspirated phones are found not only in consonant clusters before a stressed vowel, e. g. *spare, steam, school* ['speə, 'stiːm, 'skuːl], but also before an unstressed vowel (e. g. the [t] in *satisfy* ['sætɪsfaɪ]) and before a consonant (e. g. the [k] in *act* ['ækt] and the [p] in *lapse* ['læps]).

Juncture

These aspirated and unaspirated phones can be used to show juncture. If we compare the three words *spare, steam, school* with *pair, team, cool,* the aspirated phones at the beginning of the latter three ['pʰeə, 'tʰiːm, 'kʰuːl] show clearly that they are immediately preceded by a word boundary. Thus if they occur in speech with the word *this* in front of them, the listener knows from the aspiration of these plosives that the [s] in the middle of the utterance must be at the end of the syllable preceding them. In the same way if *spare, steam, school* are preceded by *the* in an utterance, there is little likelihood of confusion between a pair like *this team* and *the steam* since the unaspirated [t] in the latter is a clear indication that before the stressed vowel it can only be the second element in a consonant cluster with [s].

Distribution

The distribution of plosives in syllable-initial consonant clusters is severely restricted in English. In this position the voiced plosive phonemes /b, d, g/ can have no other consonant in front of them and the voiceless plosives can only be preceded by /s/. In clusters where the plosives are absolutely initial the second element can only be a liquid (/l, r/) or a semivowel (/j, w/), but even here some combinations are forbidden. Thus we find /p/ and /b/ combining with /l, r, j/ in words like *please, blue, pray, brood, pure, beauty* but there are no words with syllable-initial /pw, bw/.

Neutra-lization

Notice that whereas the voiceless and voiced plosives normally contrast with each other, e. g. in a minimal pair like *team, deem,* this opposition is neutralized after syllable-initial /s/. Thus in the word *steam,* where the second phoneme in the initial cluster is realized by an unaspirated phone, the phonetic difference between /t/ and /d/ here is minimal and the sound could equally well be interpreted as /d/. Only tradition prevents us from spelling the word *sdeam.* However, sometimes the spelling helps to keep two words apart even though their phonetic realizations are identical, e. g. *discussed* and *disgust.*

Allophones & Free Variants

Note that aspirated and unaspirated phones are **allophones** when syllable-initial in stressed syllables or when before consonants or unstressed vowels, since in all these positions they are in complementary distribution. However, word-finally they are **in free variation,** i. e. depending on the style of the utterance either phone can be used. In fast speech the unaspirated phones are normal: in very careful or emphatic speech the aspirated phones are often preferred, especially if the plosive is not only word-final but also sentence-final. Thus in the sentence *He's been shot* the final word would be pronounced ['ʃɒt] in normal style, but also ['ʃɒtʰ] in emphatic style.

2 Degree of Voicing

Terminology The second of the main features which characterize the phones of plosive phonemes is the degree to which they are voiced. As we shall see later, this also plays a role with the phones of fricative and affricate phonemes. We are concerned here only with voiced plosives, since the voiceless ones always remain voiceless in English. Voiced plosives may be **fully voiced, partially devoiced** or **fully devoiced.** The term devoiced refers to a sound which would normally be voiced but has had some or all of the voicing removed from it in a particular context. Although a **fully devoiced** sound is phonetically voiceless, we shall apply the term voiceless only to sounds which are naturally voiceless.

Full Voicing Voiced plosives are fully voiced, i. e. voiced from beginning to end, when the sound on either side of them is voiced. For example, the [g] in *ago* has a vowel preceding it and another following it, and since vowels in English are always voiced, the voicing which starts in the [ə] will continue throughout the whole of the [g] and on into and throughout the following [əʊ].

Partial Devoicing On the other hand voiced plosives are **partially devoiced** when one of their neighbours is voiceless or when they occur immediately after or before a pause. More exactly, they lose their voicing on the side next to the silence or voiceless neighbour but retain it on the other side. Let us take as an example the word *bread*. If said in isolation it has a silence in front of it and a silence after it. This will affect the [b] at the beginning and the [d] at the end. The initial plosive will begin devoiced after the silence and then the voicing will start a little way into the plosive since it is followed by a voiced sound [r]. In the case of the final plosive it will be the other way round. The voicing of the preceding vowel will carry on into the [d] for about half of the sound and then the second half will be devoiced because of the silence following it. Graphically we can show this in the following diagram where a straight line under the sound represents voicelessness and a jagged line under a sound represents voicedness.

Rightward/ Leftward	Two examples of words in which a voiceless neighbour causes a partially devoiced plosive phone to be used are *absence* and *obtain*. The [b] in both words is followed by a voiceless sound and will therefore be partially devoiced on that side. We can call this **rightward partial devoicing** and use the term **leftward partial devoicing** for the kind where the voicelessness or silence is on the other side.
Another Example	When two plosives which would normally be voiced occur together at the end of a word before a pause and after a vowel, the second is completely devoiced and the first is partially devoiced, retaining its voice on the vowel side and losing it on the other side. For example, in the word *robbed* the phone [b] is partially devoiced rightwards in front of the totally devoiced [d]. Although this devoiced [d] is phonetically almost exactly similar to [t] it differs in one important respect: whereas [t] is fortis, i. e. has a strong plosion, devoiced [d] remains lenis, i. e. its plosion is weak.
Comparison	If we now compare the final three segments of *robbed* and of *stopped*, we find three reasons why they are audibly quite different. First, the final plosive in the former is lenis and in the latter fortis; second, the [b] in *robbed* is partially devoiced rightwards, whereas the [p] in *stopped* is completely voiceless; and third, as we saw when we examined length in the last chapter, the vowel in *robbed* has normal length, whereas that in *stopped* is clipped, i. e. shortened, before the fortis [p]. Although the difference between devoiced plosives and voiceless plosives is phonetically very small (the build-up of air before the plosion must necessarily be very brief), native speakers can usually perceive the fortis/lenis distinction. However, it is the length of the vowel preceding these plosives which is the most important clue. In the sentence *He put it in the back* it is the clipped [æ] in *back* which signals clearly to the listener that the following sound is a voiceless fortis plosive, whereas the normal length of the [æ] in *bag* in the sentence *he put it in the bag* tells the listener that the sound following it is a lenis plosive even if partially devoiced.

Whereas partial or full devoicing only takes place before or after silence or voicelessness, no devoicing occurs where a plosive has a voiced sound on both sides of it. So if we now place the examples above in a voiced context, we find that the word-initial and word-final plosive phoneme in each case is realized by its normal fully voiced phone: e. g. the two word-initial [b]s and the word-final [d] in *some bread and butter*, the [bd] in *They robbed everyone*, and the [g] in *He put it in the bag of sweets*.

***t*-Voicing**	In American English a word-final /t/ preceded by a vowel, by /r/ or by /n/ is usually realized by a voiced phone when the next word

follows immediately and begins with a vowel, e. g. the /t/ of *but* in *but a while*, of *heart* in *my heart aches*, of *sent* in *he sent a letter*. The same phone can also be heard intervocalically or between /r/ or /n/ and a vowel in the middle of words, e. g. in *butter, hearty, center*. It sounds like a very rapid *d*. We encountered this sound when we talked about the alveolar flapped *r* which some RP speakers use intervocalically and after *th* in very careful speech. In RP it is a variant realization of the phoneme /r/, whereas in American pronunciation it is clearly a variant of /t/. The American phone can therefore be written phonetically as a [t] with a small subscript *v* for voicing below it: [t̬]. Probably as a result of the influence of the numerous American films shown on British television, this voiced *t* can also be heard sporadically in the speech of some British speakers nowadays.

3 Kind of Release

Terminology The third main feature distinguishing between the phones of plosive phonemes is their release, i. e. how and where the airstream is allowed to escape from the lungs at the plosion. Using this feature we can differentiate between three different kinds of plosive phones: **unreleased** phones, phones with **lateral release** and phones with **nasal release.** Let us consider each of these in turn.

Unreleased When a plosive phone is unreleased, the normal plosion does not take place. The speech organs are put in the correct position for the articulation of the plosive, but at the moment of the plosion, when the usual explosive burst of air should take place, the vocal cords are kept closed. In other words there is no audible release: the sound is held back for a moment. This usually happens when a plosive is found in front of another consonant, though it is not likely before [h]. For example, the first [t] in the word *resentment* when said in normal conversation will be unreleased before the following [m], whereas the final [t] will have normal release if said before a pause. Unreleased plosive phones can be indicated phonetically by placing a small raised angle after them: [˺]. This diacritic looks rather like the top right-hand corner of a door which we can imagine to be holding the plosion back. Using this sign we can now differentiate between the two phones of /t/ in the transcription of *resentment*: [rɪ'zent˺mənt]. Other examples of unreleased plosives both voiceless and voiced can be heard word-internally in *apt* [æp˺t], *blocked* [blɒk˺t], *robbed* [rɒb˺d], *redbrick* ['red˺brɪk], *dogcart* ['dɒg˺kɑːt]. In connected speech they are also found word-finally before another word beginning with a consonant, e. g. *that dog* [ðæt˺ 'dɒg], *night time* ['naɪt˺ taɪm], *don't stop* *there* ['daʊnt˺ 'stɒp˺ 'ðeə], *a black chicken* [ə 'blæk˺ 'tʃɪkɪn], *a big jug for Bill* [ə 'bɪɡ˺ 'dʒʌɡ˺ fə 'bɪl].

Like [ʔ]

Unreleased [t] and [k] sound very like the glottal stop. The listener hears the closure at the vocal cords but cannot usually see that the speaker has at the same time raised the front of his tongue to the teeth-ridge for the former or the back of his tongue to the soft palate for that latter. Unreleased [p] presents no problem since the closure at the lips is always visible.

Double Plosives

Notice that when two plosives with the same place of articulation and the same voicing occur one at the end of a word and the other at the beginning of the following word, the result in normal speech is phonetically a long consonant:

p˺ p = p:	*lamp-post, stop pulling*
t˺ t = t:	*biscuit tin, fat Tom*
k˺ k = k:	*blackcurrant, rock cake*
b˺ b = b:	*Arab boy, bob back*
d˺ d = d:	*dead duck, bird droppings*
ɡ˺ ɡ = ɡ:	*big guy, leg guard*

In very careful pronunciation the first consonant in each of these pairs may of course be said with a plosion just like the second, but this usually sounds pedantic.

Lateral Release

Phones are laterally released when their plosion takes place down the sides of the tongue instead of over it. This can only happen in the realization of the alveolar plosives phonemes /t/ and /d/ when they occur immediately after a stressed vowel and in front of a syllabic /l/. As we saw at the end of Ch. 1, it results from the reduction of a syllable with [əl] to just [l̩]. Phonetically we can mark these laterally released plosive phones by means of a small raised *l* written after the symbol for the phone, as in the following examples:

['bɒtˡl̩]	['kʰætˡl̩]	['rɪdˡl̩]	['pʰædˡl̩]
bottle	*cattle*	*riddle*	*paddle*

In all the above words we see that the laterally released plosive and the following [l̩] are at the end of the same syllable. If we have the same sequence of sounds (an alveolar plosive plus a lateral) but with a juncture between them, i. e. where the plosive is word-final or morpheme-final and the lateral is at the beginning of the following word or morpheme, the plosive is not laterally released but usually unreleased. The following examples will make this clear:

['raɪt˺ 'letəz] *write letters*	['ðæt˺ 'læmp] *that lamp*
['bæd˺ 'lʌk] *bad luck*	['red˺ 'lɒri] *red lorry*

Nasal Release

Normally in the articulation of plosives the plosion is oral, i. e. the air behind the closure escapes through the mouth. However, when the alveolar plosives /t/ and /d/ occur before syllabic [n̩] they are exploded through the nose. Like the syllabic lateral we saw above, the syllabic nasal is the usual pronunciation of a syllable which in very careful speech would be said with shwa, i. e. syllabic [n̩] results from the reduction of [ən]. The following examples show the nasally released plosive plus the syllabic nasal at the end of the same syllable:

['flætⁿ n̩]	['bʌtⁿ n̩]	['pʰɑːdⁿ n̩]	['bɜːdⁿ n̩]
flatten	*button*	*pardon*	*burden*

When /t/ or /d/ are word-final or morpheme-final and the next word or morpheme begins with /n/ they are realized by an unreleased phone instead of the nasally released one, a situation analogous to the one we saw with them in front of word-initial or morpheme-initial /l/, e. g.

[wɒt⌐ 'nɒnsəns] *what nonsense*   ['wɪt⌐ nəs] *witness*
[ðæt⌐ 'neɪm] *that name*
['bæd⌐ 'njuːz] *bad news*   ['red⌐ nek] *redneck*

Phonetically, nasal release sounds a little like coughing with the mouth closed. However, since the plosion for the [tⁿ] or [dⁿ] is made not just by suddenly opening the vocal cords as in coughing but also by lowering the soft palate, nasal release is accompanied by an audible burst of air through the nose, which is not to be heard when a person coughs.

Exception

There is one important environment in which nasal release could be expected but in fact does not take place. This is when the alveolar plosive is preceded by a nasal sound. When this happens, the shwa between the plosive and the following /n/ is usually not omitted and therefore the /n/ does not become syllabic. Thus there is no nasal release of /t/ and /d/ in the following words:

['lʌndən] *London*   ['wɒʃɪŋtən] *Washington*   ['klɪntən] *Clinton*

This environment will be discussed in more detail on page 100.

4 Place of Articulation

Preliminaries

The fourth and last phonetic characteristic distinguishing the phones of the plosive phonemes is their place of articulation. Like many other kinds of sounds, they may be affected by what immediately follows them, i. e. they anticipate the place of articulation of the following sound and adjust themselves in that direction.

Bilabials

The bilabial plosives [p] and [b] may themselves become **labio-dental** if they occur in front of one of the labiodental fricatives [f, v]. The closure is then made by placing the lower lip under the upper teeth and holding the sound until the release for the following fricative is made. We can indicate this labiodental kind of p or b by writing above or below it a small minus sign, which is used in phonetics to show a retracted sound: [p̠, b̠]. These phones are optional and occur as free variants of the normal bilabial at the end of a morpheme or word when the following morpheme or word begins with a labiodental. For example, the p in *hopeful* or in *stop fighting* and the b in *subvert* or in *club victory* may be pronounced in this way.

Alveolars

The alveolar plosives [t] and [d] may also adjust themselves to a following sound. They are usually said with the tip of the tongue between the teeth, i. e. they become **dental,** when they precede one of the dental fricatives [θ] and [ð]. This normally happens when a morpheme boundary or a word boundary separates them. The dental articulation can be shown by placing beneath them a diacritic sign which looks like a small bridge: [t̪], [d̪]. Two words in which this dental phone can be heard are *eighth* [eɪt̪ θ] and *breadth* [bred̪ θ, bret̪ θ]. Each contains two morphemes: *eight + th*, and *broad + th*. Two examples containing a word boundary between the plosive and the fricative are: *sit there* ['sɪt̪ 'ðeə] and *read this* ['riːd̪ 'ðɪs].

The alveolar plosives can also become **post-alveolar,** e. g. when they occur in front of the post-alveolar [r]. These consonant clusters are always syllable-initial in English and, as mentioned in Ch. 1, are sometimes considered as another affricate. To show that the plosive element in them is post-alveolar we can write a small inverted bridge diacritic beneath it: [t̺r], [d̺r]. Post-alveolar [t̺] and [d̺] occur freely at the beginning of words and word-medially: *train, drop, contract, address* [t̺reɪn, d̺rɒp, kən't̺rækt, ə'd̺res], but not with a word boundary or a morpheme boundary after them. In the latter case the alveolar plosive will usually be unreleased: *that road* [ðæt̚ 'rəʊd], *good riddance* ['gʊd̚ 'rɪdn̩ s].

Velars

If we look at the behaviour of the velar plosives /k/ and /g/, we find that their place of articulation is sensitive to the part of the tongue used for any vowel that follows them. If the vowel is a front vowel the plosive will be pronounced farther forward along the roof of the mouth, i. e. in a **prevelar** position; if the vowel is a back vowel the plosive phoneme will be realized farther back than normal, i. e. by a **post-velar** phone. In front of a central vowel the velar plosive will have its normal place of articulation. In other words, the three **voiceless** velar phones are in complementary distribution with one another, i. e. they are allophones, just as the three **voiced** velar phones are also in complementary distribution with one another, i. e. they too are allophones. Since the post-velar phone has a more retracted position than normal, we can show it phonetically by means of the small subscript or superscript minus sign which we used in connection with labiodental *p* and *b*. This retracted kind of velar plosive can be heard at the beginning of words like *card, curl, goose, got*: [ḵɑːdˌk̠ɜːlˌguːsˌɡɒt]. For the pre-velar plosives we can use a small subscript plus sign, e. g. in *keen, kill, get, gap*: [k̟iːn, k̟ɪl, g̟et, g̟æp]. For simplicity of presentation we have omitted the aspiration of the four initial /k/ sounds which should also be present in the above examples.

Résumé

If we now look back at all the different realizations of the plosive phonemes which we have discussed above under the headings of aspiration, degree of voicing, manner of release and place of articulation, we can choose one representative phoneme, e. g. /t/ and set it out diagrammatically with all its phones and allophones:

Phoneme: /t/

Phones/Allophones: [t] [tʰ] [t̬] [tˈ] [tˡ] [tⁿ] [t̪] [t̠]

From left to right we see the unaspirated (normal) phone, the aspirated phone found alone before a stressed vowel, the American voiced intervocalic flapped phone, the unreleased phone, the laterally released phone, the nasally released phone, the dental phone and the post-alveolar phone.

A diagram of this kind could be drawn for all the other plosive phonemes.

② Fricatives

Preliminaries

The fricative phonemes of English /f, v, θ, ð, s, z, ʃ, ʒ, h/ although more numerous than the plosive phonemes are simpler in their realizations and do not show the same wealth of phones. We can examine them more closely with regard to three main characteristics: their **distribution,** which is more interesting than that of the plosives, their **voicing,** and the **alternation** between voiceless and voiced members of pairs with the same place of articulation. Let us consider distribution first.

1 Distribution

The fricative phonemes vary considerably amongst themselves in respect of where they are permitted to occur in native English words, some (/ʒ/ and /h/) being very severely restricted.

/f, v, s, z/ The phonemes /f, v, s, z/ occur freely as single consonants at the beginning, in the middle, and at the end of words and morphemes. However, they do not behave alike in word-initial clusters. For example, although /f/ can combine with /l/, /r/ or /j/ as in *floor, fry, few*, /v/ can only combine with /j/ in this position as in *view*. On the other hand the phoneme /s/ occurs with /l/ as in *slow* and, for some RP speakers, with /j/ as in *suit*; in native English words /s/ is also found followed by one of the three voiceless plosives /p, t, k/ as in *spate, state, skate* and is the only consonant which is permitted as the first of a cluster of three consonants word-initially, as in *spray, stray, screen*. (We shall have more to say about these initial clusters of three consonants when we consider liquids and semivowels later.) Compared with /s/, its voiced counterpart /z/ is extremely restricted, for it cannot combine word-initially with any other consonant.

/ʃ, ʒ/ A similar pattern of restriction is found with the pair /ʃ, ʒ/, where the voiceless palato-alveolar fricative is found freely at the beginning, in the middle, and at the end of words or morphemes as in *ship, nation, fish*, whereas its voiced counterpart is much more restricted, usually occurring only word-medially, as in *vision, fusion, usual*, but also sometimes word-finally in words borrowed from French, e. g. in *rouge, beige, garage*. The latter word is particularly interesting as its various pronunciations show us the development from a foreign sounding word to a typically English sounding one. The American pronunciation [gəˈrɑːʒ] is perhaps closest to the original French [garaʒ], as it has retained the foreign sounding final fricative and has interpreted the French word as having stress on the final syllable, which is not usual in native English words of two syllables. French has in fact no stress, but the final syllable of a word may sound more prominent. In one RP pronunciation the stress pattern has been changed to an English one by stressing the word on the initial syllable, but the [ʒ] has been kept along with an un-English long vowel in an unstressed syllable: [ˈgærɑːʒ]. As we saw in our discussion of stress in Chapter 2, English prefers to have weakened vowels in unstressed syllables, which accounts for the [ə] in the first syllable of the American pronunciation. The next step in making the word sound more English in both varieties was to change the final [ʒ] to [dʒ], which is often found word-finally: RP [ˈgærɑːdʒ] , AmE [gəˈrɑːdʒ]. Complete anglicization has occurred in British English where not only the change of the final fricative to an affricate has taken place but also the unnatural long vowel in the final syllable has been replaced by the weak vowel [ɪ]: ['gænɪdʒ]. This latter pronunciation, which used to be frowned upon, is now quite acceptable in Britain and brings the word in line with many similar but historically much earlier borrowings from French, such as *bandage, baggage, marriage, carriage*.

Clusters

Before leaving the distribution of /ʃ/ and /ʒ/ we may note that neither is found in any native English consonant clusters word-initially and that only /ʃ/ occurs in medial or final clusters, e. g. *punishment* ['pʌnɪʃmənt], *wished* [wɪʃt]. These are, however, a different kind of cluster from the morpheme-internal ones which we have looked at so far, since in each case here /ʃ/ is separated from the following sound by a morpheme boundary: *punish+ment, wish+ed*.

/ h /

In addition to being the only English fricative without a voiced counterpart, the phoneme /h/ is also severely restricted in its distribution. We saw in Ch. 2 in connection with complementary distribution that /h/ can only be found syllable-initially, as in *horse, behave, perhaps* [hɔːs, bɪ'heɪv, pə'hæps].

/ θ, ð /

Both /θ/ and /ð/ can be found at the beginning of a word, but which of the two is used seems to depend upon the word's grammatical function. We find /ð/ at the beginning of the definite article *the*, of the personal pronoun *they, them, their*, of the conjunction *though*, and of the demonstrative pronouns or determiners *this, these, that, those* and related adverbs *then* (= at that time), *there* (= at that place), *thus* (= in this manner). At the beginning of words belonging to other word classes such as nouns and adjectives we find only /θ/, as in *thief, thigh* or *thick, thin*.
   Word-medially between vowels only /ð/ is found *(brother, rather, whether)*, whereas at the end of words both /θ/ and /ð/ are not uncommon *(truth, pith, with, soothe* [truːθ, pʰɪθ, wɪð, suːð]).

2 Voicing

/ h /

The phoneme /h/ is unique among the voiceless fricatives in having an optional fully voiced phone realizing it when it occurs between vowels. Thus in *ahead, ahoy, mayhem* we may hear either of the free variants [h] or [ɦ], where a small subscript *v* shows the voiced variant. The pronunciation of *ahead* may therefore be either [ə'hed] or [ə'ɦed].

Partial Devoicing

With the exception of /ʒ/, which as we saw can only occur word-medially in native English words and then always with voiced neighbours, the voiced fricatives behave in exactly the same way as the voiced plosives. When their left-hand or right-hand neighbour is voiceless or when there is a pause before or after them, they become partially devoiced on the side next to the voicelessness or the silence.

Final CCC Note that in clusters of three consonants at the ends of words before a pause or voicelessness, where the last two of the three consonants are fricatives, as in *shelves, valves*, both of these fricatives are fully devoiced. We can show this total devoicing diagrammatically (as we did for the partial devoicing of plosives) by drawing a jagged line under the voiced parts of a word and a straight line under the voiceless or devoiced parts. For *shelves* the diagram appears as follows:

$$\#\int e l v z \#$$

Lenis/Fortis It is important to remember that although this total devoicing should make /vz/ sound like /fs/ in this context, the former still retain their lenis articulation, i. e. they are pronounced weakly, whereas the latter are pronounced strongly since they are naturally voiceless and fortis.

Fully Voiced As is to be expected, both fricatives in this three-consonant cluster will have their normal fully voiced forms when they have voicing on both sides of them, e. g. in the sentence *She has several shelves of books* [.... 'ʃelvz əv ....], where they are preceded by [l] and followed by [ə].

3 Alternation

Background In our account of the distribution of /θ, ð/ above we had to take grammatical information into consideration, something which in the middle of the 20th century was particularly repugnant to classical American structuralist phonologists, who thought that each level of analysis should be carried out with no reference to any other level, i. e. phonology should not make any reference to grammatical, morphological or semantic facts. This notion has long since been abandoned. If we look at the behaviour of the fricative phonemes in English, we see that morphological information is needed in order to understand their distribution: the voiceless member of a pair with the same place of articulation often alternates with the voiced member when certain combinations of morphemes occur.

Example	When the plural morpheme (-s, -es) is added to certain nouns, a root-final voiceless fricative is replaced by the corresponding voiced one: the /f/ in /naɪf/ *knife* becomes a /v/ in the plural form /naɪvz/ *knive+s*, the /s/ in /haʊs/ changes to /z/ in the plural form /'haʊzɪz/ *house+s*. The context for these alternations is a purely morphological one, but if we consider the case of morphemes ending in /θ/ we discover that phonological considerations can also play a role. If the vowel preceding the voiceless fricative is short, no alternation will take place when the plural ending is added, e. g. *month+s* /mʌnθs/, *death+s* /deθs/, *fifth+s* /fɪfθs/. On the other hand when the preceding vowel is long, the voiceless fricative is often replaced by the voiced one, e. g. *path* / pʰɑːθ/, *path+s* /pʰɑːðz/; *youth* /juːθ/, *youth+s* /juːðz/. English also treats diphthongs as long vowels: so *mouth* /maʊθ/, *mouth+s* /maʊðz/ and *oath* /əʊθ/, *oath+s* /əʊðz/ behave in the same way.

🔢 Affricates

Prelimi-naries	English possesses two true affricates /tʃ/ and /dʒ/ as well as two pairs of sounds /tr/ and /dr/ which some phonologists consider also to be affricates but which are usually analysed as a plosive plus a fricative. For convenience we will consider the latter pair here only with respect to its distribution and postpone the examination of its phonetics until we come to the phones of /r/.

1 Distribution

[tʃ, dʒ; tr, dr]	Both pairs occur at the beginning and in the middle of words and morphemes, but only /tʃ/ and /dʒ/ can occur finally. Examples with the latter pair in all three positions are: *chain, Jane, wretched, rigid, rich, ridge*, and with the other pair initially and medially: *train, drain, petrol, kindred*. Note that these affricates cannot be used straddling a word or morpheme boundary, i. e. a combination of /t/+/ʃ/, /t/+/r/ or of /d/+/ʒ/, /d/+/r/ is not usually pronounced as an affricate, but with an unreleased plosive followed by a palato-alveolar fricative or by a normal voiced r- sound. Thus the juncture in *a fat wrist* [ə 'fæt 'rɪst], where the final /t/ in *fat* is usually unreleased and the initial /r/ of *wrist* is fully voiced and not fricative, makes the combination of /t/+/r/ sound quite different from the affricate combination in a phrase such as *a mattress*, where the /t/ is realized by a normally released phone and the /r/ by a partially devoiced phone which may be slightly fricative (see p.108).

Clusters	None of the affricates are found in consonant clusters at the beginnings of words or morphemes. However, at the ends, /tʃ/ and /dʒ/

do combine with /n/ and /l/ in front of them (and also with /r/ in this position in American English), e. g. *bench, hinge, belch, bulge,* and in American English also *larch, large.* These same combinations can be found word-medially when a morpheme boundary follows them, e. g. *benchmark, changeless* and in GA *largeness.*

2 Voicing

Partial Devoicing

Both /dʒ/ and /dr/ behave like the plosives and the fricatives when one of their neighbours is voiceless or when they occur after a pause, i. e. they become partially devoiced on the side next to the voicelessness or silence. However, since none of the affricates are found in consonant clusters at the beginnings of words, partial devoicing can occur here only after a pause, and then it is only the initial part of the /d/-element of the affricate which loses its voicing.

/dʒ/

At the end of a word or morpheme /dʒ/ is **unique** among the voiced phonemes of English in being realized by a **completely devoiced phone** when voicelessness or silence follows. For example, if the word *judge* is said in isolation with a pause before and after it, the final /dʒ/ will be totally devoiced, whereas the initial one will undergo leftward partial devoicing, as we would expect. Theoretically, this total devoicing of the affricate word-finally before silence should make pairs of words like *beseech, besiege; larch, large; batch, badge* sound alike, but the same two factors which we have seen several times before help the listener to differentiate. First, the naturally voiceless affricate is pronounced fortis whereas the devoiced africate still retains its lenis articulation; and second, the vowel before the naturally voiceless affricate undergoes **pre-fortis clipping,** i. e. it is shortened, whereas that before the devoiced affricate retains its normal length or may even be slightly lengthened if the word is stressed in sentence final position. Wells in his dictionary (LPD, page 136) calls this lengthening in final position **stretching.** We shall see below that the nasal consonants and the phonemes /l/ and /r/ may also undergo stretching and pre-fortis clipping.

4 Nasals

Features

Like the obstruents, the nasal phonemes can be examined with regard to their **distribution,** to the **voicing, place of articulation** and **length** of their phones, and to the fact that they can be **syllabic.**

1 Distribution

/ n, m, ŋ /

Of the three English nasal phonemes, /m/ and /n/ can be found in all positions in words and morphemes, e. g. *man, number, wonder, summer, honey, hunt*, whereas /ŋ/ never appears at the beginning, only in medial and final position, e. g. *finger, ringlet, junk, sang* ['fɪŋgə, 'rɪŋlət, dʒʌŋk, sæŋ]. Similarly, /m/ and /n/ occur word-initially or morpheme-initially in a consonant cluster with /s/ preceding them, e. g. *small, snail*, whereas /ŋ/ is never found in combination with /s/ in any position.

When we talked about neutralization in Ch. 2 we saw that if the nasal phonemes occur within a morpheme, i. e. if they are not absolutely at the beginning and not absolutely at the end of a morpheme, they are not contrastive and can be predicted from the place of articulation of the consonant following them. Thus in the examples we have just given above only the bilabial nasal /m/ is possible before the bilabial plosive /b/ in *number*, only the alveolar nasal /n/ before the alveolar plosive /d/ in *wonder*, and only the velar nasal /ŋ/ before the velar plosives /k/ or /g/ in *junk, finger*.

2 Voicing

Usually Voiced

Normally the phones realizing the nasal phonemes are always voiced but, in morpheme-initial consonant clusters with /s/ preceding them, /m/ or /n/ may have a very slight amount of devoicing on the side where the /s/ is heard, e. g. in the words *small* and *snail*. However, when /s/ combines with /m/ over a morpheme boundary in the middle of a Latinate word like *dismiss* (= *dis+miss*) the /m/ is not realized by a partially devoiced phone.

3 Place of Articulation

Preliminaries

Since the nasal phonemes are related to the plosives by having the same places of articulation, it is not surprising that they are also influenced in the same way by the neighbours which follow them.

Bilabial

Thus we find that like /p/ and /b/, when the nasal phoneme /m/ occurs in front of one of the labio-dental fricatives /f, v/, it may be **optionally** realized as a labio-dental phone, i. e. as an [m] said with the lower lip pushed a little way under and touching the upper teeth. This may occur inside a word or between words, e. g. in *emphatic* or *some fish, some vinegar*. In phonetics this labio-dental nasal is shown by adding to the right-hand side of the symbol [m] a tail curling to the left: [ɱ].

Similarly, the alveolar nasal phoneme /n/ resembles the alveolar plosives /t/ and /d/ in being realized by a **dental** phone when it precedes one of the dental fricatives /θ, ð/: it is then pronounced with the tip of the tongue between the teeth, e. g. in *tenth* [tʰen̪ θ]. On the other hand, it is realized by a post-alveolar phone, i. e. farther back along the roof of the mouth, when it occurs before the post-alveolar /r/, as in the name *Henry* ['hen̠ ri].

Because /ŋ/ can only occur either in absolute final position in a morpheme *(song, thing)*, or as the first element in a morpheme-final consonant cluster *(junk* [dʒʌŋk], *jungle* ['dʒʌŋgl]*)*, it can have a **pre-velar** or **post-velar** phone before a front or back vowel respectively (like its plosive counterparts /k/ and /g/), **only** when it is **immediately followed by a morpheme boundary**, as in *sing+ing* (prevelar) or in *strong+arm* (post-velar).

4 Length

In some respects the nasal phonemes behave a little like vowels: they are **subject to pre-fortis clipping and to stretching,** and they can be syllabic. We saw that English vowels are said shorter before a voiceless fortis sound and are normally pronounced longer when they occur at the end of an utterance and are stressed. This shortening or lengthening also applies respectively to any nasal sound which intervenes between the vowel and the voiceless fortis sound or which follows an utterance-final stressed vowel. Thus not only the vowel /aɪ/ but also the /n/ in the word *pint* are audibly shorter than in the word *pined*, and if the latter is utterance-final it is usually the nasal which is more stretched than the vowel. This same behaviour is also found in other pairs, such as *pant, panned; skint, skinned; sent, send; paint, pained.* Clipping and stretching with the other two nasals /m, ŋ/ can be heard in *ample* compared with *amble* or in *ankle* compared with *angle*, where in both cases the nasal is followed by a homorganic plosive (i. e. a plosive with the same place of articulation) and then by another consonant. Note that though /m/ occurs in the middle of words followed by a homorganic plosive (e. g. *hamper, amber*), word-finally a homorganic plosive in the spelling is not pronounced : *lamb, thumb, bomb, tomb* /læm, θʌm, bɒm, tuːm/. This does not, however, affect clipping and stretching. The word *lamp* /læmp/ has a shorter /æ/ and a shorter /m/ than *lamb* /læm/ has, and if the latter word is utterance-final these two phonemes will be realized by considerably longer phones than those heard in utterance-final *lamp*.

5 Syllabic

Prelimi-naries

In Ch. 1 (p. 46) we saw that the only English nasal consonant which commonly has a syllabic realization is alveolar /n/. The velar phoneme /ŋ/ is very rarely realized in this way, and the bilabial /m/ optionally has a syllabic phone only in the three common words *from, them, some,* which will be discussed in detail in Ch. 4 (pages 17, 19–20).

[n̩]

In all other English words, the only common syllabic nasal phone is [n̩]. Like the syllabic bilabial nasal [m̩], it too results from the omission of a preceding shwa. For example, the disyllable *button* will be pronounced ['bʌtən] in careful speech, but is usually said with a syllabic nasal in conversation ['bʌtn̩]. Syllabic [n̩] freely occurs after homorganic obstruents, i. e. after plosives, fricatives and affricates with the same place of articulation as itself. It is therefore almost always heard in words such as *question, action, basin* ['kwestʃn̩, 'ækʃn̩, 'beɪsn̩] where the preceding obstruent is alveolar, but less frequently in words like *open, bacon,* where the preceding obstruent is bilabial or velar.

Exception

As we saw on p. 90, there is one interesting exception to part of the rule given above. Although the sequence [ən] can optionally be reduced to syllabic [n̩] after an alveolar sound, the shwa must be retained in British English **if the alveolar is a plosive and itself preceded by a nasal,** as in *wanton, sentence, Clinton, London, abandon:* ['wɒntən, 'sentəns, 'klɪntən, 'lʌndən, ə'bændən]. This is also true of one RP pronunciation of the words *mountain, fountain* ['maʊntən, 'faʊntən], although these can also be pronounced ['maʊntɪn, 'faʊntɪn]. On the other hand, in GA this exception does not always apply and we often find Americans saying [wɑːntn̩, 'sentn̩s, 'klɪntn̩, 'lʌndn̩, ə'bændn̩, 'maʊntn̩, 'faʊntn̩].

5 Lateral Phoneme

/l/

In Ch. 1 we saw that the language possesses only one lateral phoneme, the voiced alveolar lateral /l/. We can examine this phoneme and its phonetic realizations under the following headings: **distribution, place of articulation,** (degree of) **voicing, fricativeness, fortis/lenis, length, syllabicity, (clear and dark) resonance.** Since fricativeness and the change from lenis to fortis go hand in hand with complete devoicing, we shall consider all three of these below under the heading 'voicing'.

 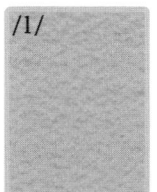

1 Distribution

General Remarks

The phoneme /l/ occurs as a single consonant freely at the beginning and end of syllables, e. g. *lift, pull, lull,* and may be found in syllable-initial clusters of two consonants as the second member after all the voiceless and voiced plosives except /t/ and /d/, e. g. *plead, bleed, clue, glue.* The only other syllable-initial two-consonant clusters in which it is heard as the second member are after the voiceless fricatives /s/ and /f/ as in *sleep, fly.* In this position it is not found after voiced fricatives nor after affricates. In native English words it forms a cluster of three consonants only after the voiceless plosive /p/ preceded by /s/, e. g. *spleen, splash, split,* though /k/ may also replace /p/ in some rather rare clusters of this length derived from Greek, e. g. *sclerotic.* In a number of words it can combine initially as the first member of a cluster with /j/, e. g. *lure, lurid, lewd, lute* /ljʊə, 'ljʊərɪd, lju:d, lju:t/ but in American English and in the pronunciation of younger generation British speakers the /j/ is usually missing.

In Final Position

At the ends of syllables, words and morphemes, /l/ combines freely as the first element of a cluster with all the plosives except /g/ *(help, bulb, halt, wild, whelk)*, with all the fricatives except /ʒ, ð, h/ *(elf, valve, filth, false, walls, Welsh)*, with the affricates /tʃ, dʒ/ *(squelch, bulge)* and with the nasals /m, n/ but not with /ŋ/ *(film, kiln).* Note that /l/ only combines with /z/ across a morpheme boundary: thus *walls = wall+s* /wɔ:l+z/; and, at least historically, the same is true of /l+θ/: *filth < foul+th, health < whole+th, wealth < well+th.*

2 Place of Articulation

Characteristics

As with all the other alveolar consonants, the /l/ phoneme in English is normally realized by a dental phone when it occurs before the dental fricatives /θ, ð/ (e. g. [wel̪θ] *wealth*, [ɔ:l̪'ðəʊ] *although*), and by a post-alveolar phone when it occurs before the post-alveolar continuant /r/ (e. g. [ɔ:l̠'redi] *already*, ['wɔ:l̠rəs] *walrus*). Note that these phones are true allophones as they occur in complementary distribution and are phonetically similar, apart from the change from the usual alveolar position to dental or to post-alveolar.

3 Voicing

Like /j, w, r/

With regard to voicing, the phoneme /l/ behaves rather like the two semivowels /j, w/ and its fellow liquid /r/.

Fully Voiced

It has its basic phonetic value when it occurs alone word-initially or word-finally or when it occurs between two voiced sounds, i. e. between two vowels, between a basically voiced consonant and a vowel, or between a vowel and a basically voiced consonant. It is then **fully voiced, lenis** and **non-fricative**, e. g. in *lead, blood, follow, bald*. Remember that the initial phoneme in *blood* is basically a voiced plosive though it may be realized by a partially devoiced phone if it is preceded by silence or a pause. Similarly, the final phoneme in *bald* is basically a voiced plosive though it may be realized by a partially devoiced phone if it is followed by silence or a pause. In each case the phone realizing the /l/ is immediately next to the voiced part of the devoiced sound and therefore itself remains fully voiced.

Fully Devoiced

However, when /l/ occurs after /p/ or /k/ in a two-consonant cluster before a stressed vowel, as in *please, pleasure, apply* or *clean, clatter, acclaim*, it is realized by a **completely devoiced** phone, which in addition is **fricative** and, rather surprisingly, **fortis.** The two liquids /l/ and /r/ and the two semivowels /j/ and /w/ are the only phonemes in English which have phones which change from lenis to fortis. When other basically voiced phonemes are realized by a completely devoiced phone, e. g. /dʒ/ word-finally before silence or voicelessness, or /d/ word-finally after /dʒ/ again before silence or voicelessness as in *bulged*, they always remain lenis.

Phonetically the completely devoiced fricative fortis phone that we mentioned above is produced by expelling air quite forcefully down the sides of the tongue while keeping the vocal cords wide apart so that no vibration of them is possible. This sound is noticeably different from the normal voiced non-fricative lenis /l/, but it should not be unfamiliar to speakers of standard German as they too have the same phonic realization of /l/ after /p/ or /k/ in their own language in exactly the same environment, i. e. in a two-consonant cluster before a stressed vowel, e.g in *Platz (= room, space)* or *klein (= small).*

Partially Devoiced

When /l/ is preceded by /p/ or /k/ in a two-consonant cluster before a non-stressed vowel as in *chaplain, necklace* or when it occurs in a cluster after another voiceless consonant as in *sleep, flight*, the phone realizing it has the kind of voicing which we would expect from the behaviour of other voiced consonants when they have a voiceless neighbour. It remains **lenis** and is only **partially devoiced,** losing its voicing on the side next to the voiceless neighbour but retaining it on the side next to the vowel. It is usually also **slightly fricative** here. This partially devoiced, lenis, slightly fricative phone is also the normal realization of /l/ in the initial three-consonant clusters /spl/ and /skl/ that we saw above in words like *splash* and *sclerotic*. In other words, the presence of the initial

/s/ in these clusters seems to prevent the rather startling change from lenis to fortis as well as the strong fricativeness accompanied by total devoicing that the we saw above for the phone of /l/ found in the two-consonant clusters /pl/ and /kl/ before a stressed vowel.

4 Length

Clipping/ Stretching

Like the nasal consonants, the English lateral phoneme is also subject to clipping before a fortis sound and to stretching at the end of an utterance-final stressed syllable. If we compare the normal pronunciation of pairs such as *pulp, bulb; fault, fold; cult, culled; bolt, bowled; false, falls* or of the alternative past tense forms *spelt, spelled* and *spoilt, spoiled*, there is a distinct difference in length between the phones realizing the /l/ in each pair: the first is short before the voiceless fortis plosives /p/ or /t/ or before the voiceless fortis fricative /s/, and the second is longer, especially if said with a pause after the word.

5 Syllabic

Like Nasals

Again like the nasal consonants, /l/ can also become syllabic when a preceding /ə/ drops out. Words such as *cattle, medal, simple, humble, wrinkle, dangle, whistle, drizzle, offal, oval, Ethel* may be pronounced either with [əl] or with syllabic [l̩] finally. This syllabic realization is the usual pronunciation in ordinary conversation, whereas [əl] is heard only in very careful speech.

In Addition

Notice that syllabicity is additional to the other features that we have described above. When the word *cattle* ['kʰæt'l̩] is said with a pause after it, in British English the /l/ is realized by a phone which is not only syllabic but which also shows leftward partial devoicing after the preceding (laterally released) voiceless phone of /t/ and it may even begin with a little friction. In other words it has the kind of voicing which we described for /l/ above under the heading of 'partial devoicing'.

American

In American pronunciation the situation is a little different. In words like *cattle* ['kʰæt̬l̩], the syllabic [l̩] shows no leftward partial devoicing, as the /t/ in front of it is realized by a voiced phone. It will be remembered that in GA this voiced [t̬] is regularly heard between vowels and thus appears in the more careful pronunciation of *cattle* with shwa before the /l/: ['kʰæt̬əl]. When in normal conversation the /ə/ is omitted, the resulting syllabic [l̩] still has a voiced neighbour preceding it and is therefore completely voiced.

If the reader is wondering why the /l/ in *cattle* in both the American and the British pronunciation does not have rightward partial devoicing before a pause (as plosives, fricatives and affricates do), it is important to stress here that the voicing of the lateral phoneme, whether the sound is syllabic or not, is never influenced by a following (or a preceding) pause: the lateral always retains its voicing on the pause side.

6 Clear/Dark

Characteristics

In the first chapter of this book where we talked about the phonetic characteristics of English phonemes, we said that there are two variants of the lateral sound, viz. clear *l* [l] and dark *l* [ɫ], and we pointed out that the dark *l* differs from the clear *l* by having the back of the tongue raised towards the velum (soft palate) as if the speaker is trying to say [uː] while producing the *l*. In Ch. 2 we saw that these two variants are allophones of the phoneme /l/, i. e. phones which are phonetically very similar and which are in complementary distribution, i. e. before vowels we always find the clear *l* and never the dark one, whereas in all other positions we always find the dark *l* and never the clear one. These two allophones occur generally throughout English, but there are some dialects of American English which use only the dark variant.

In Addition

What we have not yet mentioned is that this difference in resonance, i. e. presence or absence of velarization, occurs in addition to the changes in place of articulation, the degree of voicing, fricativeness, length and even the syllabicity of the phones of /l/ which we have described above. Thus the fully devoiced fricative fortis phone which is heard after word-initial or syllable-initial /p/ or /k/ in words like *please* or *clean*, must at the same time be non-velarized (clear) because it occurs in front of a (stressed) vowel. Similarly the clipped phone in *bolt* (before fortis /t/) and the stretched phone in *bold* (when this word is said before a pause) must both be velarized (dark) because they occur before a consonant and not before a vowel. Finally, we may note that when /l/ is found at the end of a word, whether it is syllabic or not, its resonance will change depending on whether the next word begins with a vowel or a consonant. For example, the final /l/ of *full* in the phrase *a full range* must be dark as the next word does not begin with a vowel, but it will also be post-alveolar as it is followed at the beginning of the next word by the post-alveolar sound /r/. Similarly, the final /l/ of the same word in the phrase *a full theatre* will also be dark but as it now comes in front of a dental consonant it too will be realized by a dental phone. On the other hand, if we

consider the final /l/ of *bottle* in the phrase *a bottle of rum*, in addition to being slightly fricative and partially devoiced on the side of the /t/ as well as syllabic, it must now also be clear as it occurs here before a vowel. A feature like clear and dark resonance, which is found in addition to the primary place of articulation of a sound, is usually referred to as a secondary articulation. (See Gimson, Ch. 4, p. 32).

Phoneme /r/

**Prelimi-
naries**

The post-alveolar frictionless continuant phoneme /r/ in several of its features resembles its fellow liquid, the phoneme /l/. However, there are some notable dissimilarities (sometimes due to differences between British and American pronunciation), as we shall see below when we examine it under the following headings: **distribution,** (degree of) **voicing, fricativeness, fortis/lenis, length, syllabicity, linking** /r/, and **intrusive** /r/. Since the degree of voicing, fricativeness and the change from lenis to fortis all go closely together, as was the case with the phones of /l/, we shall consider all of these below under the one heading of **voicing.**

1 Distribution

Dialects

One characteristic of the distribution of /r/ is that it divides the dialects of English into two varieties: those which are rhotic and those which are non-rhotic.

**Rhotic/
Non-Rhotic**

The **rhotic dialects** are those in which the /r/ is pronounced wherever we find the letter *r* in the spelling of a word; the **non-rhotic dialects** are those in which the /r/ is silent wherever an *r* in the spelling comes before a consonant or at the end of a word (before a pause). In most of North America the dialects are rhotic, but non-rhotic varieties can be heard in the deep south and in New England. In Great Britain, RP is always non-rhotic, but it should be stressed that this variety is associated with higher education and thus reflects the speaker's social background and not his or her geographical origin. In the regional speech of non-users of RP, there are many areas where rhotic English is quite characteristic, e. g. in the south-western and western counties of England (in the so-called 'west country'), in Lancashire, and in Scotland and Ireland.

Single /r/

If we now return from this brief excursion into dialectology and look again at the phonological aspects of the distribution of /r/, we see that as a single consonant the phoneme can freely occur both at the beginning and at the end of a syllable in rhotic English, whereas in non-rhotic English although it is often found in initial position it only occurs in syllable-final position when followed by a vowel. Thus in GA both *r*'s in the word *repair* are pronounced ([rə'peər] or [rə'per]), whereas in RP only the initial *r* is heard ([rə'peə]). On the other hand, when the suffix *-ing* is added to produce the word *repairing*, the second *r* is pronounced not only in General American, but also in RP because of the following [ɪ]. Notice that this syllable-final [r] in RP is often followed by a morpheme boundary, as in [rɪ'peər+ɪŋ], but this does not have to be the case, as we see from words like *merry, curry, herring, carrot* ['meri, 'kʌri, 'herɪŋ, 'kærət]. The parallel situation where it is followed by a word boundary will be dealt with separately below under the heading of **linking** /r/ (p. 109–110).

In Clusters

In consonant clusters at the end of a morpheme or word, the phoneme /r/ is never found as the final element in any variety of English, but as we saw above, it can be heard as the first element of a final two- or three-consonant cluster in rhotic types of English but never in this position in non-rhotic ones. So in GA we find pronunciations like [hɑːrt] and [sɜːrf] for *heart* and *surf* and, with a morpheme boundary intervening between the last two consonants, [hɜːrt+s, kɑːrd+z, bɜːrθ+s, skɑːrf+s/skɑːrv+z] for the plural forms *hearts, cards, births, scarfs/scarves* as well as pronunciations like [bɜːrp+t, əb'zɔːrb+d, sɜːrf+t, kɑːrv+d, ʌn'ɜːrθ+t] for the past tense and participial forms *burped, absorbed, surfed, carved, unearthed*. In all these final consonant clusters in RP the phoneme /r/ has no phonetic realization.

In syllable-initial clusters of two consonants, /r/ frequently combines as the second element with all the plosives *(pray, bread, treat, drag, cream, grind)*, but it is more restricted in other combinations, occurring only with the voiceless fricatives /f, θ, ʃ/ but not with /s/ *(free, thread, shrimp)* and never with the affricates /tʃ/ or /dʒ/ preceding it. In initial three-consonant clusters containing /r/, the first element must always be /s/ and the second can only be one of the three voiceless plosives /p, t, k/, as in *spray, stray, scream*. Thus in initial consonant clusters the distribution of /r/ is very similar to that of /l/.

2 Voicing

Like /l/

In regard to its realization the phoneme /r/ also closely parallels /l/ in where its phones are fully voiced, partially or fully devoiced, where they become fricative and where they change from lenis to fortis.

Fully Voiced	As a single consonant it retains its basic phonetic characteristics syllable-initially and between vowels, and is realized here as a **fully voiced, lenis, non-fricative, post-alveolar** continuant, e. g. in *rice, ray, reap, merry, arrange*. In rhotic varieties of English it is also realized in this way at the end of a syllable, e. g. in *war, here*, or before another consonant in final clusters, e. g. in *art, word.*

When /r/ occurs in an initial two-consonant cluster as the second element after the voiced plosives /b/ or /g/, it has the same characteristics as a single /r/ in initial position, i. e. it is fully voiced, lenis and non-fricative, but **after the alveolar voiced plosive** /d/, as we saw earlier when we considered affricates, it changes from non-fricative to **fricative.** Thus the fricative /r/ in the word *drain*, though also fully voiced and lenis, sounds different from that in *brain* and *grain*, where no friction can be heard. Phonetically, this voiced fricative phone somewhat resembles the phonic realization of /ʒ/, but as it is pronounced with the tip of the tongue curled back slightly just behind the alveolar ridge and not, as for /ʒ/, with the front of the tongue raised to a position farther back along the roof of the mouth, the resonance of the two sounds is different.

Fully Devoiced	In initial two-consonant clusters when /r/ is the second element after /p, t, k/ it is realized by a **fully devoiced, fortis, fricative** phone provided that the following vowel is **stressed.** We hear this kind of /r/ in words like *price, tray, creep* or *approve, attract, increase*. If we compare the first three words with *rice, ray, reap*, the difference in sound between the phones of /r/ in these two groups of words is even greater than the one we saw between the voiced fricative phone which /r/ has in *drain* and the voiced non-fricative phone which it has in *brain, grain* and *rain*. Phonetically, the fortis fricative phone is produced just like the normal lenis non-fricative kind by curling the tip of the tongue backwards slightly just behind the alveolar ridge, but the vocal cords are not allowed to vibrate and the air from the lungs is pushed quite forcefully along the back of the tongue and over the tip so that friction is generated. This is very similar to the mechanism needed for the kind of whistling which in English is usually called 'whistling through the teeth'. Indeed, when the fortis fricative is said particularly strongly it may be accompanied by a short whistling sound.

Affricates	As we saw earlier in this book, the clusters /dr/ and /tr/ are treated by some phonologists as affricates when the second element is fricative. Like /dʒ/ and /tʃ/, they are then considered to be only one sound and not a cluster of two. Notice that we can have combinations of /d/ or /t/ with /r/ in the middle of a word where a morpheme boundary comes between them, e.g *bed+room, hat+rack*. In this case, after a juncture, the /r/ is a single consonant in syllable-

initial position and therefore cannot be fricative. Thus combinations of /dr/ or /tr/ of this kind cannot be considered to be affricates. Strangely, those for whom /tr/ with a fricative second element is an affricate usually do not treat /pr/ or /kr/ in the same way, though it would be logical to do so.

Partial Devoicing

When /r/ forms an initial two-consonant cluster after any voiceless consonants other than /p, t, k/, e. g. in *frock, three, shred*, or when it clusters with /p, t, k/ before a non-stressed vowel, e. g. in *apron, hatred, sacred*, or when it is the third element of an initial three-consonant cluster beginning with /s/, e. g. in *spread, straight, scream*, it is realized by a **lenis** phone **with leftward partial devoicing** and it may be **slightly fricative.** In these three-consonant clusters /spr/, /str/ and /skr/, the initial /s/ has the same inhibiting effect as it has in the three-consonant clusters /spl/ and /skl/, which we discussed earlier in our examination of the voicing of the lateral phoneme: the change from a lenis to a fortis phone of /r/ does not take place, nor does the phone become totally devoiced or strongly fricative. This is the reason why the /r/ in *ice cream* sounds different from the one in *I scream*. In the former case a morpheme boundary separates the two words /aɪs+ˈkriːm/ and therefore the /r/ is in a two-consonant cluster with /k/ and has the fully devoiced, fortis, fricative phone, whereas in the latter case with the morpheme boundary after *I* /aɪ+skriːm/, the /r/ is in a three-consonant cluster beginning with /s/ and has the lenis, partially devoiced, only slightly fricative phone.

3 Length

Clipping

The clipping of /r/ before a fortis (voiceless) consonant and the stretching of the sound in a stressed syllable at the end of an utterance can only take place in rhotic varieties of English, as the phoneme is not found in either of these positions in non-rhotic varieties. The shortened or clipped phone of /r/ can be heard in the GA pronunciation of *heart* [hɑːrt] compared with the normal length phone in *hard* [hɑːrd].

Stretching

Similarly, the lengthened or stretched phone can be heard at the end of the word *war* in the GA pronunciation of *They went to war*. The clipping and stretching of /r/ is, of course, an extension of the clipping and stretching of the vowel preceding it. For example, both the [ɔː] and the [r] are shortened in *wart* [wɔːrt] and both are lengthened in *war* [wɔːr] at the end of the sentence quoted above. In phonetic script there is no really adequate way of showing clipping and stretching. However, we could place a breve [˘] over the symbol for a clipped vowel, e. g. [ă̆, ɔ̆ː], and a macron [¯] over the symbol for a stretched vowel, e. g. [ǣ, ɔ̄ː]. (See p. 126 for the normal use of the breve.)

4 Syllabic

Distribution

Since a consonant becomes syllabic only when it is syllable-final (or the first element in a syllable-final cluster) and only when the shwa which immediately precedes it is deleted, syllabic /r/ (like clipped and stretched /r/) appears only in rhotic kinds of English at the ends of words, e. g. in *ladder, hammer, hammered* ['lædr̩, 'hæmr̩, 'hæmr̩d]. It may, however, occur in both rhotic and non-rhotic English in the middle of a word if the following sound is a vowel. For example, the words *hammering, wondering* may be said with syllabic /r/ in fast speech ['hæm r̩ ɪŋ, 'wʌnd r̩ ɪŋ], though usually the shwa is retained. Of course, in both these cases the word has three syllables. However, in both rhotic and non-rhotic varieties, and especially in rapid pronunciation, it is common to hear only two syllables when shwa is deleted. In other words, the /r/ now becomes the initial consonant of the second syllable: ['hæm rɪŋ, 'wʌnd rɪŋ].

Compression

This reduction of the number of syllables (referred to as **compression**) also occurs with the other syllabic consonants (the nasals and the lateral phoneme). Alongside the pronunciations ['əup ən ɪŋ] and ['əup n̩ ɪŋ] for the word *opening* we also find ['əup nɪŋ]. Similarly, the three-syllable word *shortening* is often reduced to two-syllables ['ʃɔːt nɪŋ]. In the case of the lateral phoneme the fast pronunciation with the reduced syllable seems to be the most common one when it comes after a plosive, e. g. in words like *stumbling* ['stʌm blɪŋ] (from *stumble*), *rambling* ['ræm blɪŋ] (from *ramble*). Elsewhere, e. g. after fricatives, the non-reduced forms are frequently heard: *unravelling* [ʌn 'ræv əl ɪŋ] as well as [ʌn 'ræv l̩ ɪŋ], *marshalling* ['mɑːʃ əl ɪŋ] as well as ['mɑːʃ l̩ ɪŋ].

Non-rhotic

Note that in non-rhotic English, though /r/ is usually heard only in front of vowels, it does appear for some speakers before syllabic consonants, including syllabic /r/, e. g. in *current, barren, squirrel, coral, terrorist, library* ['kʌr n̩ t, 'bær n̩, 'skwɪr l̩, 'kɒr l̩, 'ter r̩ ɪst, 'laɪbr r̩ i]. This shows that the syllabic consonants of English must have a vowel-like quality about them.

5 Linking /r/

Characteristics

Linking /r/ is the name given to the /r/ which appears in RP and other non-rhotic varieties of English at the end of words when the following word begins with a vowel. These words always have a

final *r* or *re* in the spelling (e. g. *car*, *more*) which, historically, was always pronounced but which later dropped out before vowels. Thus in RP the final *r* of *car* is silent in *he shut the car window* [hi 'ʃʌt ðə 'kɑː 'wɪndəʊ], but re-appears as linking /r/ when the same word occurs in *she sold the car at Easter* [ʃi 'səʊld ðə 'kɑːr‿ət 'iːstə]. Though it is not usually referred to as an instance of linking /r/, this is, of course, the same process as we saw operating inside words: word-final /r/, though normally silent in RP in a word like *repair*, re-appears when a suffix beginning with a vowel is added (as in *repair+ing*).

6 Intrusive /r/

After /ə/

Intrusive /r/ is found only in RP and other non-rhotic kinds of English, where it is added to the end of words which historically have never had a final *r* in their spelling but which normally end phonetically in a shwa. Like linking /r/ it occurs here only when the following word begins with a vowel. Very careful RP speakers consider this pronunciation to be uneducated, but it is frequently heard in RP even in the speech of those who disapprove of it, especially when they are not concentrating on their own pronunciation. For example, in the expression *the very idea of it* the word *idea* is very often heard ending with an intrusive /r/ before the vowel at the beginning of *of*: [ðə 'veri aɪd'ɪər‿əv ɪt]. Indeed, many speakers find it difficult to pronounce this phrase without the intrusive /r/ unless they insert a glottal stop: [...aɪ'dɪə? əv ...]. The intrusive /r/ is particularly common at the end of the names of geographical entities which end in the letter *a*, e. g. *Canada, Australia, India, Africa*. So in news bulletins on radio and television we often hear readers using it in phrases like *Canada insists* ['kænədər‿ ɪn'sɪsts] or *India and China* ['ɪndɪər‿ən 'tʃaɪnə].

After /ɑː, ɔː/

Intrusive /r/ is also found in non-rhotic speech after the vowels /ɑː/ and /ɔː/, e. g. in phrases like *the Shah of Persia, law and order* or *they saw it yesterday*, which are then pronounced [ðə 'ʃɑːr‿əv 'pɜːʃə], ['lɔːr‿ən 'ɔːdə] or [ðeɪ 'sɔːr‿ɪt 'jestədeɪ]. Even though many RP speakers may unconsciously insert an orthographically unjustified /r/ after these vowels, the use of it in this position is usually very much more strongly condemned than after shwa.

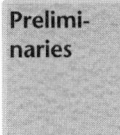 Semivowels /j/ and /w/

**Prelimi-
naries** It will be convenient for us to look at the phonemes /j/ and /w/ together, as both exhibit a number of characteristics which not only show their relatedness to vowels but which they also share with the consonants /l/ and /r/. We shall discuss these characteristics below under the headings **distribution, height, voicing** (including **fricativeness**), and **compression**.

1 Distribution

**Singly/
Initially** Both semivowels occur freely in front of almost all the vowels (monophthongs and diphthongs). However, there do not seem to be any English words beginning with /jaɪ/ or /jɔɪ/ nor with /wɔɪ/ or /wʊə/, though this may be just an accidental gap in the system. The phoneme /j/ is found in a number of words before /ɑː/, e. g. *yard, yarn*, but /w/ does not occur in this position in British English except in one RP pronunciation of the word *waft*: /wɑːft/, alongside /wɒft/. In most other words which are spelt with *wa* the RP pronunciation is either /wɒ/ (as in *wash, want*) or /wɔː/ (as in *water, warn*), but sometimes /wæ/ (as in *wax, wag, wagon*). In GA /w/ occurs before /ɑː/ in most words where RP has /wɒ/, e. g. *wash, wasp, watch*, though some of these may also have /wɒː/, e. g. /wɒːʃ/ alongside /wɑːʃ/. The cluster /wɑː/ can also sometimes be found where RP has /wɔː/, e. g. GA /ˈwɑːtər/ alongside /ˈwɒːtər/ for *water* (RP /ˈwɔːtə/).

In Clusters The distribution of /j/ and /w/ in initial clusters is somewhat complicated. The only regularly found three-consonant clusters for these two phonemes are at the beginnings of syllables, with /s/ in initial position followed by a voiceless plosive before the semivowel. However, whereas /j/ is found with all three plosives /p, t, k/, e. g. *spew, spurious, stew, skew*, /w/ appears only with /k/ and then always in the spelling *squ*, e. g. *squeeze, squat, squirt* /skwiːz, skwɒt, skwɜːt/. Occasionally, the three-consonant cluster /slj/ can be heard in the word *slew* (past tense of *to slay*), but the usual pronunciation is without the /j/, i. e. /sluː/.

**With
Plosives** In two-consonant clusters, /w/ parallels /j/ in combining with both the voiceless and voiced alveolar plosives /t, d/ *(tune, tube, dew, dune, twin, dwell)*; /w/ is common after the voiceless velar plosive /k/ *(queen, acquire)* but does not occur in native English words after /g/. The phoneme /j/ is also common after /k/ *(cure, acute)* but rare after /g/ *(argue, ague)*. Only /j/ can come after the voiceless and voiced bilabial plosives /p, b/, e. g. *pure, beauty*. The cluster /tj/ at the beginning of words like *tune* is often replaced in RP by /tʃ/ as

7 Semivowels /j/ and /w/ 111

a result of a phonological process called coalescence, which we shall describe in Chapter 4. In GA, /j/ is almost always dropped after /t, d/ (and /n/), giving rise to pronunciations like /tu:n, tu:b, du:, du:n/ (and /nu:/ for *new, knew*).

With Fricatives

In two-consonant clusters with a fricative preceding the semivowel, only /j/ can be found after /f/ or /v/, e. g. *few, view*. Both /j/ and /w/ occur after /θ/ but not after /ð/, e. g. *thew, thwack*. Whereas /w/ is quite common with the voiceless alveolar fricative /s/ preceding it, e.g. *sweet, assuage* /swi:t, ə'sweɪdʒ/, the semivowel /j/ is almost always dropped in this position in GA and in some words also by the majority of present-day RP speakers, e. g. *suit, super, sewage* / su:t, 'su:pə, 'su:ɪdʒ/. On the other hand, most speakers of RP still seem to prefer the consonant cluster in the middle of words, e. g. *assume* /ə'sju:m/, *consume* /kən'sju:m/, *pursuit* /pə'sju:t/. A cluster with a semivowel and /z/ is possible only when the voiced alveolar fricative is followed by /j/. This can be found initially in a few words of Greek origin, such as *zeugma, Zeus* /'zju:gmə, zju:s/, but here too the semivowel is always omitted in GA and sometimes in RP. As was the case with /sj/, RP seems to prefer to keep the /j/ when the cluster occurs in the middle of a word. The usual RP pronunciation of words such as *resume, presume* is therefore / prɪ'zju:m, rɪ'zju:m/, whereas in GA the /j/ is always dropped.

As far as other clusters of a fricative with a semivowel are concerned, neither /j/ nor /w/ combines with the voiceless palato-alveolar fricative /ʃ/ or its voiced counterpart /ʒ/, except in a rather rare alternative pronunciation of the word *azure* where /ʒ/ is found combined with /j/ instead of the voiced palato-alveolar being by itself, i. e. /'æʒjʊə, 'eɪʒjʊə/ for /'æʒə, 'eɪʒə/.

/hj/

We do, however, find clusters with the glottal fricative /h/ preceding both /j/ and /w/. The combination /hj/ can be heard in words such as *huge, humid, humour*, though here, unlike the cases we have just described, it is the fricative which is frequently omitted and not the semivowel, i. e. we often find /'ju:mə/ as well as /'hju:mə/. In some people's speech /hj/ may be reduced from two sounds to a single palatal fricative [ç], the sound heard at the end of the word *mich* (= *me*) in Standard German: *huge* is then pronounced [çu:dʒ]. Notice that we cannot write the latter pronunciation between phoneme slashes, as we have done for other words above, but have to use phonetic brackets, since the sound [ç] is not a regular phoneme of English but the phonetic result of the coalescence or fusion together of two phonemes.

/hw/

A cluster with /h/ before /w/ is the usual pronunciation heard in American speech when the spelling is *wh*, e. g. in words like *wheat, whistle, whisker, which*. This spelling may sometimes be pronounced in this way by an RP speaker when declaiming on the stage of a theatre or when uttering rhetorical sentences in public. However, the usual RP pronunciation is with the /w/ alone: /wiːt, ˈwɪsl̩, ˈwɪskə, wɪtʃ/. In those varieties of English where the /hw/ is common, the cluster may also undergo coalescence and be reduced to a single voiceless bilabial fricative, which can be written phonetically as either [w̥] or [ʍ]. In this case, since it regularly contrasts with the voiced semivowel /w/ to produce minimal pairs like *whine, wine* / w̥ aɪn, waɪn/ and *white, wight* /w̥ aɪt, waɪt/, it must be considered as another normal phoneme, unlike the fricative [ç] mentioned above, which also results from the coalescence of a semivowel with /h/. This [ç], however, does not contrast with /j/ in any minimal pairs and, as we shall see below when we examine the semivowels with regard to their voicing, it will have to be considered as a phone of /j/.

<table>
<tr><td>**Other
Clusters**</td><td>If we turn now to clusters containing a nasal consonant or a liquid, we see that the distribution of /j/ is very different from that of /w/. In RP the phoneme /j/ can combine easily with /m/ or /n/ but not with /ŋ/, e. g. *music, amuse, new, nuisance*, whereas /w/ forms a cluster with none of them. In GA, as we saw above, /j/ is usually omitted after /n/ but not after /m/. In all varieties of English, /w/ cannot combine with either of the liquids /l/ or /r/, and the combination of them with /j/ is limited. Thus, while a number of RP speakers and some Americans still have the cluster /lj/ in words like *lewd, lute, allude, salute*, it has been reduced to just the phoneme /l/ in the pronunciation of the majority of Americans and of many users of RP, e. g. /luːd, luːt, əˈluːd, səˈluːt/. Notice, however, that where /l/ immediately precedes /j/ but is not in the same syllable, the /j/ is always pronounced in both RP and GA, e. g. *salutation* /ˌsæl ju ˈteɪ ʃn̩ /. As for the cluster with /rj/, this is rather rare, but it can still be heard from conservative RP speakers in such words as *virulent, garrulous, ferrule*, i. e. /ˈvɪrjʊlənt, ˈgærjʊləs, ˈferjuːl/. Usually it is simplified and reduced just to the phoneme /r/. So the far commoner pronunciation of these three words is /ˈvɪrələnt, ˈgærələs, ˈferuːl/ in both American and British English.</td></tr>
</table>

2 Height

<table>
<tr><td>**/j/**</td><td>Unlike consonants, semivowels have phones which change their height, depending on the vowel following them. It will be remembered that for /j/ the front of the tongue is raised to a position a little higher than that for the front vowel /iː/ but with no contact between the tongue and the hard palate. This is the position for it when preceding the high front or back vowels, e. g. in words such</td></tr>
</table>

| | as *yeast, youth,* but when it comes in front of a lower vowel, it does not need to assume this very high position in order to be a just that little bit higher than the following vowel. So, for example, a /j/ said before the low back vowel /ɑː/ in a word like *yard* is realized by a phone which is usually noticeably lower than the one in *yeast.* |

/w/   The /w/ semivowel is also vowel-like in its production. We described it in Ch. 1 as having the lips rounded and the back of the tongue raised to a position slightly higher than for the vowel /uː/. This is its position when said with a high back or front vowel following it, but it too has lower phones in front of lower vowels. Thus the phone at the beginning of *wag* or *water* is said lower than the one at the beginning of *weak* or *wool,* though it is more difficult to perceive this because of the lip-rounding.

3 Voicing

Like /j/&/r/   The voicing of /j/ and /w/ follows a pattern with which we are already familiar from our examination of /l/ and /r/.

Single /j, w/   They both have **a fully voiced, lenis, non-fricative, basic form,** which is heard when they occur alone at the beginning of a word, as in *yes, way,* or between two voiced sounds, as in *beyond, aware* (between vowels) or *beauty, dupe, dwell, dwarf* (between a voiced consonant and a vowel, but note that after /d/ and /t/ in American English /j/ is usually dropped and /duːp/ is far commoner than /djuːp/).

After /p, t, k/   When either is found in an initial two-consonant cluster of which one of the voiceless plosives /p, t, k/ is the first element, and this cluster is immediately followed by a **stressed** vowel, then the semivowel phoneme is not realized by its basic fully voiced, lenis, non-fricative phone but by one which is **completely devoiced, fortis and fricative.** Thus for /j/ we hear this latter phone in RP word-initially, e. g. in *puke, tube, cute* [pçuːk, tçuːb, kçuːt], and word-medially in *repudiate, attune, accuse* [rɪˈpçuːdɪeɪt, əˈtçuːn, əˈkçuːz], though it is more common for GA to drop the /j/ in words like *tube* and *attune.* Similarly, the fully devoiced, fortis, fricative phone of /w/ is heard in the cluster at the beginning of such words as *twist, quit* [tw̥ɪst, kw̥ɪt] and in the middle of words like *between, acquaint* [bɪˈtw̥iːn, əˈkw̥eɪnt].

Stress?   If the reader is wondering whether there really is any stress in the monosyllabic examples we have given above *(puke, tube, cute, twist, quit),* it should be noted that (except for function words, i. e.

words whose role in a sentence is largely or entirely grammatical) most monosyllabic words in English carry primary stress, though this is omitted from the transcription when they are not in context. We should also note that when the semivowels come after a voiceless plosive, their fortis fricative phones are found not only in front of a vowel carrying primary stress, but also before a vowel with secondary stress, e. g. in long words like *pugilistic* [ˌpçuː dʒɪ 'lɪs tɪk], *repudiation* [rɪ ˌpçuːdi 'eɪʃ n̩], *Teutonic* [ˌtçuː 'tʰɒn ɪk], *cupidity* [ˌkçuː 'pʰɪd ət i], *quadrilateral* [ˌkw̥ ɒd rɪ 'læt ə rəl].

Partially Devoiced

The pattern shared with /l/ and /r/ is continued when /j/ occurs in a three-consonant cluster with /sp/, /st/ or /sk/ preceding it, e. g. in *spume, stew, skewer*, and when /w/ occurs after /sk/, e. g. in *square, squint*. Here the phone realizing each of the semivowels retains its basic **lenis** value but is **partially devoiced** on the side of the voiceless consonant and may be **slightly fricative**. The same two phones also appear after /p, t, k/ before an **unstressed** vowel *(deputy* /'depjʊti/, *opportune* /'ɒpətjuːn/, *accurate* /'ækjərət/, *adequate* /'ædɪkwət/)* and in clusters after other voiceless consonants *(few* /fjuː/, *assume* /ə'sjuːm/, *sweet* /swiːt/, *persuade* /pə'sweɪd/).*

4 Compression

Like Vowels

Whereas the semivowels show their relatedness to consonants by having phones which are able to change from lenis to fortis and from non-fricative to fricative, their relatedness to vowels is shown in the phenomenon of compression. This occurs in words such as *obvious, tedious, convenient* and *annual, strenuous, continuous* where two syllables are compressed into one either by converting the vowel [i] into [j] or by converting the vowel [u] into [w]. Thus in careful speech *obvious* and *annual* have three syllables ['ɒb vi əs, 'æn ju əl] but in rapid articulation only two ['ɒb vjəs, 'æn jwəl]. This change from a vowel which is the centre of a syllable to a semivowel which by its nature cannot be central but must be peripheral, usually only takes place in words which occur fairly frequently. In rare words the speaker is likely to be more careful with the pronunciation and to retain the vowel.

Transcription

The reader will have noticed that in the foregoing paragraphs the transcriptions of the examples have sometimes had the square brackets for phonetics around them and sometimes the slashes for phonemes. The latter were used when all the sounds inside the slashes were phonemes. On the other hand phonetic brackets were needed wherever one of the sounds under discussion was a phone, e. g. [ç] from /j/, [w̥] from /w/, and [i], [u]. As we saw in Ch. 2, it is difficult to decide whether [i] is a realization of the phoneme /iː/

or of the phoneme /ɪ/ and whether [u] belongs to the phoneme /u:/ or the phoneme /ʊ/. Certainly, neither [i] nor [u] can have the status of a separate phoneme.

8 Concluding Remarks on Consonant Phonemes

Background On page 62 in Chapter 2 we put forward some of the criticisms which have been levelled against the concept of the phoneme and phoneme analysis. Now that we have discussed the consonant and semivowel phonemes in detail and seen what their various phones are and where they occur, we are in a better position to look more critically at the problematic aspects of this approach.

Criticism Classical structural phonology (phonemics) is strictly segmental and describes each phoneme on its own merits as a unit unrelated to others that behave in the same way. Nothing in the approach shows that the phonemes /p, t, k/, for example, are any more closely related to one another than /p, s, l/ are. In our discussion above we did not adhere strictly to this principle. For example, we separated out some of the distinctive features of the phonemes /p, b, t, d, k, g/ and examined them in two groups as voiceless labials and voiced labials. Nevertheless, we were forced by the 'phoneme-and-its-phones' framework to discuss each phoneme in the group separately and to list its phones separately, which led to a fair amount of repetition. For our purposes in this book, repetition has a certain pedagogical value, but for other purposes it would be preferable to adopt a more economical approach, for example, to abandon the phoneme and its phones and to postulate a set of rules (e. g. for aspiration, for devoicing, etc.) and to show how these can be applied to groups of sounds with particular distinctive features, such as the plosives, the semivowels, etc., in certain contexts.

Criticism A further criticism of the 'phoneme-and-its-phones' approach is that it can lead to a surprisingly large array of variants which are difficult to deal with. For example, we have seen in this chapter that in different contexts the phonemes /p, t, k/ have some phones which are aspirated and others which are not, but at the same time both kinds change their place of articulation. On the other hand /b, d, g/ have phones which, depending on the context, change their place of articulation and at the same time have different degrees of voicing. How many phones do we really have here? Are the phones of /p, t, k/ really unrelated to those of /b, d, g/? A more satisfying approach might again be to discard the idea of phones and to use a set of rules operating on the group of voiceless or voiced plosives in certain contexts. In this way a rule to

adjust a sound's place of articulation to that of the sound following it would show that all the plosives /p, b, t, d, k, g/ are related.

Set of Rules

A set of such rules is given below to show how the semivowels and the liquids are related with regard to the features of voicing, fortis/lenis, fricative/non-fricative. The symbolic devices used are a simplified form of those in Transformational Generative Phonology. Compare the two rules given on page 63. The arrow points to the features each sound assumes when it occurs in the context(s) shown after the symbol / . The symbol __ indicates where each sound occurs in this context, and the symbol # is used to show where a word begins or ends.

Rule 1

j, w, l, r → voiced, lenis, non-fricative / $\left\{ \begin{array}{l} \# \_\_ \\ \text{voiced} \_\_ \text{voiced} \end{array} \right\}$

[Read: Each of the sounds j, w, l, r is *voiced, lenis,* and *non-fricative* when it is word-initial or between voiced sounds]
E.g. in the words *yes, will, love, run* /jes, wɪl, lʌv, rʌn/,
or in *beauty, dwell, glad, green* /bjuːti, dwel, glæd, griːn/.

Exception:

r → voiced, lenis, fricative / d __

[Read: r has the features *voiced, lenis, fricative* when preceded by d]
E.g. *dream, adroit, Andromeda* /driːm, ə'drɔɪt, æn'drɒmɪdə/.

Rule 2

j, w, l, r → fully devoiced, fortis, fricative / $\left\{ \begin{array}{l} p \\ t \\ k \end{array} \right\}$ __ stressed vowel

[Read: Each of the sounds j, w, l, r becomes *fully devoiced, fortis, fricative* when it occurs between word-initial p, t or k and a stressed vowel]
E.g. in the words *pure, repute* /pjʊə, rɪ'pjuːt/; *tune, attune* /tjuːn, ə'tjuːn/; *cute, acute* /kjuːt, ə'kjuːt/; *twist, between* /twɪst, bɪ'twiːn/; *queen, acquire* /kwiːn, ə'kwaɪə/; *please, deplore* /pliːz, di'plɔː/; *clean, conclude* /kliːn, kən'kluːd/; *pray, approve* /preɪ, ə'pruːv/; *try, attract* /traɪ, ə'trækt/; *cry, accrue* /kraɪ, ə'kruː/.

Exception:

If s $\left\{ \begin{array}{l} p \\ t \\ k \end{array} \right\}$ __ stressed vowel,   then Rule 3 applies

[Read: If one of the sounds j, w, l, r occurs after p, t, k preceded by s, and in front of a stressed vowel, then Rule 3 applies (not Rule 2)]

Rule 3

j, w, l, r → partially devoiced, lenis, slightly fricative /
$\left\{ \begin{array}{l} \text{voiceless} \_\_ \\ \_\_ \text{voiceless} \end{array} \right\}$

[Read: Each of the sounds j, w, l, r becomes *partially devoiced*, *lenis*, *slightly fricative*, when it occurs **after** a voiceless sound or **in front of** a voiceless sound]

E.g. in the words *few, sweet* /fjuː, swiːt/ or *filth* /fɪlθ/ or in exceptions to Rule 2 like *dispute, splendid, spray, astute, strict, skewer, squeal, discrete* /dɪˈspjuːt, ˈsplendɪd, spreɪ, əˈstuːt, strɪkt, ˈskjuːə, skwiːl, dɪˈskriːt/.

Final Note This set of rules covers most of the cases we described in this chapter in connection with j, w, l, r, but not all of them. Nevertheless, it will give the reader some idea of how another approach to the topic could be made. The rules above are similar to those found in Generative Phonology but put in a simpler form.

Vowel Phonemes and their Phones

Prelimi-naries

The vowels of English and their variants are less complicated to describe than the consonants. Some aspects, such as **distribution,** can be dealt with for the whole group; others, such as **changes in height or part of the tongue, loss of lip-rounding, free variation with other vowels,** and **compression,** can be dealt with for smaller groups or for individual sounds. For didactic reasons we will continue to use the phoneme approach and refer to variants of phonemes as phones.

Distribution

Vowels, whether monophthongs or diphthongs, form the nucleus of all syllables (except those with syllabic consonants), and all of them can occur in word-medial position. All of them are also found freely at the beginning of words but not all are found at the end. There are no words in English ending in the short monophthongs /e, æ, ʌ, ɒ/, whether stressed or unstresssed. Of the three remaining short monophthongs, /ɪ/ and /ʊ/ cannot occur word-finally stressed, but in some analyses they do appear in this position when unstressed, e. g. in words such as *happy* or *onto*. In this book we have preferred to transcribe these two unstressed sounds word-finally as [i] and [u], i. e. as shortened forms of /i:/ and /u:/, because this represents more accurately the pronunciation of most younger generation speakers of RP and GA. However, since some dialects of English and older kinds of RP have phonetic [ɪ] and [ʊ] here instead, we could argue that [i] and [u] are really higher variants of /ɪ/ and /ʊ/, i. e. phones which have a higher tongue position when word final. In Ch.2 we referred to this situation of the possible double origin of a phone as neutralization. With a few rare exceptions the other remaining short monophthong /ə/ is never found stressed in any position but can occur unstressed both at the beginning and at the end of words, e. g. *attack, drama.*

1 High Vowels

/i:, u:/

Both the long high front vowel /i:/ and the long high back vowel /u:/ show changes in their height. Word-finally in RP and in General American they are usually diphthongized, though some dialects such as Scottish and Welsh may retain a pure long vowel here. Phonetically, diphthongization means that the tongue is raised to a slightly higher position at the end of the vowel than at the beginning. The height for the final part of /i:/ now approaches that of /j/ and the height of the final part of /u:/ that of /w/. This causes a tiny off-glide /j/ to be heard when final /i:/ occurs before a word beginning with a vowel, e. g. ['θriːʲ'æplz] *three apples*. Similarly an off-glide /w/ is heard when final /u:/ appears in this same position, e. g. ['huːʷ 'əʊnz ɪt] *who owns it*. Notice that the off-glides are waning sounds, i. e. they are losing in intensity because they are at the end of a word. They thus sound different from word-initial /j/ and /w/, which increase in intensity. If the examples above were pronounced with a full /j/ or /w/ instead of the off-glide, i. e. ['θriː 'jæplz] or ['huː 'wəʊnz ɪt], this would sound rather un-English.

[i, u]

We saw in Ch. 2 that the phones [i, u] can be assigned either to the phonemes /iː, uː/ or to the phonemes /ɪ, ʊ/ and that they are found only **unstressed** either in word-final syllables, as in *funny* or *onto*, or word-medially immediately in front of another vowel, as in *radiate, radio* or *factual, continuous*. We must add here that when [i] or [u] immediately precede the phoneme /ə/, this combination may be subject to compression: a three-syllable word like *radiant* ['reɪ di ənt] then becomes reduced to two syllables ['reɪ djənt], and *factual* changes from ['fæk tʃu əl] to ['fæk tʃwəl]. No compression is found, however, when they are followed by a vowel other than /ə/: thus *radiate* and *continuation* can only be pronounced ['reɪ di eɪt] and [kən ˌtɪn ju 'eɪ ʃ(ə)n].

/ɪ, e, x/

Of the three short front vowels /ɪ, e, æ/ there is little to say about the last two except that /æ/, although always classified as a short vowel, may be realized in some contexts by a phone that is quite long. This is especially the case when it occurs in a sentence-final syllable which is stressed, e. g. *put it in the bag*. In this stretched position it may be longer than a clipped long vowel (e. g. /iː/ in *seat* in *put it on the seat*) and certainly longer than stretched /ɪ/ or /e/ (e. g. in *bin* and *bed* in the sentences *put it in the bin* and *put it in the bed*).

Details of /ɪ/

For the short front vowel /ɪ/ several phonological characteristics can be enumerated.

/ɪ/ or /ə/

1. As /ɪ/ and /ə/ are the two classical English weak vowels used to replace other vowels in unstressed syllables, it is not surprising to find that there is a considerable amount of free variation between them in many words. In some cases in RP there seems to be a difference between the generations with regard to which vowel is preferred. In the pronunciation of certain suffixes, e. g. *-less, -ness*, adjectival *-ate*, the younger generation almost always has /ə/ where some older conservative speakers may have /ɪ/. Hence, both pronunciations can be heard for words like *careless, closeness, separate* /'keələs, 'keəlɪs, /'kləʊsnəs, 'kləʊsnɪs/, /'sep(ə)rət, 'sep(ə)rɪt/. On the other hand in unstressed prefixes such as *be-* or *re-*, both

vowels can be heard from speakers of all ages, e. g. *believe* /bɪˈliːv, bəˈliːv/ or *remove* /rɪˈmuːv, rəˈmuːv/, but the commoner is /ɪ/. Note that the suffix *re-* meaning *again* always carries secondary stress and is said with the long vowel /iː/, as in *re-paint* /ˌriːˈpeɪnt/.

RP versus GA

2. In some instances of free variation between /ɪ/ and /ə/ there are differences between RP and GA. For example, for most RP speakers when the suffix *-ed* comes after /t/ or /d/ in the past tense and past participle of verbs, as in *waited, started, sounded*, it is pronounced /ɪd/, whereas in American it is usually /əd/. The same preferences are to be seen for various *-es* suffixes when they follow a sibilant sound (i. e. /s, z, ʃ, ʒ, tʃ, dʒ/): RP speakers normally have /ɪz/ here, e. g. in *kisses, roses, wishes, watches, rouges, judges*, while most Americans say /əz/. In RP the pronunciation with /əz/ is reserved for words ending in *-ers*. So RP can normally differentiate between pairs of words such as *raises, razors; watches, watchers; wages, wagers; chatted, chattered; teaches, teachers; sauces, saucers* merely by choosing /ɪ/ for the first word and /ə/ for the second, i. e. /ˈreɪzɪz/ versus /ˈreɪzəz/, etc. In GA, the problem of keeping the members of these pairs of words apart does not arise as speakers pronounce the *r* in the spelling: for them *raises* is phonemically /ˈreɪzəz/ and *razors* /ˈreɪzərz/.

In Opposition

3. Sometimes the choice between /ɪ/ and /ə/ is removed: the two sounds are then in phonological opposition and used to differentiate between the members of such minimal pairs as *allusion* /əˈl(j)uːʒn/ and *illusion* /ɪˈl(j)uːʒn/, or *accept* /əkˈsept/ and *except* /ɪkˈsept/.

/ɪ/ or /e/

4. Words beginning with one of the unstressed prefixes *em-, en-, ex-* can have an alternative pronunciation which illustrates a different case of free variation. Here /ɪ/ is replaced in some people's speech by /e/. In RP and GA this latter vowel is used as an alternative only in carefully articulated speech and in careful singing. Thus, normally, words such as *employ, enjoy, except* are pronounced with initial /ɪ/, but in the context just described they can be heard with initial /e/. However, in some varieties of English, e. g. in the northern dialects of England, the pronunciation with /e/ is the rule rather than the exception.

American

5. In some kinds of American we can sometimes hear /ɪ/ where we would normally expect /e/. This happens where /e/ in standard pronunciation is found before a nasal. Instead of the normal pronunciations /pen, sent, frend, ˈlemən, men/ for *pen, cent, friend, lemon, men* one can hear the dialect forms /pɪn, sɪnt, frɪnd, ˈlɪmən, mɪn/. These pronunciations are quite common in the singing of American pop songs. However, this use of /ɪ/ for /e/ can lead to ambiguity, as we see in the American joke about the man who

 answered his friend's request for a /pɪn/ by asking: *Do you want a sticking /pɪn/ or a writing /pɪn/?*

2 Back Vowels

Note The back vowel phonemes /ɑː, ɒ, ɔː, ʊ/ (/uː/ was dealt with on page 119) are of phonological interest mainly because several of them are found in free variation with other vowel phonemes.

/ɑː/ The long, non-rounded, low, back-central monophthong /ɑː/ heard in RP in words such as *grass, path, rather, can't, after* is normally replaced in General American by the short, low, front vowel /æ/ and in most of the non-RP dialects of Britain by the short, low, central vowel /a/. The latter will be recognized by speakers of standard German as their own vowel in words like *Mann, kalt, Last* (= *man, cold, burden*). Normally it is only heard in RP as the initial position of the glides /aɪ/ and /aʊ/.

Within RP The free variation we have been talking about here (and in the sections above in connection with other vowels) has been mainly between RP and other dialects, but there are some words in which free variation between /ɑː/ and /æ/ occurs within RP. For example, most younger speakers pronounce *plastic, elastic, substantial* with stressed /æ/, but older speakers may have /ɑː/ in place of it. In some other words the preference may be reversed: the commoner pronunciation of the word *lather* is with /ɑː/ rather than /æ/, but in the case of the word *mass* (= church ceremony) only Roman Catholics seem usually to prefer /ɑː/. Another interesting case is the word *piano*, of which the commonest pronunciation is /ˈpjænəʊ/ when the musical instrument is referred to, but which is usually pronounced with /ɑː/ by most British musicians. In the other sense of *(to be played) softly* or *a piece of music played softly* it is universally pronounced with /ɑː/.

/ɒ/ A considerable amount of variation can be found between the short, slightly rounded, low, back monophthong /ɒ/ and other vowels. Within RP this vowel is the usual pronunciation of most speakers nowadays before the fricatives /f, θ, s/ in words such as *soft, often, trough, cough, froth, wrath, cross, frost, lost, cost*, but in the speech of older conservative speakers one can also hear the higher long, rounded, mid, back vowel /ɔː/ in this position. The latter vowel was common in the first half of this century among aristocratic and upper class speakers, but its popularity among this group seems to have waned, maybe because this is also the vowel which is used here in the Cockney dialect of London. Although it does not contain a fricative, the word *gone* also displays this same variation between /ɒ/ and /ɔː/ among the same groups of speakers. It should be pointed out that not all words which in modern RP have /ɒ/ before /f, θ, s/ are subject to this replacement by /ɔː/ among older conservative users of the language: the words *scoff, moth, moss, boss, floss,* for example, are pronounced with /ɒ/ by speakers of all generations.

American In GA we normally find /ɑː/ replacing RP /ɒ/ in almost all positions, but in those words where in RP older conservative and older upper class English has /ɔː/ before a fricative, many American speakers have /ɒː/, i. e. a lengthened version of the RP vowel. Thus in GA we can hear both /sɒːft/ and /sɑːft/, /ˈɒːfn/ and /ˈɑːfn/, etc.

If we look for a moment at the historical development here, we see that the back vowel in these words has been successively lowered from /ɔː/ to /ɒ/ to /ɑː/, with one kind of American pronunciation showing the latest stage.

/ɔː/ Whereas the modern RP pronunciation of all the words we have just described above prefers /ɒ/ to /ɔː/, there are some in which the reverse situation can be observed. For example, the commoner pronunciation of many words with the spelling *al*, e. g. *alter, altar, altogether, almost, already, although, Baltic, halt, malt, salt, Walter,* is with the higher back vowel /ɔː/, but the lower back vowel /ɒ/ is very frequent here, too. In American English there seems to be a slight preference for /ɒ/ rather than /ɑː/ in such words.

Note that there are many words with the spelling *al* which do not have this pronunciation. The foreign learner should be particularly careful with such names as *Albert, Alfred, Alvin, Albion, Alsatia* and words like *algebra, alkali, alcohol,* which have an initial /æ/ in both British and American English, and never have /ɔː/ in RP or /ɒː, ɑː/ in GA.

Occasionally all three vowels /ɔː, ɒ, æ/ can be heard in the same word, e. g. *falcon* /ˈfɔːlkən, ˈfɒlkən, ˈfælkən/, though usually RP prefers the first and GA the last. (Notice that in the RP pronunciation of this word with /ɔː/ the /l/ is sometimes dropped, especially by those who practise the sport of falconry.)

GA versus RP GA regularly has /ɒ/ in a few words where the *l* in the spelling *al* is always silent, e. g. *talk, chalk, stalk, walk,* and in all other words not spelt with *al* where RP has /ɔː/ although there is no *r* in the spelling, e. g. *saw, bought, daughter, cause.* However, when the vowel is followed by an *r* in the spelling, Americans always use a higher vowel. Words such as *board, cord, horn, fourth, norm, warm* are then said with /ɔː/ as in RP but, of course, with the /r/ following it pronounced. In some of these words, however, but not in all, some American speakers use the even higher back rounded vowel /oː/, which is close to the German vowel in *Boot* (= boat), e. g. /boːrd, fo:rθ/. Such speakers may then have minimal pairs of the kind *horse* /hɔːrs/ and *hoarse* /hoːrs/, others may use /ɔː/ for both words.

/ʊ/ Unlike the phonemes which we have been examining above, the short, rounded, high-mid, back-central monophthong /ʊ/ has a variant realization which shows a difference not in tongue height but in lip-rounding. In fast or casual English of all varieties this vowel may lose its lip-rounding and be pronounced either with neutral lips or even with spread lips. This variant is not found elsewhere as a separate phoneme and therefore offers us an example of free variation between phones and not, as in most of the cases which we have so far looked at, between phonemes. Phonetically it can be written with the symbol for the second highest back secondary cardinal vowel [ɤ] (see Ch.1, p. 38).

3 Central Vowels

/ɜː/ Of the three central vowels of English /ʌ, ɜː, ə/ let us look first at /ɜː/. This long, mid, central vowel is found only where there is an *r* in the spelling. In GA the vowel may be shorter than in RP and is usually **r-coloured,** i. e. the tip of the tongue may be curled back for the /r/ during the entire articulation of the vowel. This does not happen in RP as the *r* in the spelling is silent unless followed by a vowel.

/ʌ/ The short, non-rounded, low-mid, central monophthong /ʌ/ does not show free variation within RP, but it is interesting to note that in many of the midland and northern dialects of England we hear in place of it the earlier /ʊ/ phoneme from which it is historically derived. Speakers of these dialects sometimes make mistakes when changing to an RP type of pronunciation. While correctly changing their native /ʊ/ to /ʌ/ in words such as *cut, come, country, blood, does,* they wrongly use /ʌ/ in words such as *push, butcher* which in RP are always said with /ʊ/. This phenomenon of going too far in the replacement of dialect sounds in order to achieve a more standard pronunciation is usually referred to in linguistics as **hypercorrection.**

American We noted in Ch.1 that since the beginning of this century the /ʌ/ phoneme has moved from a more back position in RP to its present mid position. This movement seems to be continuing upwards in American English where for many speakers this phoneme is now similar to RP /ɜː/, especially before /r/ in words such as *hurry, current.* The American vowel sound, however, is coloured by the /r/, i. e. the retraction of the tip of the tongue for the /r/ takes place during the articulation of the vowel. This American variant of /ʌ/ is often heard in the singing of pop songs and may even be used by British performers, who often adopt an American type of pronunciation for this purpose. Another common American pronunciation has /ə/ in place of RP /ʌ/ in words which do not contain a following /r/, e. g. /kət/ instead of /kʌt/. This vowel could also be written as /ɜ/, since short /ɜ:/ is identical with /ə/.

/ə/

The short, non-rounded, mid, central phoneme /ə/ has two realizations in RP which are important for us to note. When the sound occurs in initial or medial syllables in words, the central part of the tongue is raised to the normal mid height for this vowel, which we described in Ch.1. When /ə/ is word final, however, it is realized by a phone with a somewhat lower tongue height which may even be at the top of the low area rather than at the bottom of the mid area on the vowel chart in Ch.1. The difference between these two variants is similar to that found in standard pronunciation between the final vowels of each member in pairs of German words such as *bitte (= please)*, *bitter (= bitter)* or *Laute (= lute)* and *lauter (= louder)*. The non-final realization of /ə/ (similar to the final vowel of German *bitte*) can be heard in the first syllable of *ago, perform, contain, submit, suppose, potato* or in the second syllable of *explanation, composition, energetic*. The lower variant in word-final position (similar to the final vowel of German *bitter*) is very close to the RP vowel /ʌ/ but just a little higher.

This same variation between a lower final realization and a higher non-final realization is also characteristic of the final ə element in the diphthongs /ɪə/ and /eə/.

GA

In GA the lower variant of /ə/ occurs word-finally only when there is no *r* in the spelling (e. g. in words like *America, idea, banana*). Before word-final *r* the American vowel becomes *r*-coloured (in the same way as /ɜ:/, but as it is very short it can be analysed as a short syllabic /r/ (see p. 109).

4 Diphthongs

Preliminaries

In this section we shall take a further look at the classification of diphthongs and then turn to some of their variants in RP and GA. Of particular interest is to see how some of them are historically related.

Classification

Since a diphthong is a sound which glides between an initial vowel position and a final one, it is convenient to consider it as consisting of just these two vowels, although it passes through many other intermediate vowel positions on the way. Depending on different relationships between the initial and final vowel elements, there are **two ways of classifying** the diphthong phonemes of English.

One Way

In Ch.1 we saw that one classification was based on the direction in which the diphthongs glide. Those that move up to a final high (= close) vowel position, i. e. to either /ɪ/ or /ʊ/, are called **closing diphthongs:** /eɪ, aɪ, ɔɪ, əʊ, aʊ/. Those that move to a central vowel position, i. e. to /ə/, are called **centring diphthongs:** /ɪə, eə, ʊə/. This is the classification we shall use a little later when we look at the variants of the diphthongs.

Another Way

Another classification depends on whether the beginning of the diphthong is more prominent than the end, or vice versa. We must be careful to talk about prominence here rather than stress: a diphthong may not be stressed but the beginning may still stand out more than the end or the end more than the beginning. When a diphthong has decreasing prominence, i. e. the vowel position at the beginning (which we have loosely referred to above as its initial element) stands out more than that at the end, the diphthong is said to be a **falling** (or **diminuendo) diphthong.** This is the normal case for all the English diphthongs. For example, in the unstressed final syllable of *window* /'wɪndəʊ/ the [ə] part of the diphthong /əʊ/ stands out a little more than the [ʊ] part. On the other hand, when the final element is more prominent than that at the beginning, the diphthong is referred to as a **rising** (or **crescendo) diphthong.** These can sometimes be heard in English when either of the two phones [i] and [u] occurs before [ə] in an unstressed position in which compression could take place, i. e. where the two-syllable combination [i + ə] or [u + ə] could be replaced by [jə] or [wə]. In an intermediate stage some people reduce the two adjacent vowels to the rising diphthong [ĭə] or [ŭə]. Thus for the word *idiom* there are three pronunciations: one with three syllables and no compression ['ɪd i əm], one with two syllables in which partial compression has taken place producing a rising diphthong ['ɪd ĭəm], and one with two syllables after full compression ['ɪd jəm]. Other words in which a rising (or crescendo) diphthong can be heard are *serious, usual, gradual, vacuum* ['sɪərĭəs, 'juːʒŭəl, 'grædʒŭəl, 'vækjŭəm], for which the fully compressed forms /'sɪərjəs, 'juːʒwəl, 'grædʒwəl, 'vækjwəm/ are also found. Note that in all the transcriptions above which contain a rising diphthong we have indicated this with a breve mark [˘] above the less prominent initial element of the diphthong.

Closing

Of the closing diphthongs /eɪ, aɪ, ɔɪ, aʊ, əʊ/ only /əʊ/ requires special attention, but it is worth pointing out that all of them have variants in which the initial element is stretched when they occur stressed in word-final position. Thus, in this context, the words *pay,*

Vowel Phonemes and their Phones

pie, joy, now, know will be realized phonetically as [peːɪ, paːɪ, dʒɔːɪ, naːʊ, nəːʊ]. Variants with a clipped initial element may also be found before a fortis (voiceless) consonant, as in *hate, fight, voice, house, hope.*

/əʊ/

Within RP the /əʊ/ phoneme can be heard with its normal realization [əʊ] in words with a variety of spellings, such as *so, bone, coat, toe, know, though,* but in words where it is followed by /l/, as in *gold, mould, foal, soul,* many speakers, especially of the younger generation, have the variant [ɒʊ], where the initial element of the diphthong is the low back vowel heard in *got.*

/oʊ/

In GA the vowel in all the above words is /oʊ/, i. e. a diphthong with a higher initial element than the RP diphthong has. This initial element has the same position as the long monophthong /oː/ which we saw in one GA pronunciation of words like *hoarse* and *board.*

Centring

Like the closing vowels, the three centring diphthongs /ɪə, eə, ʊə/, which we hear in the RP pronunciation of words such as *here, dear, fierce; there, fair, wear; poor, pure, skewer,* can all have stretched realizations with a lengthened first element when they are word-final and stressed. For example, *fear* in this context would then be pronounced [fiːə] instead of [fɪə]. Similarly, they can all have a clipped initial element before a fortis consonant, as in *fierce.*

Origin

Historically, all the centring diphthongs are derived from /ɪr, er, ʊr/. In the course of time, the /r/ was vocalized to /ə/. It can still be seen in the spelling and, as we observed in our examination of the /r/ phoneme earlier in Chapter 3, it can re-appear in the pronunciation when the diphthong is word-final and the next word begins with a vowel. In GA the older pronunciation with the monophthong plus /r/ has been retained but many American speakers also have the diphthong followed by /r/: thus for words like *here, there, poor* we find both /hɪr, ðer, pʊr/ and /hɪər, ðeər, pʊər/.

/ɪə/

One set of words, this time only in RP, contains /ɪə/ as the result of the compression of the two syllables /iː + ə/. Such words as *freer* (comparative of the adjective *free*) or *reaffirm, reassure, reappear* thus have a syllable less when said with /ɪə/. Note that when the verb *reappear* is said with no compression of the first two vowels, there is a noticeable difference phonetically between these and the diphthong in the final syllable /ˌriːəˈpɪə/. On the other hand, if compression has taken place, the vowel in the first syllable and the vowel at the end are identical except for the stresss /ˌrɪəˈpɪə/.

/ʊə/

Compression is also responsible for the appearance of the diphthong /ʊə/ in some RP speakers' pronunciation of words such as *fewer, dual, jewel,* i. e. /fjʊə, djʊəl, dʒʊəl/, where others will have the non-compressed /u: + ə/, i. e. /ˈfjuːə, ˈdjuːəl, ˈdʒuːəl/.

A more interesting feature of this diphthong is that in the development of modern RP it is gradually disappearing and in many words is no longer used by the younger generations, who replace it with /ɔ:/. A fusion of three different diphthongs seems to have taken place, which were kept apart at the beginning of this century. At that time RP speakers could differentiate between *poor*, *pour* and *paw*: /pʊə/, /pɔə/ and /pɔ:/. Nowadays, most speakers pronounce all three words with /ɔ:/, though some may still keep /ʊə/ in *poor*. Whereas the replacement of /ɔə/ by /ɔ:/ has been quite general, the change from /ʊə/ to /ɔ:/ seems to have been more readily accepted by most speakers in common words of one syllable like *poor, sure*, but less so in others like *tour, moor*, especially if the vowel is preceded by /j/, as in *pure, cure*. In longer less common words like *curious, furious, tourist* the pronunciation with /ʊə/ still seems to be the commoner one, though /ɔ:/ is gaining ground.

We saw above that in almost all of the contexts where RP can have /ʊə/ before an *r* in the spelling, GA has either retained the original /ʊr/ or has /ʊər/. There are some words, however, in which beside these combinations a third American pronunciation has arisen with the *r*-coloured central mid vowel which we mentioned on page 125. Although it is a single sound we can write it as /ɜ:r/. Some American speakers will therefore pronounce *pure, sure, during* as /pjɜ:r, ʃɜ:r, 'dɜ:rɪŋ/.

CHAPTER 5 Phonological Processes

Introduction

In this chapter we shall examine the details of some of the phonological processes which operate on English words and which account for their pronunciation, especially in connected speech. Some of these processes we have already encountered several times in the preceding chapters and others were briefly enumerated at the beginning of Ch. 2. Most of the examples (words, phrases and sentences) in this present chapter will be transcribed in RP. Speakers of American English can easily convert these into their own type of pronunciation by applying the few rules given in Ch. 6 (pages 165–166). It will be convenient to discuss the phonological processes in the following order: **assimilation, coalescence, elision, epenthesis** (insertion), **compression, weakening.**

🚹 Assimilation

Definition

Assimilation is the name given to a process whereby **one sound influences the articulation of another.** When the influencing sound and the influenced sound are adjacent to each other, as is always the case in English, the process is sometimes called contiguous or contact assimilation, but in other languages we may sometimes find non-contiguous assimilation, where the two sounds are at a distance from each other. For example, the low vowel in the Old High German word *gast* (= *guest)* was raised to a mid vowel when the plural suffix *-i* was added: *gesti.* Under the influence of the high vowel in the suffix, the low vowel in the preceding syllable was assimilated and became higher.

Two Kinds

Another classification of assimilation depends on the direction of the influence. Here two main kinds of assimilation can be distinguished: (a) progressive and (b) regressive. The term progressive assimilation is used when the influence is forward to a following sound, i. e. when the second sound adjusts itself in some way to the sound preceding, e. g. either by assuming one or more features of the first sound or by modifying one or more of its own features in that direction. Regressive assimilation is the term used when the influence is backwards to a preceding sound, i. e. when the first sound adjusts itself to the sound that follows it. Note that the terms *progressive* and *regressive* refer to the direction of the influence and not to the direction of the adjustment. Examples of both kinds of assimilation will be seen below.

1 Progressive

Note

Progressive assimilation is **obligatory** in modern English when certain suffixes consisting phonetically of a single consonant are added to a word, e. g. *-s* (sometimes spelt *-es*) or *-ed*. It can sometimes also be heard optionally in rapid conversation.

-s

Let us look first at the various **-s suffixes**. These are used for the following purposes: to indicate the plural of a noun *(ships, beds, trees)*, the genitive singular *(cat's, dog's, widow's)* or the genitive plural *(cats', dogs', widows')*, the third person singular of the present tense of a verb *(jumps, runs, follows)*, or as a reduced form of *is* or *has (Pete's ill, Bob's gone, Sue's left)*. In each of these groups of three examples the suffix is added first to a word ending phonetically in a voiceless consonant, which causes the suffix also to become voiceless: /kæts͡ /, /dʒʌmps͡/, /piːts͡/. The second word in each group ends in a voiced consonant, which now makes the suffix voiced: /dɒɡz͡/, /rʌnz͡/, /bɒbz͡/. The third word in each group ends in a vowel, and as vowels are always voiced, the suffix here too will have to be voiced: /triːz͡/, /ˈwɪdəʊz͡/, /ˈsuːz͡/. In each case the suffix has been **assimilated** to the sound preceding it **with regard to the feature of voicing.** Note that assimilation does not take place when a suffix -s is added to a word ending in one of the sibilant phonemes /s, z, ʃ, ʒ, tʃ, dʒ/. In this case the suffix forms a separate syllable /ɪz/ (in GA also /əz/), e. g. *crosses, roses, dishes, rouges, ditches, judges* /ˈkrɒs ɪz, ˈrəʊz ɪz, ˈdɪʃ ɪz, ˈruːʒ ɪz, ˈdɪtʃ ɪz, ˈdʒʌdʒ ɪz/.

-ed

A similar case of progressive assimilation is found with the suffixes for the past tense and the past participle of regular verbs in English. These are usually written with *-ed*, but they are pronounced as a single consonant which is phonetically **assimilated** to the final sound of the verb root **with regard to its voicing.** When added to a verb with a final voiceless consonant, the suffix must also be voiceless: *jumped, rocked, missed, rushed, lunched, etched* /dʒʌmpt͡, rɒkt͡, mɪst͡, rʌʃt, lʌntʃt͡, etʃt͡/. When the final consonant of the verb is voiced or when the verb ends phonetically in a vowel, the suffix must then be voiced: *robbed, begged, posed, judged, lined, echoed, stayed* /rɒb͡d, beɡ͡d, pəʊz͡d, dʒʌdʒ͡d, laɪn͡d, ˈekəʊ͡d, steɪ͡d/.

Note that assimilation does not take place when the verb itself ends phonetically in /t/ or /d/. In this case both suffixes are pronounced as a full syllable /ɪd/ (in General American also /əd/): *painted, loaded* /ˈpeɪnt ɪd/, /ˈləʊd ɪd/. Particular attention must be paid to RP verb forms such as *covered, flattered, lingered*, which some foreign speakers wrongly pronounce with /ɪd/, e. g. /ˈkʌvər ɪd/, etc. Despite their spelling these forms are really phonetically

5

regular. As the verb root does not end in /t/ or /d/ the suffix cannot be pronounced /ɪd/. Since the final r in the spelling is silent, the verb ends in a vowel and the suffix must therefore be /d/. Hence the correct RP pronunciations are /'kʌvə͡d, 'flætə͡d, 'ɪŋgə͡d/. Americans also have the regular /d/ here since for them the verbs end in /r/, which is voiced: /'kʌvərd, 'flætərd, 'ɪŋgərd/.

Note also that some verbs, like *spell, smell*, have both a regularly assimilated form and an irregular unassimilated form: *spelled /* spel͡d/ and *spelt* /spelt/.

<table>
<tr><td>Optional</td><td>The relatively uncommon cases of optional progressive assimilation, which we mentioned at the beginning as sometimes occurring in rapid conversation, are found where a syllabic [n̩] comes after a bilabial plosive as in happen, ribbon or after a velar plosive as in reckon, organ. Here we find assimilation not with regard to voicing but with regard to place of articulation: after one of the labial plosives /p, b/ the syllabic alveolar nasal [n̩] may change to the syllabic bilabial nasal [m̩], e. g. /'hæpm̩, 'rɪbm̩/, and after one of the velar plosives /k, g/ rarely to the syllabic velar nasal [ŋ̩],e. g. /'rekŋ̩,'ɔːgŋ̩/. (Note: for convenience, here and in the rest of this chapter, syllabic nasals are transcribed together with phonemes between phoneme slashes, although the syllabic sounds are phones.) Progressive assimilation of this kind is usually frowned upon by careful speakers and should therefore be avoided by foreign learners.</td></tr>
</table>

2 Regressive

<table>
<tr><td>General
Notes</td><td>In modern English regressive assimilation is always optional and often found in very rapid conversation. It can be heard when a word final alveolar is assimilated to the place of articulation of the first consonant of the next word. It is important to note that the alveolar always retains its original voicing and that not every following consonant can have this assimilative influence. Before we list these influencing consonants and show the changes which they make to the alveolar sound, let us look at two examples in detail. The voiceless alveolar plosive /t/ in that guy remains voiceless, but can be influenced by the following velar plosive /g/ and is then pronounced as an unreleased /k/, i. e. /ðæt 'gaɪ/ → /ðæk͡ gaɪ/. Similarly, the voiceless alveolar fricative /s/ in this shop remains voiceless but can be influenced by the following palato-alveolar fricative /ʃ/ and then itself becomes palato-alveolar, i. e. /ðɪs 'ʃɒp/ → /ðɪʃ͡ ʃɒp/.</td></tr>
<tr><td>Where?</td><td>Before /p, b, m/:   /t/ → /p/   that pig, that box, that man
                           /ðæp͡ pɪg, ðæp͡ bɒks, ðæp͡ mæn/</td></tr>
</table>

	/d/ → /b/	red pot, bad boy, dead man
		/reb͡ pɒt, bæb͡ bɔɪ, deb͡ mæn/
	/n/ → /m/	one pen, ten bags, nine meals
		/wʌm͡ pen, tem͡ bægz, naɪm͡ miːlz/
Before /k, g/:	/t/ → /k/	that cake, that gun
		/ðæk͡ keɪk, ðæk͡ gʌn/
	/d/ → /g/	bad cold, good guess
		/bæg͡ kəʊld, gʊg͡ ges/
	/n/ → /ŋ/	ten cooks, one goat
		/teŋ͡ kʊks, wʌŋ͡ gəʊt/
Before /ʃ, tʃ, dʒ, j/:	/s/ → /ʃ/	this shirt, less cheese, this jug, this year
		/ðɪʃ͡ ʃɜːt, leʃ͡ tʃiːz, ðɪʃ͡ dʒʌg, ðɪʃ͡ jɪə/
	/z/ → /ʒ/	those sheep, these chips, these jugs, his young wife
		/ðəʊʒ͡ ʃiːp, ðiːʒ͡ tʃɪps, ðiːʒ͡ dʒʌgz, hɪʒ͡ jʌŋ ˈwaɪf/

This kind of regressive assimilation, like the optional progressive assimilation which we saw in the preceding section, sounds slovenly to careful speakers and should not be imitated by foreign learners.

3 Historical

Note

To complete our picture of assimilation we shall examine a few cases where the process has occurred historically within words and the assimilated pronunciation has usually become the regular one in modern English.

/n/ → /ŋ/

The most striking case is one we saw in Ch.2 when we discussed neutralization. We noted that inside an English morpheme a nasal sound always has the same place of articulation as the consonant that follows it: we only find words like *pump, end, think* and none like *punp, emd, thimk*. At least in the case of *n* before *k* (as in *think*) or of *n* before *g* (as in *hunger*), the homorganic nasal /ŋ/ which we now hear in the pronunciation must originally, i. e. many centuries ago, have been an allophone of /n/ resulting from regressive assimilation. **The alveolar nasal /n/ fell under the influence of the following velar plosive /k/ or /g/ and itself became realized as the velar nasal [ŋ].** Between morphemes the process is still continuing today, so that for words like *in+complete, in+capable* and *un+common, un+cover* we can hear the suffix pronounced in its original form without the assimilation as /ɪn-, ʌn-/ and also in its assimilated form as /ɪŋ-, ʌŋ-/. This is also true of the preposition *in* when it occurs in phrases like *in case*: as we would expect from the table of changes above, some speakers say /ɪn ˈkeɪs/, others /ɪŋ ˈkeɪs/. Notice that the prefix *in-* had already been assimilated to *im-* before a plosive in Latin by the Romans, before many words like *impossible, improbable, imprudent* were imported (often through Old French) into English.

Other Cases The examples we have just looked at were concerned with regressive assimilation with regard to place of articulation. There are **other cases where only voicing was involved.** In the modern pronunciation of *gooseberry, raspberry, gosling* /ˈgʊz b(ə)ri, ˈrɑːz b(ə) ri, ˈgɒz lɪŋ/ the spelling shows that an original /s/ has become voiced under the influence of a following voiced sound. Other irregularities in the pronunciation, such as the change from /guːs/ to /gʊz/ in the first word and to /gɒz/ in the third, need not concern us here. The apparent loss of /p/ in the second word will be dealt with under 'elision' below.

② Coalescence

General Notes When **coalescence** takes place, two adjacent sounds unite and fuse into one. As this fusion is the result of the two sounds influencing each other, the process is sometimes also called **coalescent (or reciprocal) assimilation.** In English the process has occurred in many words historically and the pronunciation with the fused consonant is usually obligatory nowadays. Cases of optional coalescence can be heard in modern English in rapid conversation.

Coalescence occurs **only between alveolar plosives or fricatives and a following /j/, and the resulting sound is either a palato-alveolar affricate or a palato-alveolar fricative.** The exact changes can be seen in the following table:

t + j → tʃ
d + j → dʒ
s + j → ʃ
z + j → ʒ

1 Nowadays

Examples In modern conversation coalescence is found between the final consonant of one word and the initial semivowel of the next. The following examples illustrate each of the four changes shown in the table above. The left-hand column shows careful RP pronunciation, the middle column the form that has undergone coalescence. For the sake of simplicity, we shall transcribe *you* between phoneme slashes, although it should really be in phonetic brackets since [u] is a phone and not a phoneme.

/'wɒt ju/	→ /'wɒtʃu/	*what you (need)*
/'dɪd ju/	→ /'dɪdʒu/	*did you (go)*
/'hæd ju/	→ /'hædʒu/	*had you (spoken)*
/'feɪs jɔː/	→ /'feɪʃɔː/	*face your (enemies)*
/'hæz jɔː/	→ /'hæʒɔː/	*has your (aunt come)*

Notice that in the last two examples we can also hear regressive assimilation instead of coalescence, i. e. /'feɪʃ‿jɔː/, /'hæʒ‿jɔː/.

2 Historical

Examples

In many present-day words the speaker no longer has a choice and only the pronunciation with the coalescence is acceptable. The following examples show an older, obsolete pronunciation in the left-hand column, and the modern acceptable RP pronunciation in the middle column.

/'mɪsjən/	→ /'mɪʃ(ə)n/	*mission*
/'neɪsjən/	→ /'neɪʃ(ə)n/	*nation*
/'sjʊgə/	→ /'ʃʊgə/	*sugar*
/'vɪzjən/	→ /'vɪʒ(ə)n/	*vision*
/'neɪtjʊə/	→ /'neɪtʃə/	*nature*
/'səʊldjə/	→ /'səʊldʒə/	*soldier*

3 Mixed

Note

In a fair number of other words both the pronunciation with coalescence and without it can be heard nowadays. It is often difficult to determine whether the one without the fused consonant is the original or whether it is due to what is often called **spelling pronunciation.** The latter occurs when modern speakers who hear what appears to them to be an irregular pronunciation adjust it to the spelling.

RP

In RP it is not easy to predict which pronunciation will be the commoner. Thus for the words *virtue, issue, tissue* we usually hear the pronunciations /'vɜːtʃuː, 'ɪʃuː, 'tɪʃuː/ more often than /'vɜːtjuː, 'ɪsjuː, 'tɪsjuː/. In other cases the preference seems to be the other way around: *educate, reduce, assume, Jesuit* are more common without coalescence /'edjʊkeɪt, rɪ'djuːs, ə'sjuːm, 'dʒezjuɪt/ than with it /'edʒʊkeɪt, rɪ'dʒuːs, ə'ʃuːm, 'dʒeʒuɪt/. In fact some people might even disapprove of coalescence in *reduce* and *assume.* A more com-

mon alternative in the case of the latter would be to replace /juː/ by /uː/, i. e. to pronounce it /əˈsuːm/. In RP pronunciation of words like *presume, resume*, which have a /z/ before /juː/, all three forms can be heard: the commonest is with /juː/, a little less common is with /uː/, while the form with coalescence, i. e. /prɪˈʒuːm, rɪˈʒuːm/, is uncommon and may even be considered by some people as unacceptable.

In GA the situation is less complicated. Americans always have the form with coalescence wherever this is obligatory in RP and usually also where RP has a choice. However, after /t, d, s, z/, *(tune, dew, dune, assume, presume)* the normal pronunciation is with /uː/ (/tuːn, duː, duːn, əˈsuːm, prɪˈzuːm/, though occasionally /juː/ can also be heard after /t, d, s/ but not after /z/.

🖪 Elision

1 General Notes

Definition

Elision is the phonological process in which a **sound that ought to be in a word is deleted.** It may affect both vowels and consonants.

/ə/

When we examined the nasal phonemes and the phonemes /r/ and /l/ in Chapter 3, we saw several cases of the deletion of /ə/, where either a syllabic nasal was the result or the word lost a syllable. Further examples are *quieten* /ˈkwaɪətən → ˈkwaɪətn̩/, *frightening* /ˈfraɪtənɪŋ → ˈfraɪtn̩ɪŋ → ˈfraɪtnɪŋ/, *flavouring'* /ˈfleɪvərɪŋ → ˈfleɪvrɪŋ/, *history* /ˈhɪstəri → ˈhɪstri/, *camera* /ˈkæmərə → ˈkæmrə/, *awefully* /ˈɔːfəli → ˈɔːfli/, *specialist* /ˈspeʃəlɪst → ˈspeʃlɪst/.

Consonants

The elision of a consonant can sometimes be heard in words like *almost, always* where /l/ is elided after /ɔː/, but this pronunciation should not be imitated by foreign speakers. By far the most common kind of consonant elision, and the one which we shall look at in detail below, occurs when **the middle plosive in a series of three adjacent consonants is deleted.** We shall refer to this as **middle-consonant elision.** There are historical cases where the pronunciation resulting from the elision is obligatory nowadays, and there are present-day cases where the process is optional. As with assimilation and coalescence, these optional cases usually occur in casual or rapid conversation and not in careful speech.

2 Historical

handkerchief — A number of words in modern English owe their apparently irregular pronunciation to **middle-consonant elision followed by assimilation.** Perhaps the most striking example of this is the word *handkerchief.* It looks as if it ought to be pronounced /'hænd,kɜːtʃɪf/ (a kerchief for the hand), but if we look more closely at the phonetics of this word, we see the series of consonants /ndk/, where the middle one is a plosive. By the process of elision the /d/ was dropped leaving /nk/. Then the /n/ came under the influence of the velar plosive /k/ and by regressive assimilation was converted into the velar nasal /ŋ/. The modern pronunciation /'hæŋkətʃɪf/ is therefore not at all deviant but the regular product of two phonological processes. Even the weakening of stressed /ɜː/ to /ə/ was a logical phonological process, once people no longer recognized the word *kerchief* in the pronunciation. It should be noted that until the beginning of this century most people could neither read nor write and were therefore not influenced in their pronunciation by spelling.

Other Cases — A less spectacular example can be seen in the word *raspberry,* where the first element *rasp* in 16th century English was the original name of this fruit. When later the word *berry* was added, the series of three consonants /spb/ arose, which by elision of the middle plosive was reduced to /sb/. This then became /zb/ by regressive assimilation when the /s/ fell under the influence of the following voiced plosive /b/ and itself became voiced.

Another interesting case is the word *mustn't* in which the sequence /stn/ has undergone elision of the middle plosive /t/ and is always pronounced /sn/. Since the /s/ does not become assimilated to the /n/ with regard to voicing, as we might have expected, the pronunciation of the word is always /'mʌsnt/. Two similar cases are the verbal expressions *supposed to* and *used to,* in both of which the middle /t/ in the sequence /ztt/ is almost always elided and the /z/ subsequently assimilated to the voicelessness of the final /t/, producing /sə'pəʊs tu/ and /'juːs tu/.

3 Nowadays

Elision of /t, d/ — Present-day middle-consonant elision is **always optional.** It is very frequently heard between words, but may also occur in the middle of a compound word between its component morphemes. It differs from historical elision in being **reversible,** i. e. the elided plosive can be restored in careful pronunciation. Furthermore, whereas the elided middle consonant in historical elision could be a plosive other than /t/ or /d/ (e. g. /p/ in *raspberry*), these two **alveolar plosives are the only ones which can be elided nowadays.** There are also some restrictions on the kinds of consonants which can occur in first or last place in the sequence of three. The following diagram gives the rule for elision and shows which consonants permit elision to take place when they come before and after /t/ or /d/.

Rule: C^1 + /t, d/ + C^3 → C^1 + C^3

C^1 = /m, n, ŋ/ C^3 = /m, n/
        /l/   /l, r/
        /p, b, t, d, k, g/   /p, b, t, d, k, g/
        /f, v, s, z, ʃ, ʒ, θ, ð/   /f, v, s, z, ʃ, ʒ, θ,ð/
        /tʃ, dʒ/   /tʃ, dʒ/
                                        /w/

Let us first look at a few examples and then discuss the restrictions on the consonant preceding and following the alveolar plosive before it can be elided.

Between Words

A very common case of elision between words is with **past tense or past participle forms** of verbs **before a word beginning with a consonant.** For example, in the /mdd/ of *calmed down* the middle /d/ is often elided, producing /md/ and making the past tense phonetically identical to the present tense. Similarly in *wronged them* the /d/ in the sequence /ŋdð/ can be dropped and again the past and the present tense sound alike. For young English and American children learning to read and write, this kind of elision can lead to difficulties with the spelling. If they always hear *mashed potatoes* pronounced without the middle /t/ of the sequence /ʃtp/, it is not surprising if they write *mash potatoes* without the *-ed* in an essay on 'What I had for lunch today'.

Inside Words

Examples of compound words which have internal optional elision between their components are less frequent but several can be found **with a nasal as the first consonant.** For such words as *grandfather, grandmother, granddaughter, grandson* most people prefer the elided form, but may pronounce the /d/ in careful speech. In the case of *landscape, landmark, windscreen, handbag* both pronunciations can be heard. Words with a fricative as C^1 are not so numerous, but a common one, which seems almost always to be said without the /t/ in the middle is *Christmas*. Others which are as common with elision as without are *software, postcard*.

Forbidden Cs	We should note that some sequences of three consonants are not possible because of the distribution of English phonemes. C^1 cannot be /h/ as there are no morphemes in English with this fricative in final position or in a final cluster with /t/ or /d/. Similarly, since /ŋ/ cannot be morpheme-initial, this nasal is never found as C^3.
C^1+ /t, d/ + /h/	Sometimes there are phonetic reasons for the restriction. For example, elision does not normally take place when C^3 is /h/ and the middle plosive is /t/, as in *worked hard, kept hold*, because the /h/ merely makes the /t/ sound aspirated, in which case we would then have only two consonants [kt^h, pt^h] instead of a sequence of three /kth, pth/. Probably a similar reason also accounts for the absence of elision when /d/ is the middle consonant here. It will be remembered that word-final /d/ becomes partially devoiced before word-initial /h/. We therefore have the voiceless part now sounding as if it were aspirated so that again the sequence is more like a cluster of two consonants than the sequence of three necessary for elision.
/n, l/ + /t/ + C^3	In combinations where /nt/ or /lt/ occur before another consonant the /t/ is usually pronounced **unreleased and not elided**, e. g. *aren't they* is heard as [ˈɑːntʃ ðeɪ] and not as /ˈɑːn ðeɪ/, and *malt beer* as [ˈmɔːltʃ bɪə] and not as /ˈmɔːl bɪə/. Notice, however, that the /t/ element in /tʃ/ as well as the /d/ element in /dʒ/ are regularly elided after /n/ by some British and American speakers in words like *lunch, change*. Here the affricates seem to have been re-analysed as clusters of two consonants, i. e. /t + ʃ/ and /d + ʒ/. After elision the words are pronounced /lʌnʃ/ and /tʃeɪnʒ/.
C^1 + /t, d/ + /j/	In careful pronunciation word-final /t/ and /d/ after another consonant are usually kept before a following /j/, but in more rapid speech they may **coalesce** with the /j/ to give /tʃ/ and /dʒ/. Thus *helped you* and *told you* can be heard as /ˈhelptʃu/ and /ˈtəʊldʒu/.
asked	As a final curiosity, we may note that in casual speech the /k/ of *asked* is often elided although it is not an alveolar plosive, i. e. people say /ɑːst/ instead of /ɑːskt/. Perhaps the elided form represents an older pronunciation; however, this cannot be a case of historical elision as we defined it above, because historical elision has always produced pronunciations which are nowadays obligatory, and this is not true of *asked*, which is equally acceptable when pronounced with the /k/.

4 Epenthesis

Epenthesis is the phonological process of inserting a sound into a word. This has happened historically with obligatory results for present-day pronunciation and is continuing today as an optional process. In modern English it is sometimes found with vowels, as when an unmotivated /ə/ is inserted into the word *athlete* /'æθəliːt/ (a pronunciation which foreign speakers should avoid), but it is far more common and acceptable with consonants. The usual case is when a **plosive** which is not in the spelling **is inserted** into a word **between a nasal and another consonant**. The plosive must be **homorganic with the nasal**, i. e. have the same place of articulation, and it **must agree with the sound following it in respect of voicing.**

1 Nowadays

Rule

In present-day English, whether British or American, the consonant after the nasal in a cluster which undergoes epenthesis is always a voiceless fricative or a voiceless plosive. So we could write the modern rule as follows:

Rule: C^1 + C^2 → C^1 + homorganic plosive + C^2

C^1 = Nasal C^2 = Voiceless Fricative
                          Voiceless Plosive

/ns/ → /nts/

Numerous examples of the insertion of /t/ between /n/ and /s/ can be found, especially in words ending in *-anse, -ense, -ance, -ence, -ince*, e. g. *expanse* /ɪk'spænts/, *dense* /dents/, *chance* /tʃɑːnts/, *fence* /fents/, *rince* /rɪnts/. It must be stressed that both pronunciations are equally acceptable, but for foreign learners the one without the epenthetic /t/ is to be preferred, since it helps to keep apart the members of many pairs, like *chants, chance; dents, dense; scents, sense; tents, tense; prints, prince*, where the two words sound identical after epenthesis has taken place.

Note that between the alveolar nasal /n/ and the voiceless fricative /s/, the only possible epenthetic plosive is the voiceless alveolar /t/. It is interesting that this particular case of epenthesis works in exactly the opposite direction to modern middle-consonant elision: here epenthesis inserts a /t/ between two consonants where originally there was not one, while elision in the same environment drops a /t/ which should really be present. Other cases of epenthesis do not show this interaction with elision.

Other Cases

If we examine words with a cluster consisting of a bilabial nasal plus a voiceless plosive, e. g. /mt/ in *dreamt*, we find that the epenthetic plosive here must be bilabial like the nasal and voiceless like the following plosive, i. e. /mt/ → /mpt/. Many people who use this irregular past tense form instead of the regular one *dreamed* /dri:md/ will therefore pronounce the word /drempt/. Others, who make no use of epenthesis, will say /dremt/. It is worth observing that this last pronunciation contains the combination bilabial nasal plus alveolar plosive, which in our discussion of neutralization in Ch.2 we saw to be an uncharacteristic cluster inside a single English morpheme. It is true that the nasal and the plosive are separated here by a morpheme boundary *(dream+t)*, but there is still an uneasy feeling about this combination in a single syllable. Epenthesis is a way out of this problem: when the /p/ has been inserted, the nasal has a homorganic plosive following it and is now part of a kind of cluster which English prefers. Other cases of this kind of epenthesis but with a fricative following the bilabial nasal are *warmth* /wɔ:mpθ/ where /mθ/ → /mpθ/, and *triumph* /ˈtraɪʌmpf/ where /mf/ → /mpf/. The cluster /mθ/ has arisen in the former word because of a morpheme boundary between the adjective *warm* and the noun-forming suffix *-th*; in the second word the cluster /mf/ was imported via Old French from Latin and is not an original English one. With the epenthetic /p/ both these words sound more comfortably English.

A comparable development has occurred in words containing a velar nasal plus a voiceless fricative, e. g. *length, strength*. Here the epenthetic plosive must be velar like the preceding nasal and voiceless like the following fricative, i. e. /ŋθ/ → /ŋkθ/. So for these two words we hear both /leŋθ, streŋθ/ and /leŋkθ, streŋkθ/. Again there is a morpheme boundary between the nasal and the fricative *(long+th, strong+th)*, justifying an otherwise un-English word-final cluster of consonants, and again the pronunciation with epenthesis sounds more comfortable.

2 Historical

In words in which epenthesis has taken place historically, the epenthetic plosive is now part of the spelling. Unlike epenthesis nowadays, the historic insertion took place not just between a nasal and a plosive that was voiceless but **also between a nasal and a voiced sound.**

For example, the modern word *nimble* is derived from the Middle English *nemel*. Here, when the second vowel was weakened and dropped out, the bilabial nasal /m/ came together with the voiced lateral, and a plosive was inserted having the same place of articulation as the nasal and the same voicing as the lateral, i. e. /ml/

→ /mbl/. The same epenthetic /b/ can be heard in *thimble, tumble, humble,* though each of these words has a different history. *Thimble* derives from Old English *thȳmel,* whereas *tumble* came into Middle English from Middle Low German *tummelen,* and *humble* was imported from Old French (being derived ultimately from the Latin word *humilis*). Another borrowing from Old French, *chamber,* shows an epenthetic /b/ which had already been inserted into a Latin word (Latin *camera* → Old French *chambre*). A similar case, but this time with the change /nr/ → /ndr/, can be seen in the word *tender,* where Latin *tener* became the Old French *tendre,* which was then borrowed into Middle English. Predictably, the epenthetic /d/ took its place of articulation from the preceding alveolar nasal and its voicing from the following voiced /r/.

C³ Voiceless

Some historical examples where the epenthetic plosive is voiceless can be observed in the English family names *Thompson (Tom+son)* and *Sampson (Sam+son)*. Speakers of German will also recognize an epenthetic /t/ in such words as *namentlich, ordentlich, eigentlich* in their own language.

5 Compression

Definition

Compression is a phonological process in which two syllables become compressed into one. Having encountered several different cases of it in Ch.3, we can now pull the threads together. We should note first that it is more common in fast or casual speech and that it is less usual in rare words than in ones which are used frequently.

Examples

Let us look at the details of some of the more characteristic cases of this phonological process.

/ən, n̩/→/n/
/əl, l̩/→/l/

One case of compression affects syllables with **potential syllabic nasals** or **potential syllabic laterals,** and operates in both British and American English. We saw that words such as *threatening* or *rattling,* when carefully spoken, have three syllables and can be pronounced in two ways. Either the /ə/ before the nasal or the lateral is retained or else it is elided and the nasal or the lateral becomes syllabic, e. g. /ˈθret ən ɪŋ, ˈθret n̩ɪŋ/ and /ˈræt əl ɪŋ, ˈræt l̩ɪŋ/. In faster or more casual speech the three syllables can be compressed into two and the words are then pronounced /ˈθret nɪŋ, ˈræt lɪŋ/.

/i/ → /j/
/u/ → /w/

Another case of compression which we noted earlier, and which is also found in both British and American English, affects **high vowels.** When one of the two phones [i] realizing /iː/ or [u] realizing /uː/ occurs before an unstressed vowel, it is frequently replaced by the corresponding semivowel /j/ or /w/ respectively. Though this is not really consistent, for convenience we shall write these phones between phoneme slashes in the following transcriptions. Examples of this kind of compression can be heard in the pronunciation of such words as *obedient* /ə 'biː di ənt/ → /ə 'biː djənt/, *genius* /'dʒiː ni əs/ → /'dʒiː njəs/ and *conspicuous* /kən 'spɪk ju əs/ → / kən 'spɪk jwəs/, *tenuous* /'ten ju əs/ → /'ten jwəs/.

/iː + ə/
→ /ɪə/

/uː + ə/
→ /ʊə/

A third case of compression is found only in RP. It occurs in some words that have a **long vowel followed by shwa.** This combination is replaced by a diphthong beginning with a vowel position slightly lower than that of the original long vowel. In this way the two syllables /iː + ə/ are reduced to monosyllabic /ɪə/, e. g. in *foreseeable* /fɔː 'siː ə bl̩/ → /fɔː 'sɪə bl̩/, *agreeable* /ə 'griː ə bl̩/ → /ə 'grɪə bl̩/, and more commonly /uː + ə/ to monosyllabic /ʊə/, e. g. in *cruel* /'kruː əl/ → /kruəl/, *steward* /'stjuː əd/ → /stjʊəd/. Note that compression of this kind can produce some diphthongs which are not otherwise found in English, e. g. /ʊɪ/ in *Jewish* /'dʒuː ɪʃ/ → /dʒʊɪʃ/, *blueish* /'bluː ɪʃ/ → /blʊɪʃ/.

/aʊ + ə/
→ /aə/

The final case of compression which we need to examine is also restricted to RP. If, as most phonologists do, we analyse the combination /aʊə/ not as a monosyllabic triphthong but as two syllables, i. e. as a diphthong plus a vowel, then the reduction of this combination in fast or casual speech to monosyllabic /aə/ is an example of compression. It can be heard in such words as *nowadays, power, flour*, which instead of /'naʊ ə deɪz, 'paʊ ə, 'flaʊ ə/ are then pronounced /'naə deɪz, paə, flaə/. Indeed, there are some RP speakers who reduce this diphthong even further to /aː/. Foreign speakers should be able to recognize these compressed forms, but they should not imitate them. Notice that with words like *towel, bowel, trowel*, where an /l/ follows the diphthong plus shwa, the compression to /taəl, baəl, traəl/ is less common than to /taʊl, baʊl, traʊl/, forms which are produced by the elision of /ə/. The pronunciation with just /aː/ does not occur here.

If we analyse /aʊə/ as a monosyllabic triphthong, the reduction to /aə/ must then be considered to be a case of weakening and not of compression.

6 Weakening

General Notes

One of the most characteristic features of English pronunciation is the weakening of the vowels in unstressed syllables to either /ə/ or /ɪ/, as in the most common pronunciation of *possible* /'pɒsəbl/ and *message* /'mesɪdʒ/. Sometimes both /ə/ and /ɪ/ are equally frequent as in *captain* /'kæptɪn, 'kæptən/. We can see that /ə/ and /ɪ/ are weakened forms of strong vowels, because people often

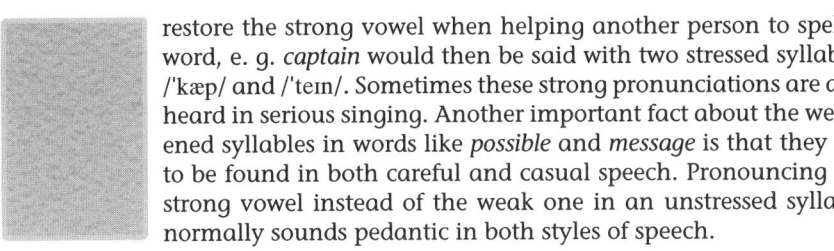

restore the strong vowel when helping another person to spell a word, e. g. *captain* would then be said with two stressed syllables /'kæp/ and /'teɪn/. Sometimes these strong pronunciations are also heard in serious singing. Another important fact about the weakened syllables in words like *possible* and *message* is that they are to be found in both careful and casual speech. Pronouncing the strong vowel instead of the weak one in an unstressed syllable normally sounds pedantic in both styles of speech.

1 Weak Forms

Function Words

Another form of weakening affects whole words and can be found in all styles of speech except in extremely careful enunciation. There are a number of very common **function words** in English **(monosyllabic conjunctions, prepositions, pronouns, determiners, auxiliary verbs)** which occur in two forms: a strong form with a full vowel, and a weak form with a weakened vowel or a syllabic consonant. Let us take the conjunction *and* as a common example first and then look at the members of each of these groups of function words in turn.

and

If I point to the word *and* on a page and ask any native speakers of English how it is pronounced, they will always say /'ænd/. This is the normal form of the word when we talk about it in isolation. It is stressed and has its full vowel /æ/ because it is the topic about which we are now thinking. However, when we use it in context, it is an unimportant little linking word. The items it joins together are now the important elements in the conversation. It is not surprising, therefore, to find that *and* in context normally has the weak vowel /ə/ instead of /æ/ and usually loses the final /d/. So in a fish shop I would ask for some /'fɪʃ ən 'tʃɪps/ *(fish and chips)* and I could take them home to /'dʒɒn ən 'meəri/ *(John and Mary)*. Notice that the loss of the final /d/ is not surprising, as it is the regular result of the phonological process of middle-consonant elision, in which we saw earlier that /t/ or /d/ as the middle consonant in a sequence of three is usually dropped. What is a little surprising is that in casual or fast speech *and* is frequently reduced to /ən/ even when there is no sequence of three consonants and it precedes a word beginning with a vowel, e. g. *Sue and Ann* /'su: ən 'æn/. This may be because in a case like this, if the /d/ were pronounced, there could then be some confusion between the names *Ann* and *Dan*. However, since most cases with a following vowel do not show this ambiguity, it is more probable that owing to the high frequency of middle consonant elision the pronunciation without the /d/ has been generalized to all contexts where *and* is unstressed.

Often in rapid speech the weak form /ən/ is further reduced by elision of the shwa and becomes just syllabic [n̩]. Thus, instead of the pronunciation given above for *fish and chips*, we also often hear /ˈfɪʃ n̩ ˈtʃɪps/. This reduction to the syllabic alveolar nasal does not take place, however, after another nasal or a lateral sound. So it will not be found in expressions like *John and Mary* or *Bill and Jane*, where *and* can only have the weak form /ən/.

Summarizing, we can show the behaviour of *and* in the following formula, where 'SF' equals 'strong form' and 'WF' equals 'weak form':

> *and*:   SF /ˈænd/   →   WF /ən/ → [n̩]

2 Conjunctions

Like *and*

Other conjunctions like *and* which have a strong and a weak form are *as, but, than, that*. Let us take each word in turn and show how and when each form is used.

as

The conjunction *as* has the following strong and weak forms:

> *as*:   SF /ˈæz/   →   WF /əz/

As with *and*, the strong form of *as* is comparatively rare and is usually heard only when we talk about the word or point to it in a text. The strong form is thus used when the word is compared or contrasted with another, e. g. *I didn't say 'as', I said 'and'* /aɪ ˈdɪdnt seɪ ˈæz, aɪ ˈsed ˈænd/. **With a few exceptions** which we can discuss when we come to prepositions and auxiliary verbs, **strong forms are always stressed.**

The weak form of *as* can be used wherever the word is not stressed, e. g. in *Jane is as tall as Tom* /ˈdʒeɪn ɪz əz ˈtɔːl əz ˈtɒm/ or in *It's broken, as you know* /ɪts ˈbrəʊkən, əz ju ˈnəʊ/. When *as* is the first word in a sentence and introduces a clause, it may be either weak or strong. If it is strong it will, of course , be stressed. For example, *As you all know, Albert is a doctor* /əz ju ˈɔːl ˈnəʊ, ˈælbət ɪz ə ˈdɒktə/ or /ˈæz ju ˈɔːl ˈnəʊ .../

but

The conjunction *but* has the following forms:

> *but*:   SF /ˈbʌt/   → WF /bət/

The word is almost always unstressed and therefore usually found in its weak form in conversation, but sometimes it does occur stressed before a strong dramatic pause, e. g. *I could help you,* **but** ... /aɪ ˈkʊd ˈhelp ju, ˈbʌt .../. Examples of the weak form can be seen in *I like cheese but not meat* /aɪ ˈlaɪk ˈtʃiːz bət ˈnɒt ˈmiːt/ and *No one but Alfred came* /ˈnəʊ wʌn bət ˈælfrɪd ˈkeɪm/.

than

The conjunction *than* resembles *and* in having two weak forms, one with a weakened vowel and one with a syllabic nasal.

than: SF /ˈðæn/ → WF /ðən/ → /ðn̩/

The weak form /ðn̩/ is commoner but both can be used everywhere, e. g. in sentences such as *Cathy is older than Alice* /ˈkæθi ɪz ˈəʊldə ðn̩ (or: ðən) ˈælɪs/ and *I'd like tea rather than coffee* /aɪd ˈlaɪk ˈtiː ˈrɑːðə ðn̩ (or: ðən) ˈkɒfi/.

that

The last of the conjunctions with a strong and weak form is the word *that*, which introduces a clause after verbs of saying, thinking, knowing, etc.

that: SF /ˈðæt/ → WF /ðət/

The strong form is rarely used in connected speech as it has very little semantic content. It is the rest of the clause which contains the message for the hearer. Even in careful pronunciation the weak form is usually preferred. Examples are *This proves that they told a lie* /ˈðɪs ˈpruːvz ðət ðeɪ ˈtəʊld ə ˈlaɪ/ and *Daphne thought that it might help* /ˈdæfni ˈθɔːt ðət ɪt ˈmaɪt ˈhelp/.

Unrelated to the conjunction, are the relative pronoun *that* as in *the girl that won the prize* and the demonstrative *that* as in *that's right, that book's torn*. The relative pronoun has a weak form exactly like that of the conjunction: /ðə ˈɡɜːl ðət ˈwʌn ðə ˈpraɪz/, whereas the demonstrative is never weakened, even if it is not stressed: /ˈðæts ˈraɪt/, /ðæt ˈbʊks ˈtɔːn/. All three words can be heard in the sentence: *Dan thinks that that book that you bought is boring* /ˈdæn ˈθɪŋks ðət ðæt ˈbʊk ðət ju ˈbɔːt ɪz ˈbɔːrɪŋ/.

3 Prepositions

General Notes

Not all prepositions undergo weakening. With the exception of *into* and *onto*, all prepositions of two or more syllables remain unchanged though they may often be unstressed, and even some monosyllabic ones have only one pronunciation, e. g. *through, up, down, off, on*. Weakening does occur, however, with the following:

at: SF /ˈæt/ → WF /ət/
for: SF /ˈfɔː(r)/ → WF /fə(r)/
from: SF /ˈfrɒm/ → WF /frəm/ → /frm̩/
of: SF /ˈɒv/ → WF /əv/
to: SF /ˈtuː/ → WF /tu/ before a Vowel
　　　　　　　　　　/tə/ before a Consonant

at, of

The first four of these prepositions do not need much comment, but we will come back to *for* and *from* below. We can hear the weak form of each of them in the sentence: *At last they asked for instructions from the captain of the team* /ət 'lɑːst ðeɪ 'aːskt fər‿ɪn'strʌkʃnz frm‿ðə 'kæptɪn əv ðə 'tiːm/.

for

Notice that both the strong and the weak form of *for* has linking /r/ before a vowel. The weak form with linking /r/ can be seen in the sentence which we have just transcribed and also in expressions like *for example* /fər‿ɪg'zɑːmpl̩/, *for ever* /fər‿'evə/ or *for Easter* / fər‿'iːstə/. The strong form with linking /r/ before a vowel can often be heard, when the preposition receives contrastive stress, as in *This book isn't **for** Ian but **by** Ian* /ðɪs 'bʊk ɪznt ˋfɔːr‿'iːən bət ˋbaɪ 'iːən/. Examples of the weak form without linking /r/, i. e. where no vowel follows, can be seen in '*This is for May and that's for Jason* /'ðɪs ɪz fə 'meɪ ən 'ðæts fə 'dʒeɪsn̩/.

from

Of the two weak forms of the preposition *from*, the one with the syllabic nasal /frm̩/ is commoner than the one with shwa. Another example of it is: *Joe's just had a letter from my aunt* /'dʒəʊz 'dʒʌst hæd ə 'letə frm̩ maɪ 'ɑːnt/.

to, into, onto

The situation with *to* and the related prepositions *into* and *onto* is a little more complicated. *To* has a strong form with a long vowel /'tuː/, which is normally used only when the word is stressed. *Into* and *onto* can never be stressed on the *-to* syllable and therefore never have a long final vowel. This vowel always behaves like the vowel in the weak form of *to*, whether these prepositions are stressed or not. In other words, their final syllable, like weak *to*, is /tu/ before a vowel and /tə/ before a consonant or a semivowel. The following examples illustrate the use of all these weak forms.

I want to see your letter to Oliver /aɪ 'wɒnt tə 'siː jɔː 'letə tu 'ɒlɪvə/.

Angela drove first into Oxford and then into the forest /'ændʒələ 'drəʊv 'fɜːst ɪntu 'ɒksfəd ən 'ðen ɪntə də 'fɒrɪst/.

They walked onto the veranda of a house that looked onto a lake / ðeɪ 'wɔːkt ɒntə də və'rændə əv ə 'haʊs ðət 'lʊkt ɒntu ə 'leɪk/.

SF or WF

There is one context in which the strong and the weak form can both be used with no change in the emphasis or the meaning. This is when the preposition comes immediately in front of a personal pronoun. When the strong form is used here, it is unusual in having no stress on it. Examples: *Ted's looking at it* /'ted z 'lʊkɪŋ æt ɪt (or: ət ɪt)/.

Sally's going to wait for you /'sæli z 'gəʊɪŋ tə 'weɪt fɔː ju (or: fə ju)/.
(Other cases of unstressed strong forms can be seen on pp. 157–158.)

4 Pronouns and Determiners

General Notes

Some of the most frequently used words in the language are pronouns and determiners. The latter are words such as the definite and indefinite articles, which are used to introduce noun phrases. Both grammatically and semantically they are the least important words in such phrases and are therefore almost always weakened. In the case of the pronouns, their semantic content is normally already known from the context; so they too are almost always weakened in connected speech. Let us look first at the personal pronouns. Those that have strong and weak forms are alphabetically: *he, her, him, his, me, she, them, us, we, who, you*. For convenience, we shall deal with them in groups which show similar behaviour.

you, who

These two pronouns have a long vowel in the strong from and are then usually stressed. The weak form is never stressed. It is formed by shortening the long vowel and not by replacing it with shwa. Note that the vowel in the weak form is not /ʊ/, which is lower and farther forward in the mouth.

you: SF /'ju:/ → WF /ju/
who: SF /'hu:/ → WF /hu/ → /u/

An example of *you* in the strong form with contrastive stress is *Did* **you** *go or did* **Alan?** /dɪd ˈjuː ˈgəʊ ɔː dɪd ˈælən/. Far more common is the unstressed weak form: *When you heard it, did you laugh?* /wen ju ˈhɜːd ɪt ˈdɪd ju ˈlɑːf/. Sometimes a weak form /jə/ is found in sentences like the latter, but it is not recommended to learners of British English, where it usually sounds rather slack.

The word *who* can be either the relative pronoun or the interrogative pronoun. When it is the former, it is normally weak as in *the man who bought it* and has the vowel of the strong form shortened /ðə ˈmæn hu ˈbɔːt ɪt/. However, like all words which have **strong and weak forms that begin with** /h/, the relative pronoun *who* **may lose this** /h/ **when weak,** as in the example we have just had /ðə ˈmæn u ˈbɔːt ɪt/, or in *the girl who smiled* /ðə ˈgɜːlu ˈsmaɪld/. The interrogative pronoun is invariable and always pronounced /hu:/ whether stressed or unstressed.

he, me, she, we

This group of pronouns behaves like that in the previous section: the weak form is formed from the strong form **by reducing the length of the vowel** and not by replacing it with /ə/. This shortened vowel is not /ɪ/ but a little higher and farther forward.

he: SF /'hi:/ → WF /hi/ → /i/
me: SF /'mi:/ → WF /mi/
she: SF /'ʃi:/ → WF /ʃi/
we: SF /'wi:/ → WF /wi/

As *he* begins with /h/, it can drop this fricative in casual and rapid speech, **except after a pause or as the first word in a sentence**. The dropping of /h/ in weak forms is always optional. Examples:

He thinks he's very clever /hi 'θɪŋks i z 'veri 'klevə/.

Did he find the one he'd lost? /'dɪd i 'faɪnd ðə 'wʌn i d 'lɒst/.

Examples with the other pronouns:

She told me she likes you /ʃi 'təʊld mi ʃi 'laɪks ju/.

We know she'll miss you /wi 'nəʊ ʃi l 'mɪs ju/.

him, his, her Of these three words, *him* is always a pronoun, but *his* and *her* can be either a pronoun or a determiner. As a pronoun *his* is always stressed and therefore appears only in the strong form. As determiners, i. e. before a noun in a noun phrase, both *his* and *her* usually have the weak form, but they can be found in the strong form when they are contrastively stressed. The weak form of all of them optionally loses its initial /h/ except before a pause or right at the beginning of a sentence.

> *him:* SF /'hɪm/ → WF /hɪm/ → /ɪm/
>
> *his:* SF /'hɪz/ → WF /hɪz/ → /ɪz/
>
> *her:* SF /'hɜ:(r)/ → WF /hə/ or /ɜ:/ → /ə/

If *him* or *his* do not lose their initial /h/, the weak form differs from the strong form only in not being stressed. An example of *him* with contrastive stress can be found in the sentence: *Don't play with* **him**, *play with* **me** /'dəʊnt 'pleɪ wɪð ˋhɪm, 'pleɪ wɪð ˋmi:/. An example containing the weak forms of both *him* and *his* is: *They arrested him in his own garden* /deɪ ə'restɪd ɪm ɪn ɪz 'əʊn 'gɑ:dn̩/. *His* can have a weak form here because it is a determiner in the noun phrase *his own garden*. If we compare this with *We both have gardens but his is bigger* /wi 'bəʊθ hæv 'gɑ:dnz bət 'hɪz ɪz 'bɪgə/, in this latter sentence we now see *his* as a pronoun, which cannot have a weak form.

The weak forms of *her* need a little more explanation. It will be remembered that the vowels /ə/ and /ɜ:/ are both mid central vowels and therefore, despite the different symbol which we use for each, /ə/ can be thought of as a shortened form of /ɜ:/. It seems more accurate then to say that the weak form /hə/ is derived by shortening the long vowel of /hɜ:/ according to the principle which we have seen several times above, rather than to think of the long vowel as merely being replaced by /ə/, although of course the result is the same in each case. This weak form with the /h/ can be used in all unstressed positions, i. e. sentence-initially or after a pause or elsewhere, as in *Her sister entered the room and gave Jane, her cousin, a book for her birthday* /hə 'sɪstər̩ˌentəd də 'ru:m ən 'geɪv 'dʒeɪn, hə 'kʌzn̩, ə 'bʊk fə hə 'bɜ:θdeɪ/. If *her* is a pronoun the /h/ of the weak form is frequently dropped: *I gave her the money and told her to pay* /aɪ 'geɪv ə ðə 'mʌni ən 'təʊld ə tə 'peɪ/. However, if *her* is pronounced /ə/ when it is a determiner in a noun phrase, it is likely to be confused with the indefinite article *a*, e. g. in *Mary lost her purse yesterday*; so here it almost always takes the form /ɜː/: /'meəri 'lɒst ɜː 'pɜːs 'jestədeɪ/.

us, them

Two other common pronouns which undergo weakening when unstressed are *us* and *them*. As neither contains a long vowel in the strong form, the weak form is formed with /ə/, as we would expect, and in the case of *them* the shwa can be elided to produce a syllabic nasal.

> *us:*   SF /'ʌs/   → WF /əs/
> *them:* SF /'ðem/ → WF /ðəm/ → /ðm̩/

As usual, the weak form with the syllabic nasal is far more common than the one with shwa. Examples:
She gave us the letters and we posted them later /ʃi 'geɪv əs ðə 'letəz ən wi 'pəʊstɪd ðm̩ 'leɪtə/.
We saw them with them in the park /wi 'sɔː ðm̩ wɪð ðm̩ ɪn ðə 'pɑːk/.

some

Let us turn now from the personal pronouns and examine the important word *some*. It is a pronoun when used by itself, e. g. *We'd like some*, but a determiner when used in a noun phrase before a noun, e. g. *We'd like some cheese*. As a pronoun, it is always found in the strong form but not always stressed. As a determiner, it may have only a strong form or it may have both a strong and a weak form, depending on its meaning. The weak form contains either a shwa or a syllabic nasal.

> *some:* SF /'sʌm/ → WF /səm/ → /sm̩/

The weak form is most frequently found when *some* is partitive, i. e. when it means *a small or a certain amount of (something)* or *a small or a certain number of (things)*, e. g. *some cheese, some bread* or *some apples, some chips* /sm̩ 'tʃiːz, sm̩ 'bred, sm̩ 'æplz, sm̩ 'tʃɪps/. We can see both the unstressed partitive determiner and the unstressed pronoun in the following sentence: *If you'd like some meat they'll give you some* /ɪf ju d 'laɪk sm̩ 'miːt ðeɪl 'gɪv ju sʌm/.

Notice that when *some* is a pronoun and followed by the preposition *of*, it is always strong and stressed: *I want some of them now* /aɪ 'wɒnt 'sʌm əv ðm̩ 'naʊ/. When contrasted with another pronoun or noun, or even with another *some*, it is also always strong and stressed, both as a pronoun and as a determiner, e. g. (as a pronoun). **Some** *like them,* **some** *don't* /'sʌm 'laɪk ðm̩, 'sʌm 'dəʊnt/ and (as a determiner). **Some** *people drank beer,* **others** *wine* /'sʌm 'piːpl̩ 'dræŋk 'bɪə, 'ʌðəz 'waɪn/. The contrast is often only implied, as in *Some guests dislike French onions but we've cooked some nevertheless* /'sʌm 'gests dɪs'laɪk 'frentʃ 'ʌnjənz bət wi v 'kʊkt sʌm ˌnevəðə'les/. Here the first *some* is implicitly contrasted with *other (guests who do like French onions)*. Notice too that the second *some* (referring to *onions*) is not contrastive and is therefore not stressed, but as it is a pronoun it has the strong form.

Other Cases We were careful above to limit the weak form of *some* to its partitive use as a determiner. There are some other meanings of this word for which the weak form is never used. One of these is in the expression *some ... (or other)* referring to a person or thing that is not known or not specified. Unlike the partitive determiner, this *some* can be used with a singular countable noun, e. g. *She's married to some politician (or other)* /ʃiː z 'mærɪd tə sʌm ˌpɒlə'tɪʃn (ɔːr ˈʌðə)/. With this kind of *some*, the words *or other* are often omitted. Another kind expresses approval or admiration and, as in the use we have just described, it can often be found with a singular countable noun but is always stressed: *He's certainly some dancer!* /hi z 'sɜːtnli 'sʌm 'dɑːnsə/. The last kind of *some* we need to look at has the meaning of *almost, approximately* and is used before numbers. It usually has the strong form unstressed but the weak form is sometimes found too, e. g. *They bought some 50 books with the money* /ðeɪ 'bɔːt sʌm (or: sm̩) 'fɪfti 'bʊks wɪð ðə 'mʌni/.

Before we leave *some*, we should note that all the compounds containing this word such as *somebody, someday, somehow, someone, somewhere, sometimes* can never contain the weak form, as they are all stressed on the first syllable and weak forms can never be stressed.

a, the We saw above that some words function only as pronouns and have both strong and weak forms, whereas others function both as pronouns and as determiners and then usually have the strong form for the pronoun and the weak form for the determiner. There are two words, the indefinite and the definite articles, which can only be determiners but which have both strong and weak forms. Although the weak forms for all the classes of words which we have been dealing with above are very characteristic of native English pronunciation, foreign learners quite often learn only the strong forms. With the articles, however, this situation is reversed and it is usually the strong forms which are neglected. Note that *the* has two weak forms depending on the kind of sound following it, while the indefinite article has two strong and two weak forms differentiated in this way:

the: SF /'ðiː/ → WF /ði/ before a Vowel
/ðə/ before a Consonant
(Before a Consonant) *a*: SF /'eɪ/ → WF /ə/
(Before a Vowel) *an*: SF /'æn/ → WF /ən/ → [n̩]

The strong form of *the* is heard when someone stresses the word in order to emphasize that some person or thing is the only one of its kind, e. g. *Mabel is **the** expert on making wine* /'meɪbḷ ɪz 'ðiː 'ekspɜːt ɒn 'meɪkɪŋ 'waɪn/. Normally, however, the article is not stressed, e. g. *The house at the end of the road is the oldest* /ðə 'haʊs ət ði 'end əv ðə 'rəʊd ɪz ði 'əʊldɪst/

The strong forms of *a, an* are not common, but /'æn/ has to be used when we talk about *an* as a word. Strangely, when *a* and *the* are referred to, e. g. by linguists and language teachers, they often appear in the weak form, which is then stressed because it is out of context, e. g. *Use 'a' in this sentence, 'the' is wrong!* /'juːz 'ə ɪn ðɪs 'sentəns, 'ðə ɪz 'rɒŋ/. This is one of the very rare cases in English in which the weak vowel shwa can be heard with stress on it. Of course, we could also use the strong forms /eɪ/ and /ðiː/ in this example.

The weak forms of *a* and *an* can be heard frequently in all kinds of English and from all kinds of speakers. Note, however, that the weak form of *an* with the syllabic nasal is **not** found **after another nasal or after** /l/; here /ən/ must be used. The following examples show all these cases:

At the foot of a hill he met a man carrying a sack /ət ðə 'fʊt əv ə 'hɪl (h)i 'met ə 'mæn 'kæriɪŋ ə 'sæk/.

With an almighty shout he seized a sword and waved it in a circle above his head /wɪð n̩ ɔːl'maɪti 'ʃaʊt (h)i 'siːzd ə 'sɔːd n̩ 'weɪvd ɪt ɪn ə 'sɜːkl̩ ə'bʌv (h)ɪz 'hed/.

She gave Jane an orange and offered Bill an apple /ʃi 'geɪv 'dʒeɪn ən 'ɒrɪndʒ n̩ 'ɒfəd 'bɪl ən 'æpl/.

Finally, let us mention **one use** of the strong form of *a* which **foreign learners should not imitate.** This is sometimes heard in formal interviews and in formal speeches, where the weak form would sound very much more natural, e. g. *There is a certain stigma about this usage of which a linguist would disapprove* /ðeəɹ̩ɪz eɪ 'sɜːtn̩ 'stɪgmə əbaʊt ðɪs 'juːsɪdʒ əv wɪtʃ eɪ 'lɪŋgwɪst wəd ðɪsə'pruːv/. People who use the strong form in this way probably think that it lends weight to the utterance.

5 Auxiliary Verbs

General Notes

Another very common group of words on which weakening operates are the **primary auxiliary verbs** *be, have, do* (which are used to form the tenses and aspectual forms of other verbs) and the **modal auxiliary verbs** *can, could, shall, should, will, would, must* (which are used before a lexical verb to show the speaker's attitude towards certain features of his utterance, such as possibility, uncertainty, obligation, etc.). We will deal with each primary auxiliary separately and treat the modal auxiliaries in groups.

| **be** | The verb *be* functions as an auxiliary verb when it is used for the continuous tenses or the passive forms of a lexical verb, as in *We are playing, She was talking, John was stopped by a policeman.* It can also be a lexical verb itself, e. g. when it precedes a noun phrase, an adjective or an adverbial expression of place: *They are students, Emily is tired, She was at the market.* The verb *be* is exceptional in having weak forms not just as an auxiliary verb but also as a lexical verb. The parts of *be* which have strong and weak forms are: *be, am, are, was, were, is.* (*Is* will be dealt with separately below.) |

> *be*: SF /'biː/ → WF /bi/
> *am*: SF /'æm/ → WF /əm/ → /m̩/ after pronoun *I*
> *are*: SF /'ɑː(r)/ → WF /ə(r)/
> *was*: SF /'wɒz/ → WF /wəz/
> *were*: SF /'wɜː(r)/ → WF /wə(r)/

The strong forms are normally heard if the word is being talked about or if it is used with contrastive stress. An example of the latter with lexical *be* is the sentence: *He doesn't want to* **seem** *happy, he wants to* **be** *happy* /hi 'dʌznt wɒnt tə ˈsiːm 'hæpi, hi 'wɒnts tə ˈbiː 'hæpi/. The weak form of lexical *be* can be heard in the simple sentence *She'd like to be a nurse* /ʃi d 'laɪk tə bi ə 'nɜːs/, and of auxiliary *be* in *I must be going now* /aɪ 'mʌst bi 'gəʊɪŋ 'naʊ/. (Note that the /t/ of *must* may be omitted here as the result of middle-consonant elision.)

| **am** | The weak form of *am* is usually the non-syllabic nasal /m/, as in *I'm dreaming* /aɪm 'driːmɪŋ/, but when *am* precedes *I* in questions it takes the form /əm/, as in *Am I right?* /əm aɪ 'raɪt/, or it can be stressed: /'æm aɪ 'raɪt/. |

| **are** | Both forms of *are* (and also of *were*) have linking /r/ in RP when they come before a word beginning with a vowel. The strong form occurs, for example, in *The men* **are** *eating* /ðə 'men ɑːrˈiːtɪŋ/, contradicting someone who has said that they were not. The weak form with linking /r/ appears in *My arms are aching* /maɪ 'ɑːmz ər 'eɪkɪŋ/. Without the linking /r/, this weak form is identical with the weak form of the indefinite article *a*, as we see in *The men are digging a hole* /ðə'men ə 'dɪgɪŋ ə 'həʊl/. Note that in the combinations *we're, they're, you're* compression always takes place and the weak form of *are* becomes part of the diphthong, i. e. instead of / wi + ə, ðeɪ + ə, ju + ə/ we find /wɪə, ðeə, jʊə/, and often /jʊə/ is further reduced to /jɔː/, e. g. *You're talking too fast* /jɔː (or: jʊə) 'tɔːkɪŋ tuː 'fɑːst/. |

| **was, were** | Stressed *was* and *were* are also frequently found in contradictions. If somebody says that he was not responsible, we could contradict this claim by saying: *Yes, you* **were** *responsible* /'jes ju ˈwɜː rɪ'spɒnsəbl̩/ |

or *Yes, he **was** responsible* /'jes i ˋwɒz rɪ'spɒnsəbl̩/. In most other contexts only the weak forms will be used, as in *Pamela was cooking and the girls were playing chess* /'pæmələ wəz 'kʊkɪŋ ən ðə 'gɜːlz wə 'pleɪŋ 'tʃes/, and with linking /r/ in *We were only teasing you* /wi wər‿'əunli 'tiːzɪŋ ju/.

is

The word *is* has three weak forms, two of which we have already seen when we dealt with the assimilation of different kinds of suffixed *-s*.

    is: SF /'ɪz/ → WF /ɪz/ after /s, z, ʃ, ʒ, tʃ, dʒ/
                     → WF /s/ after voiceless sound
                     → WF /z/ after voiced sound

When *is* is emphatic, contrastive or used metalinguistically (i. e. when we talk about it as a word), it requires the strong form; otherwise one of the three weak forms is used in the contexts shown above. Note that after a sibilant sound the weak form differs only from the strong form in not being stressed. An example of the strong emphatic form can be seen in: *Oh thank you, that **is** kind of you* /əu 'θæŋk ju, ðæt ˋɪz 'kaɪnd əv ju/. Examples of the weak forms are: *This is what it's all about* /'ðɪs ɪz 'wɒt ɪt s 'ɔːl ə'baʊt/ and *If the judge is right, Keith's in danger and Joe's lost his job* /ɪf ðə 'dʒʌdʒ ɪz 'raɪt, 'kiːθ s ɪn 'deɪndʒər‿ən 'dʒəu z 'lɒst (h)ɪz 'dʒɒb/. (If a pause is made after *danger*, the linking /r/ shown in the transcription will not be used in RP.)

have

The auxiliary verb *have* is found in the following strong and weak forms:

    have: SF /'hæv/ → WF /həv/ → /v/ after *I, you, we, they, who*
                              → /əv/ elsewhere
    had: SF /'hæd/ → WF /həd/ → /d/ after *I, you, he, she, we,*
                                  they, who
                              → /əd/ elsewhere
    has: SF /'hæz/ → WF /həz/ → /əz/ after /s, z, ʃ, ʒ, tʃ, dʒ/
                              → /s/ after voiceless sound
                              → /z/ after voiced sound

The strong forms occur in the usual contrastive, emphatic and metalinguistic contexts, but the weak forms need further explanation. For all three words the weak forms with initial /h/ can be used everywhere, providing that the word is not stressed. They sound a little more careful than those with shwa or with a single consonant. In the case of *have* and *had*, the single consonant form (/v/ and /d/ respectively) is usual after personal pronouns which end in a vowel and after the pronoun *who*. These contracted weak forms are usually indicated in the spelling, e. g. *we've, who'd*, but even when the auxiliary is written in full, the contracted weak form is often used in reading aloud. Otherwise the forms with shwa (/əv/ and /əd/) are used, except after a pause or sentence-initially (e. g. in questions). As with all weak forms that can lose the initial /h/, only the form with the /h/ is permitted at the beginning of a sentence or after a pause. The following examples illustrate some of these different forms:

Examples

*They **have** made a mess, haven't they!* /ðeɪ ˈhæv meɪd ə ˈmes, ˈhævnt ðeɪ/. (The first *have* here is emphatic, the second *have* obeys the rule which says that all auxiliary verbs which are written as one word with contracted *not*, e. g. *wasn't, weren't, isn't, hasn't*, etc., must be stressed and therefore cannot have the weak form.)

They've left, so they might have finished /ðeɪ v ˈleft, səu ðeɪ ˈmaɪt (h) əv ˈfɪnɪʃt/.

She'd noticed that Grace had brought some clothes that had been washed by her mother /ʃi d ˈnəutɪst ðət ˈgreɪs (h)əd ˈbrɔːt sm ˈkləuðz ðət (h)əd biːn ˈwɒʃt baɪ hə ˈmʌðə/.

His cash has run out and his health's got worse /hɪz ˈkæʃ (h)əz rʌn ˈaut ən hɪz ˈhelθ s ˈgɒt ˈwɜːs/. *He's lost everything* /hi z ˈlɒst ˈevrɪθɪŋ/. (Note that the weak form of *has* is identical with that of *is* after a voiceless or voiced sound, but not after a sibilant. In the latter case, the weak form of *has* is always /(h)əz/, never /ɪz/.)

do

The auxiliary verb *do* has only two forms which are weakened:

do: SF /ˈduː/ → WF /du/ → /də/
does: SF /dʌz/ → WF /dəz/

When *do* and *does* are used in emphatic sentences they must always have the strong form, as they then have to be stressed. On the other hand, when these words are used to make questions the weak forms are necessary. Emphatic example: *I **do** like that coat!* /aɪ ˈduː laɪk dæt ˈkəut/. Questions: *Do you think she's married?* /du (or: də) ju ˈθɪŋk ʃi z ˈmærid/. *When does he arrive?* /ˈwen dəz i əˈraɪv/.

Notice that in the formula *how do you do*, which is used by a person who is being introduced to another and which is repeated by the other person in reply, the first *do* may be reduced just to /d/ before the semivowel /j/ or even coalesce with it to form /dʒ/ if said very rapidly: /ˈhau du (or: də) ju ˈduː/ → /ˈhau dʒu ˈduː/. In slack English the pronoun may be further weakened to: /ˈhau dʒə ˈduː/. The second *do* in this expression is not an auxiliary verb but a full or lexical verb like *think* and *arrive* in the other examples with *do* above.

can, could

The strong and weak forms of *can* and its past tense *could* are:

can: SF /ˈkæn/ → WF /kən/ → /kn̩/
could: SF /ˈkud/ → WF /kəd/

You can find the word 'can' many times in that article /ju kn̩ 'faɪnd ðə 'wɜːd 'kæn 'menɪ 'taɪmz ɪn ðæt 'ɑːtɪkl /.
If they could show us the place, we could help them /ɪf ðeɪ kəd 'ʃəʊ əs ðə 'pleɪs, wi kəd 'help ðm̩/.
I could have sworn he was there /aɪ kəd (h)əv 'swɔːn (h)i wəz 'ðeə/.

These two modal auxiliaries may be written in full (*I shall, I will*) or both may be contracted to *'ll*, as in *I'll*. In reading, non-contracted forms on the written page are often pronounced weak, if they are unstressed. The strong and weak forms are as follows:

shall: SF /'ʃæl/ → WF /ʃəl/ → /ʃl̩/
will: SF /'wɪl/ → WF /l/ after *I, you, he, she, we, they, who*
/wəl/ → /wl̩/
/əl/ → [l̩] except after /l/ or a vowel

The strong form of *shall* is sometimes heard in utterances where one person determines the behaviour of another, e. g. *He shall go, even if he protests*, but this usage is rather old-fashioned nowadays. In the future tense the weak form of *shall* is common in British English after the pronouns *I* and *we* in both the forms /ʃəl/ and /ʃl̩/, but in American English is usually replaced by one of the weak forms of *will*. This latter usage is becoming increasingly popular in British English too. It should be noted that when the weak form follows one of the personal pronouns or *who*, it is almost always /l/ and that it is not syllabic: contractions like *he'll, you'll, they'll, who'll* consist of a single syllable, not of two. In all other contexts the usual weak form is /wəl/, which may optionally be reduced to /wl̩/ with syllabic [l̩]; in rather more casual or fast speech we may also find the weak forms /əl/ or just syllabic [l̩], except after another /l/ or after a vowel, where only /əl/ can be heard. Sometimes, however, in less casual speech, the strong form of *will* without any stress on it replaces all the weak forms we have described above.

I shall ring them up tomorrow, if they'll give me their number /aɪ ʃl̩ 'rɪŋ ðm̩ ʌp tə'mɒrəʊ, ɪf ðeɪl 'gɪv mi ðeə 'nʌmbə/. (*I shall* could be replaced by the monosyllable /aɪl/ *I'll* here.)
I don't think Jill will be able to take you, but Joe'll drive you there, I'm sure /aɪ 'dəʊnt θɪŋk 'dʒɪl əl bi 'eɪbl tə 'teɪk ju bət 'dʒəʊ əl 'draɪv ju 'ðeə, aɪm 'ʃɔː/. (In fast casual speech only /əl/ is possible here as *Jill* ends in /l/ and *Joe* ends in a vowel.)
If you do that, the shelves will get wet and the books will be ruined! /ɪf ju 'duː: 'ðæt, ðə 'ʃelvz l̩ get 'wet ən ðə 'bʊks l̩ bi 'ruːɪnd/. (In more careful style both instances of [l̩] in this sentence could be replaced by /wəl/ or /wl̩/, and in very careful style even by unstressed /wɪl/).

would, should, must	Let us take these last three modal auxiliaries together, as they do not present any great problems. Their strong and weak forms are:

would: SF /'wʊd/ → WF /d/ after *I, you, he, she, we, they, who*
 /wəd/ → /əd/
should: SF /'ʃud/ → WF /ʃəd/
must: SF /'mʌst/ → WF /məs(t)/.

Would, like *had*, is pronounced /d/ when it follows *who* or a personal pronoun ending in a vowel and is not stressed. In other unstressed positions the weak form /wəd/ is normal, but this may be reduced to /əd/ in fast conversation. *Should* has only one weak form of importance for foreign learners /ʃəd/, though occasionally further reduced forms such as /ʃd/ and /ʃt/ may be heard from native speakers. These should not, however, be imitated. *Must* has a weak form /məst/ when it is unstressed, but this may lose its final /t/ by the process of middle-consonant elision when the next word begins with a consonant. We saw earlier in this chapter that the negative form *mustn't* /'mʌsn̩t/ obligatorily loses its middle /t/ for the same reason.

Examples

Although he hated it, she **would** *call him Georgie* /ɔːl'ðəʊ ɪ 'heɪtɪd ɪt, ʃi ˈwʊd kɔːl ɪm 'dʒɔːdʒi/. (Emphatic *would* here suggests that she persistently used this name for him. Both *he* and *him* could be said with initial /h/ in more careful pronunciation.)

If you'd just sit down, your head would be better /ɪf ju d 'dʒʌst sɪt 'daʊn, jɔː 'hed wəd bi 'betə/. (In very casual rapid speech the second *would* could be /əd/ and the final /t/ of *just* could be elided.)

They knew she would protest, but they thought the present would please her /ðeɪ 'njuː ʃi wəd prə'test, bət ðeɪ θɔːt ðə 'preznt wəd 'pliːz hə/. (In all styles except the most careful, the first *would* could be reduced to /d/ after the pronoun *she*, although this is not indicated in the spelling. On the other hand, the second *would* could only be reduced to /əd/ in very casual pronunciation.)

You must be mistaken! The children must have been at home then / ju 'mʌs(t) bi mɪ'steɪkn̩, ðə 'tʃɪldrn̩ 'mʌst əv biːn ət 'həʊm 'ðen/.

You must inform them at once! /ju məst ɪn'fɔːm ðm̩ət 'wʌns/.

Initial Aux

We observed above that at the very beginning of a sentence the conjunction *as* introducing a clause can be optionally weak or strong. All the primary and modal auxiliary verbs we have examined above also behave in this way when sentence-initial. We saw one example under *am (Am I right?)* with either strong stressed /'æm/ or weak unstressed /əm/. Other examples with other auxiliaries are:

Have we seen it? /'hæv wi (or: həv wi) 'siːn ɪt/. (Remember that / həv/ cannot lose its initial /h/ here because at the beginning of a sentence it comes after a pause.)

Do you smoke a pipe? /'duː ju (or: du ju) (or: də ju) 'sməʊk ə 'paɪp/.
Can they come at six? /'kæn ðeɪ (or: kn̩ ðeɪ) 'kʌm ət 'sɪks/.
Shall I tell them? /'ʃæl aɪ (or: ʃəl aɪ) (or: ʃl̩ aɪ) 'tel ðm̩/
Must we go now? /'mʌs(t) wi (or: məs(t) wi) 'gəʊ 'naʊ/.

SF + ∅

There is one environment to which we must pay particular attention. Some words like the **auxiliary verbs** and the **prepositions**
are not normally intelligible unless they are completed by another
word. If I suddenly tell you *I can*, you will want to know *can what?*
and in answer I would have to supply the missing infinitive verb,
e. g. *swim* or *pay*. Similarly, prepositions normally combine with
noun phrases. If somebody tells me *He is sitting at*, the sense is
incomplete: I must know *at what?* And the answer could be *at the
table*. We saw above that when an auxiliary verb is used with an
infinitive, or a preposition with a noun phrase, it is almost always
found in the weak form when unstressed. What we have not yet
examined are those cases where one of these words makes sense
although the **verb or noun which should be following it** has
either been **moved to another part of the sentence or been
omitted.** The reason for the omission may be that the word has
already been mentioned or that the context makes it quite clear
to the listener what has been left out. When a preposition or an
auxiliary verb is left **stranded** in this way it **must always have
the strong form.** The preposition is unusual here in that this is
one of the rare cases where a strong form is found with no stress
on it. On the other hand, the strong form of the auxiliary does
usually carry stress when stranded, though there are some situations which require it to have none.

Prep + ∅

Let us look first at a sentence with a stranded preposition. In questions that begin with interrogative words like *who, what, where*, a
preposition is often separated from its object and must then have
the strong form:
What are you looking at? /'wɒt ə ju 'lʊkɪŋ æt/. (Note that the same
question with the preposition in front of its object sounds rather
unnatural in English: *At what are you looking?* /ət 'wɒt ə ju 'lʊkɪŋ/).
Who did he give it to yesterday? /'huː dɪd i 'gɪv ɪt tuː 'jestədeɪ/.
Where did she come from this time? /'weə dɪd ʃi 'kʌm frɒm 'ðɪs 'taɪm/.
(The two last sentences show clearly that the strong unstressed
form of the preposition does not have to be sentence-final, as is
sometimes claimed: it can be followed by other words. Note that
in the first sentence *to* does not go with *yesterday* but with *who* at
the beginning; and in the second sentence *from* goes with *where*
and not with *this time*.)
Prepositions also have the unstressed strong form when they
occur in relative clauses from which the relative pronoun that
should come after them has been omitted, e. g.

I know the book you are looking for (= for which you are looking)
/aɪ 'nəʊ ðə 'bʊk ju ə 'lʊkɪŋ fɔː/.
That's the one you were thinking of (= of which you were thinking)
/'ðæt s ðə 'wʌn ju wə 'θɪŋkɪŋ ɒv/.

Aux + ∅

Examples of auxiliary verbs with a zero infinitive that can be supplied from the previous part of the sentence or from the context are:

It will be hard to succeed but I know I can (= can succeed)
/ɪt ̩l bi 'hɑːd tə sʌk'siːd bət aɪ 'nəʊ aɪ 'kæn/. (Here the auxiliary is stressed because of the contrast between *hard to succeed* and *can succeed*.)

(Do you think you'll succeed?) - I know I can! /aɪ 'nəʊ aɪ kæn/. (In this sentence the contrast is between *think* and *know* and therefore the word 'can' does not need to be stressed.)

(Are you going?) - Yes, I am. (= am going) /'jes aɪ 'æm/.

(Would she like some cake?) - Yes she would (= would like) /'jes ʃi 'wʊd/.

In these last two examples, the auxiliary verb must be stressed as it is the only verb in the reply. Compare the last example with:
I think she would /aɪ 'θɪŋk ʃi wʊd/, where *think* can now take the stress and *would* can be left unstressed.

6 Final Remarks

Résumé

To conclude our survey of the phonological process of weakening in English, let us turn our attention away from function words and broaden our perspective. We have seen that weakening occurs first within words: with very rare exceptions, only syllables carrying primary or secondary stress have full vowels in English; all others are weakened. Secondly, we saw that words which have little semantic content but which are necessary for the grammatical functioning of a sentence, the so-called function words, are also weakened. Characteristically, these are almost always monosyllables and the weak forms are very much more common than the strong forms. We have noted that when function words are given more content or importance, e. g. by being contrasted, compared, emphasized or talked about, the weak forms are out of place and the strong forms are needed.

Titles of Address

With this overall picture in mind, we should not be surprised to discover that there are a few other types of word which because of their relative unimportance in a certain context also undergo weakening. One of these is titles of address. When the words *Sir* or *Saint* are used with a person's name, e. g. *Sir Winston Churchill* or *Saint Joan*, it is the name which is important and not the title. In

British English (but not in American, which always uses the strong forms /sɜːr/ and /seɪnt/) these are always said with the weak forms /sə/ and /sn̩t/ respectively: /sə ˈwɪnstn̩ ˈtʃɜːtʃɪl/ and /sn̩ t ˈdʒəʊn/. If the name begins with a vowel, linking /r/ will be heard with *Sir*, e. g. *Sir Oliver* /sər‿ˈɒlɪvə/. In some people's speech, the final /t/ of *Saint* may be elided before a name beginning with a consonant (middle- consonant elision), but usually the /t/ is pronounced with an unreleased phone in this position except before a vowel: [sn̩tˀ ˈdʒəʊn], but *Saint Agatha* [sn̩t ˈægəθə].

says

Let us finish this chapter with one other type of word which is weakened (this time optionally) when unimportant in a context. This happens when the actual words of a person are quoted and then *says* is used followed by the name of that person. Alongside the normal pronunciation /sez/ we may sometimes hear the weakened form /səz/, particularly when conversation is being read aloud from a book, e. g. in *"Wipe your eyes, child!" says Mary, as she gives the boy a handkerchief* /ˈwaɪp jɔːr‿ˈaɪz ˈtʃaɪld, səz ˈmeəri, əz ʃi ˈgɪvz ðə ˈbɔɪ ə ˈhæŋkətʃɪf/.

Scripts and
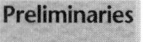**CHAPTER** # Transcriptions

Preliminaries Now that we have examined the sounds of English on two levels, the phonetic and the phonemic levels, and in the last chapter seen some of the phonological processes which affect words in context, we can conclude this little book by returning to phonetic scripts and transcriptions and by looking at how different kinds of script have been used to represent words in context. We shall first take a quick look at the past of RP transcriptions, which will enable the interested reader to interpret the scripts used in some of the older phonetic and phonological literature, especially older dictionaries. We can then examine briefly how American linguists and dictionary-makers have coped with this same problem. Finally, we will give a summary of the main correspondences between RP sounds and those of General American. This will permit speakers of the latter type of English to convert easily any RP transcriptions which they may encounter in their reading of phonetic and phonological literature, and will in particular enable them to deal with the RP transcriptions throughout this book (especially in Chapter 4) which for reasons of space have not been given American equivalents.

❶ Transcriptions

Narrow First some general words about transcriptions. It is important to understand the difference between a narrow transcription and a broad one. The term **narrow** is applied to transcriptions which contain a certain amount of phonetic detail: the narrower a transcription is, the more phonetic detail it contains and the more diacritic signs and special symbols it requires. This kind of transcription, **phonetic transcription,** is placed between phonetic brackets ([.....]).

Broad On the other hand, a **broad** transcription shows an absence of phonetic detail. The broader it is, the smaller the number of diacritics and of special symbols. The broadest of all transcriptions is thus one which contains only phonemes. This is referred to as a **phonemic transcription** and is written between phoneme slashes (/...../). For example, almost all the transcriptions for the sentences in the last chapter were written in this way. We were not interested in the phonetics of these sentences, but in the phonological processes operating on the phonemes of English. All the symbols we used represented phonemes, with the exception of [i] and [u] (which are not phonemes but the phonetic realizations of two phonemes) and with the exception of the syllabic consonants [n̩, m̩, l̩] (which are realizations of the phonemes /n, m, l/ when a /ə/ preceding them has been elided).

Mixed The inclusion of phones in a phonemic transcription produces a slightly mixed script which can therefore be described as a little narrower than purely phonemic. Notice that when we had to deal with phones such as the unreleased [t˺] in *Saint Joan* on page 159, we used phonetic brackets as we were now more interested in the phonetic realization of the phoneme than in the phoneme itself. Note too that this distinction in terminology between 'phonetic transcription' and 'phonemic transcription' is often not upheld and the term 'phonetic transcription' is used loosely to refer to any transcription of a language, even to a purely phonemic one.

② Scripts

1 British

IPA Script In Chapter 1 the reader was introduced to the phonetic symbols of the International Phonetic Association (IPA) and throughout the book we have used the most recent version of these to show both phones and phonemes. If the reader turns to other British books on phonetics and phonology or to any of the British dictionaries of English for foreign learners (see part 2 of the Bibliography, pages 168), he will find that they all make use of the IPA symbols to indicate pronunciations.

Dictionaries The IPA script is also used by many of the British dictionaries intended for native speakers of English. Even the renowned Oxford English Dictionaries have now abandoned their old system of showing pronunciation which used various diacritic signs above the spelling. The recent Second Edition of the large Oxford English Dictionary and the latest edition of the Oxford Concise English Dictionary both now use the simpler IPA script, though for the final unstressed vowel of words like *any* the OED has retained the symbol for the older pronunciation /ɪ/, whereas OCED uses the more modern /i/. Rather surprisingly, OCED transcribes the final diphthong of words like *aware* as /ɛ:/, while OED has the more accurate /ɛə/. It will be remembered that most of the modern British didactic dictionaries have replaced /ɛə/ with /eə/, the form we also have used in this book. This has been done to make it look more like /eɪ/, a replacement which is less accurate phonetically but more convenient for the printer. Other surprising transcriptions in OCED are /ʌɪ/ and /ʌɪə/ for the vowels in *bite, fire* instead of the usual /aɪ/, /aɪə/ found in OED and most other British didactic dictionaries.

OALD

These variations between different dictionaries, between different editions of the same dictionary, and between textbooks can be very confusing for students of British English. Since they mainly concern vowels, it will be helpful to look at the two characteristics of vowels, i.e. length and quality, which have played a role in the development of the scripts for RP and to see how these have been used in various editions of the Oxford Advanced Learner's Dictionary (OALD).

Vowels

In our discussion of the phonetics of English vowels at the beginning of this book, we saw that some of the vowels occur in pairs. Each pair consists of a short and a long vowel, the long vowel being higher than the short one. The following words illustrate these four pairs in RP: *sit, seat; cot, caught; but* (in its weak form), *Bert; pull, pool*. If we refer to the length of a vowel as **its quantity,** and the difference in height as its **quality,** it is clear that we need only one of these features to differentiate each member of each pair. For example, we can say that *sit* contains the high front vowel that is short, while *seat* contains the one that is long: therefore in our script we could use the same symbol for each but keep them apart by using the colon of length after the long one.

Quantitative

This **quantitative transcription,** which shows differences in the length but not in the quality of the vowels, was in fact the kind used in the earlier editions of OALD. For example, in the second edition (1963) our pairs above were transcribed as follows:

| /sit/ *sit* | /kɔt/ *cot* | /bət/ *but* | /pul/ *pull* |
| /siːt/ *seat* | /kɔːt/ *caught* | /bəːt/ *Bert* | /puːl/ *pool* |

Qualitative

When the third edition appeared in 1974 it was decided to change to a **qualitative transcription,** which ignored length but used different symbols for the high and low member of the pairs. This was felt to be necessary as it had been observed that many foreign learners who used the dictionary (especially speakers of Romance languages, in which no differences in quality occur between long and short pairs of vowels) had been misled by the old script into thinking that the only difference between the members of the pairs was their length, i.e. that the vowel in *sit*, for example, was merely a short version of the vowel in *seat*. The qualitative transcription of our pairs was now written as follows:

| /sɪt/ | /kɒt/ | /bət/ | /pʊl/ |
| /siːt/ | /kɔt/ | /bɜt/ | /pul/ |

This change of script provoked protests from users of the dictionary all around the world, who had become confused by the fact that the transcriptions /sit, kɔt, pul/, which until 1974 had represented *sit, cot, pull*, now stood for *seat, caught, pool*.

Mixed

The result was that when the 14ᵗʰ edition of Everyman's English Pronouncing Dictionary (EEPD) was revised by Professor A.C. Gimson in 1977, it was decided to use a script which was both quantitative and qualitative. As EEPD was the most authoritative dictionary on British pronunciation at that time, this new script was adopted for the fourth edition of OALD in 1989. The reader will recognize it as the one which we have been using throughout this book, where a different symbol is used for each member of a vowel pair and additionally the long vowel is shown by placing a colon after it. A script of this kind, in which both quantity and quality are shown, is often referred to as a **mixed transcription.** Our pairs now appear transcribed as follows:

/sɪt/	/kɒt/	/bət/	/pʊl/
/siːt/	/kɔːt/	/bɜːt/	/puːl/

[i], [u]

To complete the history of the script used for monophthongs in OALD we may note that in the fifth edition (1995) the use of the phones [i] and [u] was also adopted from EEPD to indicate the unstressed vowel sounds which we hear word-finally in *happy* and the weak form of *you*, or in pre-vocalic position in words such as *variation* or *actual*. For convenience the dictionary writes these two sounds between phoneme slashes, as we too have done in this book. Previous editions of the dictionary had used /ɪ/ and /ʊ/ here, a practice which is still found in the latest editions of many other British dictionaries.

Diphthongs

The history of the transcription of diphthongs is less complicated. Until the 14ᵗʰ edition of EEPD (1977), most of the didactic British dictionaries and the textbooks on phonetics and phonology had followed the usage of the International Phonetic Association, which transcribed the RP diphthongs as follows:

/ei/ as in *bay*	/iə/ as in *beer*	/au/ as in *now*
/ai/ as in *by*	/ɛə/ as in *bare*	/əu/ as in *know*
/ɔi/ as in *boy*	/uə/ as in *poor*	

In 1977 EEPD revised the script for the diphthongs, replacing /i/ with /ɪ/, and /u/ with /ʊ/. Additionally, as we saw above, the phonetically more accurate transcription /ɛə/ was replaced with /eə/ to help the printers. This script was then adopted by all the learners' dictionaries, including OALD, where the diphthongs now appear in the form we know:

/eɪ/	/ɪə/	/aʊ/
/aɪ/	/eə/	/əʊ/
/ɔɪ/	/ʊə/	

As many of the monolingual dictionaries which use the IPA script show slight differences among themselves, it is always advisable to consult the explanatory pages at the front of each dictionary before searching for a word and its pronunciation.

2 American

Consonants For the representation of consonants, most American scripts used in textbooks have the same symbols as the IPA, except that in place of IPA /ʃ, ʒ, tʃ, dʒ/ we usually find /š, ž, č, ǰ/ respectively, and often /y/ is used where IPA has /j/.

Vowels American phoneticians have a longer tradition of using different symbols to distinguish the high and low members of the pairs of vowels we looked at above. A qualitative script is usually used, i.e. **the colon for length is omitted.** Thus we find /ɪ, i/ and /ʊ, u/ as in IPA, and often /ə, ɜ/. Sometimes the latter two are written with a right-hand hook at the top of each symbol to show /r/-colouring /ɚ, ˈ/ i.e. to show that they are pronounced with the tongue already in position for a following /r/. The symbol /ɜ/ may sometimes be used where RP has /ʌ/. The RP pair /ɒ, ɔː/ is not treated as a pair in American since the first of these two vowels is pronounced like British /ɑː/. Some American scripts use the symbol /a/ for this vowel, others /ɑ/. The second vowel, which always occurs before /r/, is usually written /ɔ/, but (as we saw in Ch. 4, p. 123) in some words (e.g. *four, port*) some Americans have a higher vowel which is written as /o/: we thus find both /fɔr, pɔrt/ and /for, port/.

Diphthongs One of the biggest differences between American and British scripts is in the transcription of diphthongs. The Americans treat the diphthong as a vowel plus a semivowel, an analysis which has a long tradition going back to the beginning of the 19th century. Thus the usual American equivalents of the British closing diphthongs are:

/ej/ as in *bay*   /aw/ as in *now*
/aj/ as in *by*   /ow/ as in *know*
/ɔj/ as in *boy*

Some scripts use the IPA symbols for all these diphthongs, some write the three front closing diphthongs as /ey, ay, ɔy/ and some treat /ow/ and /ej/ as monophthongs, writing them as just /o/ and /e/. Whereas the latter symbol is used in IPA for the monophthong heard in the word *bed*, American scripts normally use /ɛ/ for this sound. So there is no confusion if *laid* is transcribed /led/ and *led* is transcribed /lɛd/. It should be noted that the centring diphthongs of British English /ɪə, eə, ʊə/ are normally represented as a monophthong plus /r/ in American books, e.g. *beer* /bɪr/ or /bir/, *bare* /bɛr/ or /ber/ and *poor* /pʊr/ or /pur/.

Dictionaries Let us conclude this survey of phonetic/phonemic symbols used in America by pointing out that though they are employed in the specialist literature, they are not usually found in American dictionaries. Strangely, American lingui sts have not produced any monolingual dictionaries for foreign learners, where the use of a phonetic script for pronunciations is essential. All the monolingual dictionaries are aimed at native speakers of English and, like many of the British ones of this kind, indicate pronunciation by placing diacritical marks over the spelling. It is therefore even more important here to consult the front matter of each dictionary before use in order to discover what the diacritics mean and how pronunciations are represented.

🖪 American English in IPA Script

RP → GA For the reader of this book who is interested in seeing how the IPA script can be used to transcribe American pronunciation, this final section will be devoted to giving a few rules for converting British Received Pronunciation into General American.

American /t/ The **consonant symbols** present no problem, as RP and GA share the same sounds. We do, however, need to show the American voiced /t/, which does not occur in RP:

RP /t/ between vowels → GA [t̬] : *better* /'bɛt̬(ə)r/
RP /t/ after /n/   → GA [t̬] : *winter* /'wɪnt̬(ə)r/

Note that if the /ə/ is dropped after the American voiced /t/ the following /r/ will become syllabic. Note too that we are now including a phone (voiced [t̬]) in an otherwise phonemic transcription.

Vowels For the **vowels** we shall need a number of rules, as it is here that the two varieties of English differ most. Quite a few of these differences arise because American English has retained the /r/ after a vowel, whereas British English has either lost it or vocalized it to /ə/.

RP /ɒ/ → GA /ɑː/ : *hot* /hɑːt/, *John* /dʒɑːn/
RP /ɑː/ → GA /æ/ : *last* /læst/, *rather* /'ræð(ə)r/
        → GA /ɑː/ before /r/ : *part* /pɑːrt/, *charm* /tʃɑːrm/
RP /ɔː/ → GA /ɒ/ : *caught* /kɒt/, *ought* /ɒt/, *law* /lɒː/
        → GA /ɔː/ before /r/ : *war* /wɔːr/, *court* /kɔːrt/
RP /ɜː/ → GA /ɜːr/ : *hurt* /hɜːrt/, *heard* /hɜːrd/

RP /əʊ/ → GA /oʊ/ : *go* /goʊ/, *below* /bə'loʊ/
RP /ɪə/ → GA /ɪr/ or /ɪər/ : *here* /hɪr/ or /hɪər/
RP /eə/ → GA /er/ or /eər/ : *care* /ker/ or /keər/
RP /ʊə/ → GA /ʊr/ or /ʊər/ : *poor* /pʊr/ or /pʊər/

Exceptions

Occasionally there are exceptions to these correspondences, e.g. GA has /ɑ:/ in *father* /'fɑ:ð(ə)r/, although the vowel is not immediately followed by /r/. For GA speakers who have a higher vowel than /ɔ:/ before /r/ in some words, this can be written with /o:/, as in *four* /fo:r/ and *court* /ko:rt/. Another place where Americans can have two vowels corresponding to a single RP one is in words like *dog, cloth, frost, trough, office*, which except for *dog* all have a fricative after the vowel: though for some Americans the correspondence between RP /ɒ/ and GA /ɑ:/ applies here, many have the vowel /ɒ:/ in these words. The reader is warned that the British learners' dictionaries give only one RP and one GA pronunciation in the transcription we are describing here. For information on variant pronunciations both in RP and GA it is advisable to consult a good pronouncing dictionary such as Wells' LPD or Roach & Hartman's EPD.

/r/-coloured Vowels

One final word must be said about the transcription of /r/-coloured vowels. We mentioned above in connection with the scripts used in America that the sounds which are written as /ə/ and /ɜ:/ in RP are pronounced with the tip of the tongue curled back for /r/ when they occur before this consonant. As this /r/-colouring is spread over the whole vowel, some phoneticians prefer to use a different symbol. In place of the /ɜ:r/ which we have written above and which is used in EPD, one can also find /'/, e.g. in LPD, where *hurt* and *heard* are transcribed /hɝt/ and /hɝd/ respectively. Similarly, instead of /(ə)r/ we also see /ɚ/, e.g. in EPD whereas LPD prefers /ᵊr/. In the latter notation the small raised shwa, like our normal-sized shwa in parentheses, shows that this vowel can be omitted and the remaining /r/ then becomes syllabic. Notice that /r/-coloured shwa and syllabic /r/ are two names for the same thing.

Sample Texts

For comparison three sentences are given here in GA and RP using the IPA script. Alternatives are placed in parentheses.
1. *No, the news George heard last week was not important.*
GA: /'noʊ, ðə 'nu:z 'dʒɔ:rdʒ 'hɜ:rd 'læst ('læs) 'wi:k wəz 'nɑ̤tɪm'pɔ:rtn̩t (ɪm'pɔ:rtn̩t)/'
RP: /'nəʊ, ðə 'nju:z 'dʒɔ:dʒ 'hɜ:d 'lɑ:st ('lɑ:s) 'wi:k wəz 'nɒt ɪm'pɔ:tn t/
2. *The girls were all sobbing and the boy was hiding his tears behind a large handkerchief.*
GA: /ðə 'gɜ:rlz wər 'ɒ:l 'sɑ:bɪŋ ən ðə 'bɔɪ wəz 'haɪdɪŋ ɪz (hɪz) 'tɪrz ('tɪərz) bə'haɪnd ə'lɑ:rdʒ 'hæŋkərtʃɪf/

RP: /ðə 'gɜːlz wərˌɔːl 'sɒbɪŋ ən ðə 'bɔɪ wəz 'haɪdɪŋ ɪz (hɪz) 'tɪəz bɪ'haɪnd ə 'lɑːdʒ 'hæŋkətʃɪf/

3. *Don't your letters take a long time to go from here to America!*

GA: /'dount jʊr (jʊər, jɔːr, joːr) 'leɾ(ə)rz 'teɪk ə 'lɒːŋ ('lɑːŋ) 'taɪm tə 'goʊ frm̩ 'hɪr ('hɪər) tu ə'merɪkə/

RP: /'dəʊnt jɔː (jʊə) 'letəz 'teɪk ə 'lɒŋ 'taɪm tə 'gəʊ frm̩ 'hɪə tu ə'merɪkə/

 Conclusion

Final Notes

Our short survey of English phonetics and phonology is now at an end. The reader has been introduced to the basic concepts of articulatory phonetics and has seen how these work for British and American English. Using the phoneme theory we have shown how these sounds function in English, how they are distributed and what variants they can have. We have also discussed the main phonological processes which affect sounds when they occur in context and especially when they are used in casual or rapid speech. Where necessary we have also given a little historical background information for the better understanding of certain phonological phenomena. Finally we have shown the reader what kind of scripts he may encounter in British and American books on English phonetics and phonology.

Further Reading

With this basic knowledge the reader should now be in a position to find his way with relative ease through the phonetic information given in the dictionaries and to tackle more detailed books and ones with other approaches to phonetics and phonology, e.g. Abercrombie, Catford, Gimson, Ladefoged (phonetics);
Giegerich, Harris, Lass, Scherer & Wollmann (English phonology);
Couper-Kuhlen, Cruttenden, Crystal (prosody and intonation);
Chomsky & Halle, Kenstowicz & Kisseberth, Durand (generative phonology);
Goldsmith, Hogg & McCully (autosegmental and metrical phonology)
Kaye (cognitive phonology);
Anderson & Ewen (dependency phonology);
Wells (varieties of English);
Crystal, McArthur (reference works for quick overview).

Bibliography

General

ABERCROMBIE, David: *Elements of General Phonetics*. Edinburgh: Edinburgh University Press 1967.

ANDERSON, John M. & C. Ewen: *Principles of Dependency Phonology*. Cambridge: Cambridge University Press 1987.

CATFORD, John C.: *A Practical Introduction to Phonetics*. Oxford: Clarendon Press 1988.

CHOMSKY, Noam & Morris Halle: *The Sound Pattern of English*. New York: Harper & Row 1968.

COUPER-KUHLEN, Elisabeth: *An Introduction to English Prosody*. London: Edward Arnold 1986.

CRUTTENDEN, Alan. *Intonation*. Cambridge: Cambridge University Press 1986.

CRYSTAL, David (Editor): *Dictionary of Linguistics and Phonetics. Third Edition*. Oxford: Blackwell 1991.

CRYSTAL, David: *Prosodic Systems and Intonation in English*. Cambridge: Cambridge University Press 1986.

DURAND, Jacques: *Generative and Non-Linear Phonology*. London: Longman 1990.

GIEGERICH, Heinz: *English Phonology. An Introduction*. Cambridge: Cambridge University Press 1992.

GIMSON, Alfred C.: *An Introduction to the Pronunciation of English. Fourth Edition, revised by Susan Ramsaran*. London: Edward Arnold 1989.

GOLDSMITH, John: *Autosegmental and Metrical Phonology*. Oxford: Blackwell 1990.

HALLE, Morris: *The Sound Pattern of Russian*. The Hague: Mouton 1959.

HARRIS, John: *English Sound Structure*. Oxford: Blackwell 1994.

HOGG, Richard & C. McCully: *Metrical Phonology. A Coursebook*. Cambridge: Cambridge University Press 1987.

KAYE, Jonathan: *Phonology: A Cognitive View*. Hillsdale, N.J.: Erlbaum 1989.

KENSTOWICZ, Michael & C. Kisseberth: *Generative Phonology*. New York: Academic Press 1979.

LADEFOGED, Peter: *A Course in Phonetics*. Chicago: Chicago University Press 1982.

LASS, Roger: *Phonology. An Introduction to Basic Concepts*. Cambridge: Cambridge University Press 1984.

MCARTHUR, Tom (Editor): *The Oxford Companion to the English Language*. Oxford: Oxford University Press 1992.

SCHERER, Günther & A. Wollmann: *Englische Phonetik und Phonologie. 3. Auflage*. Berlin: Erich Schmidt Verlag 1986.

WELLS, John C.: *The Accents of English. Volumes 1–3*. Cambridge: Cambridge University Press 1982.

Dictionaries

[CED] *Collins English Dictionary. Third Edition*. Edited by Patrick Hanks. Sydney, Auckland, Glasgow: Collins 1995.

[CIDE] *Cambridge International Dictionary of English*. Edited by Paul Procter. Cambridge: Cambridge University Press 1995.

[COB] *Collins COBUILD English Language Dictionary*. Edited by John Sinclair. London: Collins 1987.

[EEPD] *Everyman's English Pronouncing Dictionary. Thirteenth Edition*. Edited by Daniel Jones, revised by Alfred C. Gimson. London: Dent 1967.

[EPD] *English Pronouncing Dictionary. Fifteenth Edition*. Edited by Daniel Jones, revised by Peter Roach & James Hartman. Cambridge: Cambridge University Press 1997.

[LPD] *Longman Pronunciation Dictionary*. Edited by John Wells. Harlow: Longman 1990.

[LDCE] *Longman Dictionary of Contemporary English. Third Edition*. Edited by Della Summers. Harlow: Longman 1995.

[OALD] *Oxford Advanced Learner's Dictionary of Current English. Fifth Edition*. Edited by Jonathan Crowther. Oxford: Oxford University Press 1995.

[OCED] *Oxford Concise English Dictionary. Ninth Edition*. Edited by Della Thompson 1995. Oxford: Clarendon Press.

[OED] *Oxford English Dictionary. Second Edition, Volumes 1–20*. Edited by John Simpson & Edmund Weiner. Oxford: Clarendon Press 1989.

Subject index